In The Money

2023

The Right Options Strategy to Make Profit From the Market

DISCLAIMER

The ideas and strategies in this book are simply describing what has worked – and what hasn't worked - for me. The information in this book is for educational purposes only and is not investment advice. I am not a financial advisor or investment adviser and advise that you consult a licensed financial advisor to determine the suitability of any investment.

While I have spent many hours checking and rechecking the figures in the book, I make no representation as to the accuracy or completeness of the information and will not be liable for any errors or omissions.

The author assumes no responsibility or liability for trading and investment results, losses, injuries, or damages. It should not be assumed that the ITM strategies will be profitable and will not result in losses. It is not a replacement for professional financial and investment advice.

Contents

Introduction

Years ago, as I was buying yet another book promising to reveal stock market secrets and make me fabulously wealthy, I had the niggling doubt: why are you writing this? Why aren't you sipping vintage champagne on your yacht and partying with the rich and famous?

You, dear reader, are probably having exactly the same thoughts right now about this book. Let me set your mind at ease.

I am not going to show you how to become a millionaire overnight. I don't know how to do that, and I don't know anyone who does. What I *am* going to do is show you a very simple strategy to trade the stock market which has brought me double-digit returns over the past years, and it can do the same for you.

You can do the In The Money (ITM) strategy from anywhere with an Internet connection, and that's practically everywhere these days. You want to spend 4 months this summer drifting through France and Italy? No problem! In fact, that's what I am going to be doing. You can choose when you want to 'work' and how much time you spend on it. You can even do it in your pyjamas if you want to!

It is absolutely the best 'job' in the world. I love it and want to show you how to do it too. Everything starts with a first step. Congratulations on taking the first step on the way to becoming wealthy and financially free.

Prologue

You've read the motivational books, checked out the get-rich-quick websites, and watched the success videos. You've recited affirmations, manifested, and made motivation boards. You know that you can be whoever you want to be and do whatever you want to do. It's all in your mindset. If you believe it hard enough it will magically happen.

But, deep down, do you really believe it?

I don't. How many people do you know who really have it made? How many people do you know who are still reading books about 'fulfilling their potential' or 'living their dream'? I bet you know WAY more people who are still searching or who have just given up. Motivational books and courses are great to get you fired up but that's about it. They will all tell you to 'take action' but are very vague on what action you should take.

Let's face it, not many people get to 'live their dream'. It's not because of a lack of energy or intelligence or drive. ***It's because of lack of money***. They don't have a practical strategy to actually make money. They don't know where to start.

Trying to live the dream without money? It's just not going to happen! Money gives you freedom. Money means you don't have to worry. Money means you don't have to do things you don't want to do. Money means you get to do the things you DO want to do.

I know this because for many years I wanted what I (rather vulgarly) called 'F U money'. Despite having a high-flying career in IT, I always had to defer to the CEO, who could make my life miserable by making bad decisions that I had to implement. So many times, I just wanted to be able to say: ***F U, I am out of here***. But I couldn't. Not then. I needed the pay cheque.

Fast forward to today. I don't work for anybody else and haven't for years. I don't do things I don't want to do (like cleaning the house for a start!). I do things that I do want to do like traveling – business or first class of course. I have time to enjoy my life. I don't worry about the future. I know I have enough money, and I know that I will make lots more. I am free to live my life the way I want, and that is a wonderful feeling.

This book will show you how to do it too. You will learn to trade the market safely, and with returns that are double or triple the market. The trading strategy (ITM) that I am going to show you only takes about 10 minutes a week, and it is something I love to do. It's not a chore in any way. In fact, I love checking my accounts every day and updating my wealth spreadsheet.

So, buckle up for an invigorating journey to your wealthy future. A journey where you will learn to make money and be on your way to becoming financially free to live the life that you want.

Chapter 1. Monkeys and Markets

The stock market is a lot of fun if you know what you are doing and are on the right side of it. Checking your accounts and finding you are $1K, $10K, or $50K richer than yesterday really gives you a nice, safe, warm feeling inside. You feel proud of yourself. You've made money, but more importantly, you know HOW to make money.

The stock market is a totally miserable place to be if you don't know what you are doing, and it is going against you. When you are losing money, seeing your hard-earned capital disappear – well, that's guaranteed to spoil your day! You feel helpless. You watch your balance go down, not knowing what to do except to sell in a panic. That gives you a cold, shaky, panicky feeling. I know. I've been there. It's horrible. And I am never going there again.

If you have been there too, then you'll know how little fun it is, and it's the main reason why most people stop playing the market. It's a very common situation, not just for newbies, but also for stock market 'experts'. Now for the good news: I am going to show you how to never be in this position, and how to keep yourself safe while you make profits in the market.

Before we start let's look at how the so-called 'market experts' actually perform. If you think that they know what they are doing you are in for a big surprise. In fact, their performance is guaranteed to shock you!

Why a Monkey can beat the Market

Did you know that a blindfolded monkey throwing darts at a newspaper's financial pages can select a portfolio that does just as well as one carefully selected by experts?

That's not a joke. It's actually correct. The claim was made in the 1972 book *A Random Walk Down Wall Street* and has been tested and found to be true. OK, it wasn't tested by real monkeys wearing real blindfolds. Instead of real monkeys, they used people who selected 100 random 30-stock portfolios. And yes, you guessed it, the randomly-selected portfolios did better!

This wasn't a one-off experiment either. They repeated the process of replicating 100 monkeys throwing darts at the stock pages every year from 1964 to 2011 and tracked the results. Each year, an average of 98 of the 100 monkey portfolios beat the average of all the stocks.

How could a blindfolded monkey pick stocks better than highly trained and highly paid experts? There is a very easy answer: because the experts don't do it very well at all. In fact, most 'expert' stock pickers perform worse than the average of all stocks, which is usually the benchmark they are trying to beat.

Yet, we keep on giving our money to experts who can't even match the market! Are we crazy? The short answer is yes, we are. Warren Buffet, the well-known investor, has said that Wall Street is the only place where people ride in their Rolls Royce to get advice from people who take the subway. How badly do the experts perform? Very badly indeed. Did you know that fewer than 1 in 5 beat the average?

How Bad are the Experts?

That means that *4 out of 5 experts underperform the market.* Morningstar, the investment research and management firm, found that in 2016 only 18% of fund managers beat the market. To make it even worse, the fund managers who beat the market one year rarely did it 2 years in a row. How can this be?

There are thousands of 'expert' fund managers and many thousands of managed funds. Most investment management firms will have lots of different funds. This isn't just to give their customers a choice, but of course that's what they say in the glossy brochures. Oh no! It is so that they can cover all bases.

By the law of averages, some of the funds will perform well, some funds will perform badly, and some will be just average. But the investment management firm will be able to point to a few well-performing funds and publicize the performance of the best ones, while conveniently ignoring the funds that performed badly.

What happens to the funds that perform badly? They will be quietly killed off. Funds are killed off quite regularly. 30% of the poorest performing funds in the 5 years to March 2012 had disappeared by March 2017.

To get a feel of what is happening and to keep things simple, let's assume that all these thousands of funds are made up of 30 equally-weighted stocks. These stocks have been carefully selected by the expert fund managers because they think that they will go up in price.

So, let's think about the thousands of funds, each with a portfolio of 30 stocks. Obviously, some portfolios will perform better than others. In some, all 30 stocks might go up. In others, all 30 stocks might go down. Most will be in the middle somewhere, with some stocks going up and some stocks going down. By chance alone, half of the stocks will go up and half will go down.

(To make things simple we are assuming that it is equally likely that a stock will go up or down. In a bull market more stocks will go up; in a bear market more stocks will go down. In this case, the distribution will be skewed

but there will still be funds that outperform and funds that underperform.)

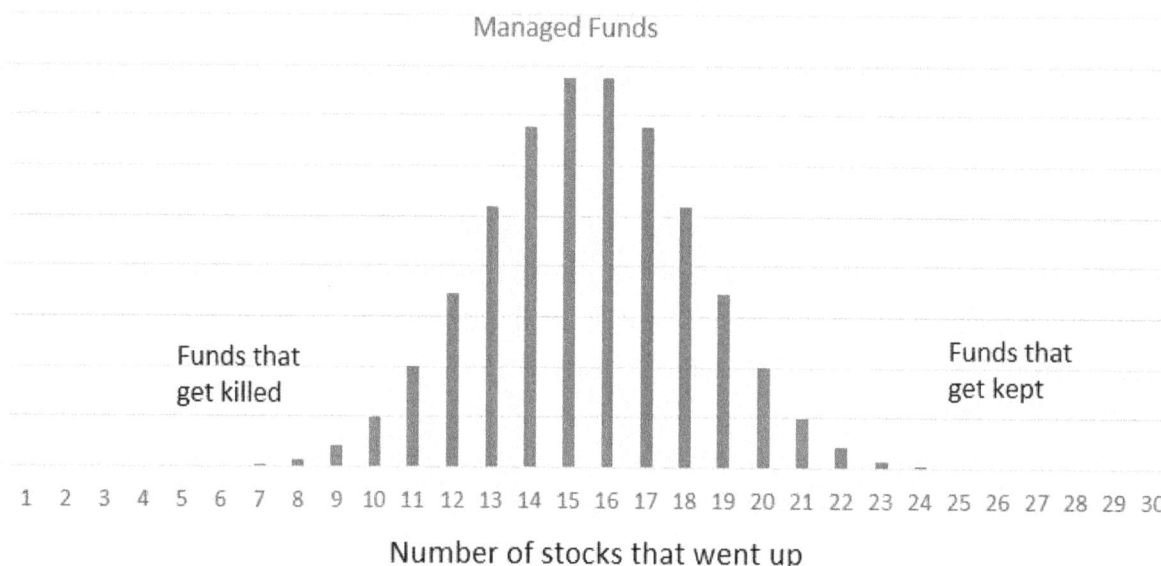

Managed Funds

Funds that
get killed

Funds that
get kept

1 2 3 4 5 6 7 8 9 10 11 12 13 14 15 16 17 18 19 20 21 22 23 24 25 26 27 28 29 30

Number of stocks that went up

The distribution of funds will be as in the diagram, a Bell or normal curve. There will be some good performers and some terrible performers, but most will be around the middle. No prizes for guessing which ones will be the keepers and which ones will quietly disappear!

Picking a Winning Fund

Everyone wants to pick a fund that is going to do well, but how can they know which ones are going to win? Unfortunately, there is no sure way to choose a fund that is going to be successful. If there was, everybody would do it.

You will have seen the warning *past performance is no indication of future performance*. Well, that's absolutely right. Studies have shown that if you pick a fund from the top 25% best-performing funds for one year, then the chances of it being in the top 25% the next year are – wait for it – 25%! In other words, no better than chance. How many were still there the next year? 4%. The year after? 0.5%. The year after that? 0.3%. So, the next time someone is telling you how well their funds under management are doing, just smile politely and say that you are delighted for them. You know better!

We've seen that picking a winning fund is a loser's game. It can't be done. So, what are we going to do?

Einstein had a Point

The good news is that you don't have to be a rocket scientist to win on the stock market. In fact, you don't even have to know a lot about it. People can spend their entire waking hours following it and reading about it, but that doesn't generally help them be successful in the market.

Some people do spend all their time looking at it. It is addictive. I know. I've personally wasted way too many days in front of a screen convinced that there was an answer in there somewhere if I worked hard enough at it. Realizing that hard work did not translate into success was hard to accept.

Why I - and everyone else who spends hours and days researching - didn't win was because what I ended up with was knowledge. A lot of knowledge, but that wasn't enough. What I needed was wisdom. What's the difference?

> ➢ **Knowledge** is knowing that a tomato is a fruit.

> ➢ **Wisdom** is not putting it in a fruit salad.

That said, you DO have to know all about the bit of the market that we are going to play in. I am not suggesting that you stumble in blindly. I am going to work on the Einstein principle:

Everything should be made as simple as possible, but not simpler.

The good news is that the part of the market you need to know about it is only a very small part of the stock market information that is floating around. Most of that information is just 'noise' and you can safely ignore it. In fact, I recommend that you do.

Just imagine that the stock market is a lovely big apple pie – but you only have a small slice that you need to know about. Let other people worry about the rest of it. You don't need to.

The Market and the Beach

If you listen to journalists and stock market experts you are guaranteed to end up confused and misinformed, which is not good. You need a clear head and to be able to look past all that noise, because noise is just what it is.

I always think that the stock market is a bit like the ocean and the tides. If the tide is coming in some waves are bigger than others and travel further up the beach making a new 'record'. Some waves do not even make it to where the last wave did, maybe a lot less. But soon afterward another wave comes that will end up further up the beach. And that happens again and again.

If you start watching the waves, then you can become fascinated by them. "Oh look, that one is the biggest so far, I bet the next one will get even further up the beach". Then it doesn't. You are disappointed. What to think?

Smart people know that you keep your eye on the tide, not the waves.

Some waves are always going to go higher than others. Some aren't going to reach a previous high. But if the tide is still coming in you don't bet against the tide.

Of course, at some stage, the tide is going to change and start going out. We know that. Just like the stock market will stop going up and start to go down. We know that too. But I will show you how to recognize the 'turn of the tide' so that you don't get caught.

Clickbait and Listicles

So why is there all this noise? Every day you are bombarded with articles that scream *Market Crash Imminent!* or *Dow to Double in Next Year!* or some such rubbish. And woe betides you if you click on any of these headlines. You will be bombarded with even more rubbish articles.

Why do journalists and 'experts' do it? *Because that is how they get paid.* Journalists get paid by getting as many people to click on their articles as they can. The more clicks, the more they get paid, and the more of an expert they are. It's not like the days of paper newspapers, where there was little feedback about how many people read a particular article. With online news, every click is tracked so that they know exactly how many people are reading it.

Let's say you are writing a news article and you only get paid if you reach 50,000 clicks. Clearly, you want as many clicks as you can get. What do you think people are going to click on?

Markets pretty normal, same as yesterday
OR
Expert says market crash starting this week!

Of course, the second one is going to get more clicks. Who wants to read that yesterday was quite normal, much the same as the day before? That's a 'meh'. On the other hand, if the market is going to crash, they definitely want to know about it, especially if it is an 'expert' saying so. So, they click.

It's not just for articles on the stock market. We all recognize the type of headlines.

The sure-fire cure for back pain doctors don't want you to know!
80-year-old woman looks 25. You'll never guess her secret!
Young Mum lost 50kg in 2 weeks with this simple little trick.

We've all clicked on these headlines. I definitely have. What is annoying is that if you have clicked on a headline about, say, luggage then you are going to be bombarded with more of the same for weeks, even after you have bought your new travel bag.

Some of the stock market headlines you are almost guaranteed to see are:

World's richest man warns of stock market meltdown!
Stock market overvalued; experts say sell now!
Experts predict imminent stock market crash!

It is always amusing to look at the articles from one or more years ago. You will see hundreds of shocking headlines that never came true or even came remotely close to coming true.

As well as clickbait, there are listicles, a word made up of 'list' and 'articles'. These are incredibly popular and get lots of clicks.

9 things you didn't know about Kim Kardashian.
7 shocking reasons you'll never eat airline food again.
5 secrets to a better sex life.

Listicles are especially popular with finance reporters who know absolutely nothing about, and have had no experience of, the stock market. Some headlines you will have seen:

Warren Buffett's 7 secrets that can make you rich!
5 stocks to buy right now.
11 mistakes most stock market traders make.

Why am I showing you these? *Because you have to learn to ignore them.* This is very, very important. You can't stop seeing the headlines, but you don't have to respond to them. Remember why they are being written. Someone wants you to click on them so that they will be paid. They don't care if they are giving you good information or not. They just want you to click.

So. Don't. Click.

Keep a clear head. Avoid having your mind getting cluttered up with the rubbish they are writing and get on with making money. If they knew how to do that, they wouldn't be writing clickbait headlines!

Remember the beach.
The 'experts' are talking about the waves. We keep an eye on the tide.

The Rich Get Richer

The saying goes: *the rich get richer, and the poor get poorer*. If you want to be rich (and let's face it, you wouldn't be reading this book unless you did!) then you need to follow what the rich people do, not what the poor people do. So, let's look at the differences.

Let's think of an average person, not rich but not poor. Let's call her Katy. Katy does not own any stocks directly, but she has a retirement fund. She is not involved in making decisions about where the fund invests her money. In fact, she has no idea what she is invested in. Someone else manages that for her, she just looks at the statement once a year and hopes that it is bigger than the year before. Which it usually is, although nowhere near as much as she would like it to be.

Katy would like to have more money. She thinks it would be lovely not to have to worry about it all the time. She would love to be financially free. But there's a problem. She doesn't know how to do it! She doesn't know anything about the stock market or how to start trading it. In fact, she doesn't even know anyone who does.

Katy is not alone. Most people don't own shares and don't know anyone who does. In fact, more US families own cats (30%) than stocks (14%), according to a CNN report. The statistics for American Households in 2017 show that

➤ 51% own no stock

➤ 35% indirectly own stock (retirement accounts)

➤ 14% directly own stock

This is for the total population. When you look at WHO owns the stocks the picture becomes much clearer. Stock ownership is a "rich peoples' thing". It's the rich who own the stocks:

➤ The richest **1%** own over **40%** of stocks

➤ The richest **10%** own **84%** of stocks

➤ The richest **20%** own well over **90%** of stocks

That's the rich, and they are doing very well. Guess what? It's the rich who get richer! We all know that. There's a saying *It takes money to make money* and to some extent that is true. The more money you have the more money you can make.

If you have $1,000 and you increase it by 5% you get $50. If you have $1,000,000 and you increase it by 5% you get $50,000. A big difference! But I am going to show you a strategy where you can get started with very little money, but really magnify your profits.

So that's the rich. What about everyone else? Well, that's not so pretty:

➢ The bottom 60% own just 1.8% of stocks

➢ The bottom 80% own just 7% of stocks, *including their retirement accounts*

So, you can see that Katy not knowing anyone who invests in the stock market is not unusual. In fact, it would be **more** unusual if she **did** know someone who actively invested.

Shark Attacks and Ice Cream

How do the rich get richer? Well, most of that is due to the stock market. Property is right up there also as a rich person's investment, but it is not really practical for many people. If you are going to own investment properties, then you need a large investment to get started and you may not see a profit for some years.

We can see from the figures above that rich people own stocks. People who are not rich tend not to own stocks. Is there a correlation? In my opinion that is a resounding YES! However, we need to be careful about assuming that just because two things correlate (i.e., they move in tandem) that one causes the other.

For example, rich people tend to have more expensive cars, but just buying an expensive car will not make you rich. It is probably going to do just the opposite! Every statistician knows:

Correlation is not Causation (but it can be!)

What do they mean by this? It means that just because 2 things move together it doesn't mean that they are related. For example, the number of smartphones has increased in recent years and so has the incidence of obesity. Perhaps one could draw some sort of inference that both correlate with our increasingly sedentary lifestyles, but no one would seriously suggest that smartphones cause obesity.

Likewise, shark attacks are highly correlated with the amount of ice cream sold. Clearly, anyone attacked by a shark is not more likely to go and buy an ice cream, and anyone eating an ice cream is not suddenly going to be more attractive to sharks, especially if they are on dry land. The probable explanation is that shark attacks and ice cream are both correlated with summer. In summer, more people are likely to be in the ocean where shark attacks can occur, and in summer people tend to eat more ice cream.

Hence, we have correlation but not causation. However, people confuse the two all the time and become convinced that one *causes* the other. If you want to have a laugh and see some totally ridiculous connections just google '*spurious correlations*'.

Rich people invest in stocks because they produce wealth, unlike expensive cars which reduce wealth, and hence they get richer. If you don't own stocks, then you are missing out on something that could make you wealthy. However, I am not suggesting that you run out and buy some stocks. Definitely not, that's way too risky. There are smarter ways of making money than owning stocks outright, which is what this book is about. But remember:

If you want to get rich - legally - the stock market is the way to do it.

We are going to use a strategy that is simple and elegant and guaranteed to beat the market. If the market goes up by 10%, you will make 20%. If the market goes up 20% then you will be 40% up. Way better than the 'experts' we were looking at earlier!

What Katy Did

Let's get back to Katy. Katy is aware of the stock market but has no idea how to make money from it, although she definitely wants the freedom that money can give her.

One day Katy was reading some statistics on a website. She saw that 94% of rich households have significant stock holdings (over $10K). But she didn't know anyone who owned stocks. Katy knew about property. She knew a lot of people who were buying their own homes – and they were often mortgaged up to their eyeballs!

And that is why the middle class isn't rich. Not because they own their own home or have a mortgage, but because they don't have anything else. Most people in the middle class have all their wealth tied up in their homes. It's their biggest asset. *For the richest Americans, only 7.6% of their wealth is tied up in their house.*

So why do the rich get richer, and the poor get poorer? The answers are in the figures above!

Now I am not saying that you shouldn't try to own your own home. I do, and I can understand anyone wanting to own their own place. What I *am* saying is that it is not enough. You need an extra plan if you want to be financially free. And that extra plan should be the stock market. So, let's start with a crash course on how the stock market really works.

Bulls and Bears

Fund managers, stock pickers, market analysts, financial gurus. The one thing they all have in common is that they love having people think that they are smarter than the average bear.

That was an in-joke. Couldn't resist it. You probably know the expression 'bulls and bears' but let's just go over it anyway so that there is no confusion.

➤ A **Bull** is someone who thinks the market, or a stock, is going **UP.**

➤ A **Bear** is someone who thinks the market, or a stock, is going

DOWN.

Why are they called bulls and bears? The most common explanation is to think of their method of attack:

> ➢ Bulls lower their head then toss UP.

> ➢ Bears raise their paws and crash DOWN.

There is another story about how we got the expressions, all about trappers selling bearskins, but it seems a bit obscure. Let's go with the obvious explanation.

The Difference Between Bulls and Bears

There is a saying about the bulls and the bears which is very true:

> ➢ Bulls walk up the stairs

> ➢ Bears jump out the window

What do we mean by that? It means that markets tend to go up slowly, often quite steadily, which makes it easier to trade because it is predictable. When markets are going up it is called a ***bull market.***

Typical Bull Market

On the other hand, when markets go down, they can go down with breathtaking speed. For example, the COVID bear market of 2020 lasted 27 days, and the market dropped 34%. Terrifying!

Bear markets often catch unprepared people by surprise, and they panic and sell, usually at the worst possible time. Anything to stop the pain of watching their profits, or even their capital, disappear before their eyes!

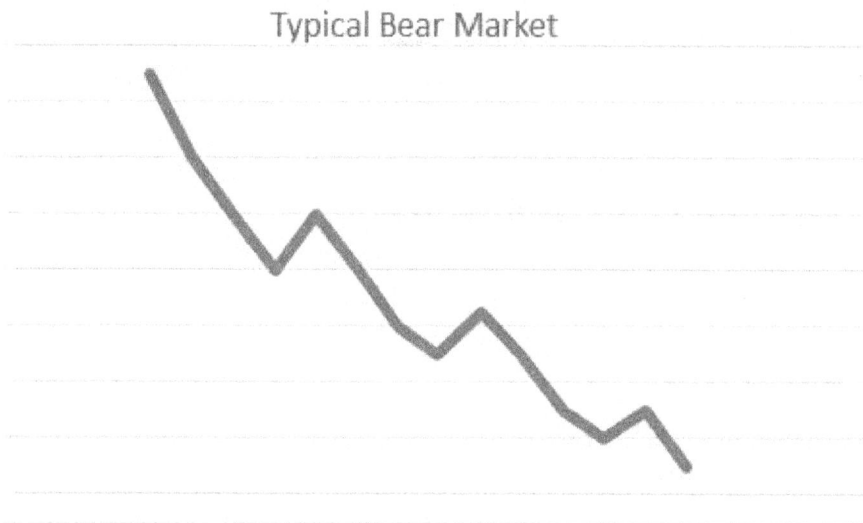

Typical Bear Market

On the way down, markets often stop for a few pauses on the way. Everyone thinks 'Whew, thank goodness that's over!' and there is what is called a 'relief rally' where people pile back into the market again driving the prices up. It's more picturesquely, but rather heartlessly, called a 'dead cat bounce'.

As people buy back in, they often buy back their stocks at a higher price than they sold them during the panic. Then the bear market resumes, there is another drop, and the same thing happens again. And again. The diagram above is what a bear market typically looks like. It goes down, but not straight down. It is more like a sawtooth than a straight line.

Finally, the market bottoms out and starts to rise again. It always has. It always does. It always will.

How do I know if it's a Bull or a Bear Market?

When I started writing the first edition of this book, we were in a bull market. When I finished the first draft, we were still in it. Then something big happened. Coronavirus (or COVID 19 if you prefer) happened.

The market plummeted, ending the long bull market. What followed was a very sudden and very painful bear market that no one saw coming. It was unusual because it was an event not caused by the economy or financial conditions, but a pandemic that closed down most of the world. The extent of the closing down really was unprecedented. This was the quickest, most sudden bear market ever.

The post-GFC (Global Financial Crisis) bull market had been going on for quite a long time, over 10 years, although during that time there had been some major reversals, like at the end of 2018 when it plummeted by 20%. There had been headlines for some years saying it was the longest bull market ever, although this depends on your definition (we will look at that later in the book.)

What I wrote in January 2020 is still valid, so we will look at it and address the covid effects later in the book. It is discussed in more detail in the companion book *In The Money: Bear Market Strategy*. The rules I am going to show you about how the stock market works are still correct and will guide you safely through incredible events such as a pandemic and the worldwide lockdown.

All bull markets end sometime, and successful traders - that's you (when you have finished reading the book) and me – need to know how to recognize a market top. Not the exact date, of course, no one knows that. But we need to know when it is getting close.

There is a saying **they don't ring a bell at the top!** But the signs of a bull market petering out are obvious when you know what to look for. We'll go through these signs so that you will recognize them. Then, once we have recognized that we are near the top of a bull market what do we do? We get out of our positions, slowly and carefully, at a nice profit. We don't dump them in a mad panic.

Then we look at how we make money on the way down. You can make money in both a bull and a bear market. The only difference is that you can make more money more quickly in a bear market, simply because the market moves more quickly. *This book does not cover the bear market strategy*. The next book in this series, **In The Money: Bear Market Strategy,** is all about how to trade a bear market.

Remember, the bulls go up the stairs, the bears jump out the window!

What a Market Top Looks Like

During a bull market people make money. Some more than others (and you are going to be one of the ones who makes more). After a while, everyday people start to notice what's happening.

They read about people who have made enough money to buy a nice house, send their children to college, go on great vacations, and so on. Then they start to hear about someone's friend who bought this stock, and guess what? The next day it went up 10 times, and they bought a yacht! Then it's on the TV news, and there are adverts everywhere for 'systems' that are guaranteed to make you money and courses to show you how to beat the stock market.

The headlines scream at you:

Dow Makes Another All-Time High!

Sixteen-year-old trader makes $1 million in 1 week!

Homeless man now a Millionaire!

It seems to be everywhere. People are gripped with FOMO: Fear Of Missing Out. They figure if other people can do it then they can too. So, they sign up with some 'education' or 'financial advice' company offering them a sure-fire way to picking stocks that are going to double or triple, and they jump in. Usually right at the wrong time, just when the market is peaking.

Market Top signs to look out for:

➢ Headlines and news are mostly positive.

➢ Lots of adverts for free courses about trading.

➢ Lots of adverts about 'black box' systems guaranteed to identify stocks that are going to go up.

➢ People you know are buying stocks for the first time.

➢ You hear about people who have borrowed to invest in stocks.

➢ Taxi / Uber drivers start giving you stock tips.

➢ You hear someone say: ***This time it's different.***

My personal experience of the Global Financial Crisis of 2008 was terrifying because all around I saw people losing their life savings and their houses. I had no idea when it would finish, no one did, so I was waiting for a bottom like everyone else.

Luckily, I personally didn't lose any money in my trading accounts although I did in my managed funds (never again!). I had seen the signs and was prepared. The tipping point was when I read an article in August 2007 about how the stock market could never crash again, and I didn't understand what the writer was trying to say. It seemed like gobbledygook to me. But I **did** recognize what the headline meant. It was really saying 'This Time It's Different'.

I realized that the other signs were all around as well, so started to close down my positions. I was a little early (August / September 2007), so I had to endure the pain of seeing the market keep on going up while I was sitting on the sidelines. So much so that I started to doubt myself and think that I had got it wrong and everyone else was right. Everybody else was still making money and crowing about it. I felt like a bit of an idiot. A lot of an idiot, actually.

But I was only out by a month or two. The market peaked in October 2007 then started sliding and did not reach the bottom until March 2009 by which time it had lost 57% of its value. Luckily, being out of the market I was not affected, other than the retirement money I had in managed funds which froze all withdrawals, leading me to vow never to let anyone else manage any of my money ever again. Sadly, however, many people lost their life savings.

A famous investor, Sir John Templeton, once said:

Bull markets are born on pessimism, grow on skepticism, mature on optimism and die on euphoria.

This sums it up nicely. So where are we right now, in December 2021? We have had an amazing bull market since the end of the COVID bear. As I mentioned, the COVID bear market only lasted for 27 days, the shortest bear market on record but it was a severe bear market. The definition of a bear market is that it drops 20% from its highs. The Covid bear dropped 34%. Nasty.

Since late March 2020, the bull market has gone up steadily with only minor dips. In fact, since the depths of the bear market, it has more than doubled in value. Can this continue? Of course, not; all bull markets come to an end, and this one will also. But it is not all bad news: bear markets also come to an end as well. But let's have a quick look at what happened in the last 2 years.

In January 2020, the press was mostly negative and stock ownership was not widespread so I would have said that we were still in the skepticism phase. We were not even close to the levels of direct stock ownership that we have seen before:

➢ 1989: 13.1%
➢ 2001: 21.3%
➢ 2007: 18%
➢ 2017: 13.8%

At that time, my call was that the bull market was still running and had a way to go before it turned into a bear market. Then came Covid, the coronavirus, and by early February it was obvious that we were in uncharted territory. The last major pandemic was almost a century ago when the world was hit by the Spanish Flu. The world and the stock market were quite different then, so we didn't know exactly how it was going to play out.

What I found strange was that initially the markets shrugged it off and did not seem to realize the seriousness of the situation. Then, of course, all of a sudden it did, and the market dropped like a stone.

Between the 19th of February and the 23rd of March, it lost 34% of its value. For people watching their investments and retirement funds disappear before their eyes it must have been terrifying.

Would our strategy have kept you safe? Yes, it would. If you were following the ITM (In The Market) rules you would have sold. I followed the rules, so I got out before I lost too much money. They kept me safe, so I was watching with horror - but from the sidelines. A much more comfortable place to be!

Chapter 1 Highlights

At the end of each chapter, we will review the major points so that you can check that you haven't missed anything.

➢ Experts are not good at getting results – most underperform the market. Managed funds don't perform any better.

➢ The market direction (trend) is like the tide, the daily fluctuations (noise) are like the waves. We are going to trade with the tide and ignore the waves.

➢ The news is full of market noise. We have to learn to read the mood, but not get sucked into believing the headlines and experts.

➢ Rich people get rich because they own stocks. Poor people stay poor because they don't.

➢ Bull markets are when stocks are on an uptrend. Bear markets are when stocks are in a downtrend. We need to know which one we are in to be able to trade safely.

And finally, some more words of wisdom from Sir John Templeton:
When people are desperately trying to sell, help them and buy.
When people are enthusiastically trying to buy, help them and sell.

◆ ◆ ◆

Chapter 2. The Rollercoaster

Right now, you're thinking 'OK, I want to start now, let's just cut straight to the strategy!' Fear not, we will get there as promised, but first, we have to dispel a few myths and look at WHY people generally lose money on the stock market. Forewarned is forearmed. You need to know what to expect so that you can handle it with equanimity, and not panic and freak out because you don't know what is 'normal'.

Why People Lose Money on the Stock Market

Almost everyone has a horror story about the stock market. How they lost their shirt, or their friend lost theirs', or their friend's friend, or someone they heard about somewhere. These poor people had their life savings wiped out and lost their house, now they are working two jobs to make ends meet.

The sad thing is that these stories are probably true. People who don't know what they are doing often lose everything. The stock market is not a place for people who are not sure what they are doing, and it's not for the faint-hearted.

But these disasters are not going to happen to you. You are going to be able to trade knowing exactly what you are doing and how much money you are going to make. You will be able to glance at one figure (SPY, but more of that later) on the financial pages and know exactly how much your account has just gone up by and how much money you have made without even looking at your account. And crucially, you are going to be able to recognize the end of a bull market when it comes, so that you can switch to a different method of making money, one that works in a bear market.

The psychology of why people lose money on the market is really quite simple, and very predictable. When things are quiet most people are not interested in the stock market. It's not on their radar. Most people who do make money in the stock market are generally quiet about it and go about their business of making money without telling other people about it. This is a good rule to follow, and something I discuss later in the book.

Above The Radar

Of course, most of the time stock markets go up, and sooner or later journalists start to notice and write about it. At first, they do the 'doom and gloom' stories about how a crash is imminent and how we are going to plunge into recession, but after months or even years without a crash, the journalists start to change their tune.

We start to see 'human interest' stories about ordinary people who have done amazing things. How a single mother put her 5 kids through college by trading the stock market at night after her day job stacking shelves. About the 15-year-old boy wonder who has made enough money to buy himself a Ferrari that he's not old enough to drive. About the old couple who have been poor all their life but thanks to the stock market have just bought themselves a waterfront mansion.

As these stories continue, the stock market creeps into everyone's consciousness. Round the (pre-covid!) watercooler people are discussing shares and telling stories of someone they know who has made a heap of money. Maybe they are even bragging about a trade they have done themselves where they got a windfall profit (people rarely talk about the money they lose). People who aren't in the market start to feel left out.

The papers and websites are full of 'expert opinions' about why the stock market will keep on going up and why 'this time it's different'. Investor Clubs start up, like book clubs except that instead of talking about books they talk about which stocks to buy, and usually the club itself has a flutter on the market.

They hear more and more stories about ordinary people making fortunes and so they feel like they should be doing it too. It seems that there is a party going on and they're not part of it.

'FOMO' starts. It means Fear of Missing Out.

People scramble to get into the market, and there are lots of 'experts' offering to help them – for a fee of course. These 'experts' are going to make a lot of money, not on the stock market, but on helping other people lose their shirts on the stock market!

Courses spring up claiming to teach you how to make millions, easily, with no risk, in 2 minutes a week by 'just following this simple system' or buying this 'pick a winner' software. Or, for the more technically minded 'momentum' trading or 'sector rotation' or 'trend following' or any of the myriads of systems that spring up. Not that I was any different. In my time, I have fallen for a fair number of these 'experts' and always ended up wishing I had never heard of them.

So, people get into the market without really knowing what they are doing. Most are relying on the 'expert' to tell them what to buy and when, but some adventurous souls may even do their own analysis. Just so that you know what we mean by this let me explain. There are 2 main types of stock market analysis:

➤ **Fundamental Analysis** - looking at the company financials

➤ **Technical Analysis** - looking at the stock chart of the company

People jump into the market, ill-prepared, with no experience behind them and no perspective. Worse, they have no understanding of what stock markets do! For a while it goes well, and they congratulate themselves on their financial acumen and perspicacity. They start to plan what they are going to do with all this lovely money. They join in all the financial chat around the water cooler. They modestly let slip how much money they made last week. They brag about how much their favorite stock has gone up. They're part of the party at last!

Nothing Is Forever

Then it comes to an awful, grinding halt. Suddenly, the market drops, and they see all their lovely money disappearing before their eyes. Markets drop much more quickly than they rise, so the speed with which they are losing money takes their breath away. With their profits gone, they start to panic. Now they are losing their capital! Soon they can't take the pain anymore, so they sell their shares, recouping a fair bit of their original investment although all their profits are gone. They heave a sigh of relief. They're out. The pain has stopped.

Then the market stages a 'relief rally' and starts climbing again. Our poor people. The pain comes back, but now it's a different level of pain. Now it's the pain of being wrong combined with FOMO. They hold out for a bit, then capitulate. They buy back their shares at a higher price than they sold them, confident that they will soon be out of the red.

Almost as though it knew, the market immediately drops again. The pain starts again as they watch their capital being eroded. Mindful of their last experience they decide to tough it out and hold their stocks, watching as their money disappears. Eventually, the pain becomes too much, and they crack. They capitulate. They sell again.

As is the way of the market, there is another relief rally. The pain of being wrong starts again, and FOMO. Now they have an additional motivation: *revenge*. They want revenge on the market, which seems to have it in for them personally. They are determined to get their own back, to prove themselves right, and punish the market by winning back their capital **and** their profits. They buy their shares back – again at a higher price than they sold them.

Of course, the market drops again. The pain starts again. They are now underwater, with most of their original investment gone. They surrender. They sell while they still have a little money left.

They don't like this game; they are not playing anymore. They're out. They watch smugly as the market falls a bit more. They congratulate themselves on getting out while they could. But, of course, the inevitable happens. The market turns positive again and starts going up. And up. And up.

The Stock Market Roller Coaster

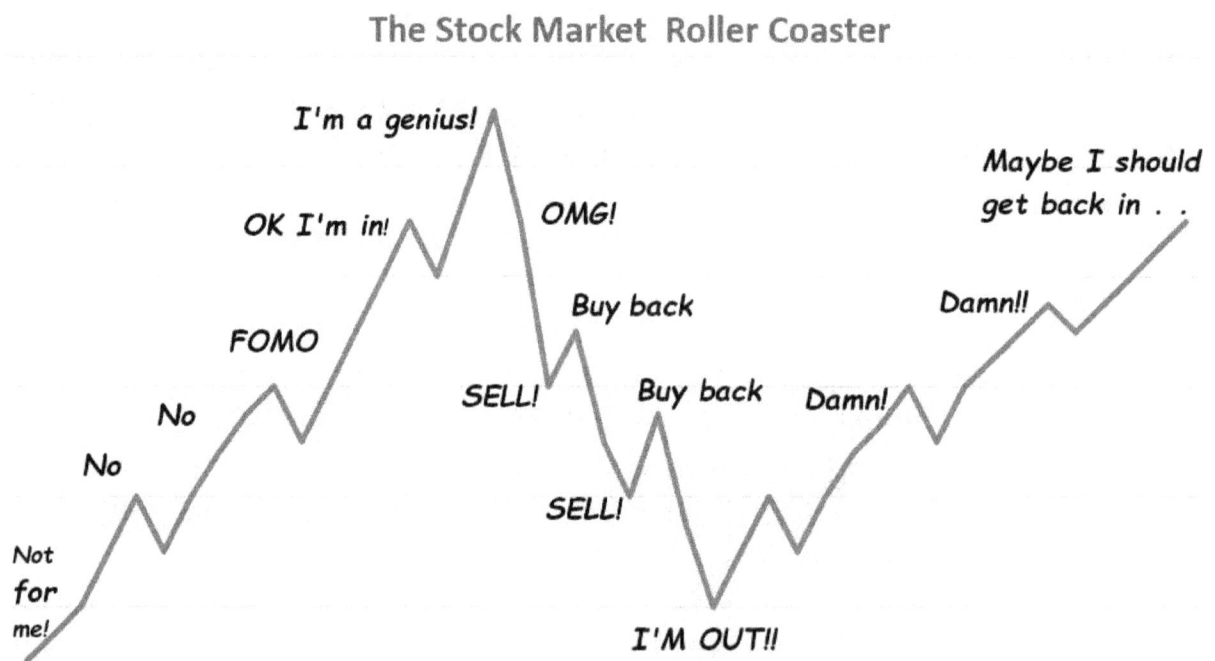

Of course, most people who have had this experience are not tempted to get back in. They didn't like it. They can do without the pain, and their money has pretty well all gone anyway.

They start to warn other people of the dangers of the stock market and dissuade them from entering it. They look for stories about people like them who have lost money, and confirmation bias kicks in. Get back in the market?

No way! Not for them. They're out.

But traders make money – don't they?

Well, no, actually. The great majority of studies point to the same conclusion: trading is hazardous to your wealth! OK, I didn't make up that phrase, although I wish I had. It came from a paper published some years ago that looked at the stock trading account data of over 60,000 households and analyzed whether they had made any money or not. Overwhelmingly, they hadn't.

They also noted that those households that traded more frequently had the worst performance.

A recent study went through tens of millions of trades, between 1992 and 2006 and found that 80% of active traders LOST money. They managed to lose, even when the market itself went up 12% on average during this period, and there was only one negative year (2002). That takes some doing! In fact, they found that only 1% were ***predictably*** profitable, and any others who made money only did so on short-term winning streaks. In both cases, the profits were wiped out by transaction fees, commissions, and taxes.

There ***are*** people who make money from active trading, but it's not the people who actually ***do*** the trading. It's the people who sell tools to other wannabe traders. All the information courses, stock trading newsletters, tip sheets, 'how-to advice', stock charts, technical analysis, trading clubs, investment advice, stock-picking systems, and so on. These are the people who make the money, just as long as they don't actually trade!

Never Go Naked

Of course, you will hear people telling you of someone else who has done really well, even given up their day job for full-time day trading. That they have a sure-fire system for picking winners. How often have I heard that!

My advice is not to take it at face value. Smile politely, say that is wonderful for them, but don't take any of it on board. Don't mention that you know all traders have short-term winning streaks. Don't tell them that 99% of traders LOSE money.

If you listen to people who tell you things like this, it will (a) make you feel inadequate and - even worse - (b) it will disrupt your thinking. Especially, avoid trading chat rooms and trading clubs - these are populated with people giving tips and warnings for their own nefarious purposes to people gullible enough to listen to them. Don't go near them – they rot your brain!

There is also longevity. The average life span of a professional trader is between 2 and 5 years. I can't find any studies and figures for non-professional traders, but I have met hundreds over my 20 years in the markets, going to lots of seminars and courses. From personal observation, I would say that the life span for a non-professional is a lot shorter, probably because they are trading their own money and run out of it more quickly.

I remember sitting next to a relatively new trader at breakfast at one seminar. She was white and shaking, absolutely devasted. She had lost her entire capital of $26,000 overnight on a 'safe' trade on gold. Obviously, it wasn't 'safe', although it was touted as such.

She was following a strategy that involved selling naked puts, which is something you should never do. Not ever. (I will explain later in the book what that means) The strategy relied on the stock or commodity not making a sudden drop, and – you guessed it – it did. She was wiped out. Completely.

Of course, it recovered in the next couple of days and if she had been using a safe strategy, she would have been OK, but it was too late for her. That was the end of her trading career. And she was terrified of going home and explaining to her husband that she had lost their nest egg.

Who Should You Listen To?

Over the years I have seen first-hand many stories like this and heard of lots more. The sad thing is that not only do these people lose all their money, but it also affects them personally. It hurts to lose money, and it hurts a lot to lose ALL your money.

When people are forced out of the market, it really rocks them. All their dreams of financial freedom disappear before their very eyes. It is quite horrible to watch, and I want to make sure that it NEVER happens to you - which it won't if you follow the ITM strategy.

People who have been forced out of the market tend to become the doom and gloom merchants who will tell you how dangerous it is. Again, commiserate and agree with them (don't make them feel worse!) but do not take it on board. That's not going to happen to you.

Always think about who you listen to and take advice from. Guard against being swayed by opinions from those who failed at what you are trying to do.

Would you take beauty advice from someone who looks 10 years older than their age? Diet advice from an obese person? Parenting advice from someone with appallingly-behaved children? Of course not. So why would you take investment advice from someone who has lost all their money?

Think about who you should listen to about trading – someone who has made money on the stock market or someone who has lost money on the stock market?

Dinosaurs and Decisions

The stock market is all about people. In fact, the stock market *is* just a huge group of people, making decisions about what to buy and what to sell. This gives us a big clue about how to recognize and trade the tide.

Most people think the stock market is all about the business and the companies listed on the stock exchange. It's not. It's about what people *feel* about the companies and the market. Notice I said 'feel' not 'think'. That's not a typo. The stock market is just one big mass of people with feelings of hope, fear, and greed, and when you realize this, it becomes easier to understand. It's important to realize that humans make decisions based on emotion and justify them afterward with rationalization.

To really understand the stock market, you have to know how people make decisions. Most people have no idea why they make the decisions they do but will always have an explanation for why they did it. This explanation is not the real reason but what the person thinks is a good rationalization of why they did what they did. To explain this, let's have a very quick look at how the human brain works.

One of the most useful models for understanding how the brain works is in terms of its evolution, with some parts developing before others. In this model, the brain has three separate and distinct sub brains. These sub brains do not operate independently, they are interconnected. And that is where things get interesting.

First, there is the oldest sub-brain, the reptilian brain. It controls vital functions such as breathing, heart rate, body temperature, and balance. It's called the reptilian brain (or sometimes the 'dinosaur brain') because it includes the main structures found in a reptile's brain, the brainstem, and the cerebellum. The dinosaur brain is very reliable and controls vital bodily functions like heart rate, breathing, body temperature, and balance. You don't have to remember to breathe or to tell your heart to keep beating. The reptilian brain does all that for you. It tends, however, to be rigid and compulsive. For example, it doesn't think up innovative ways for your heart to beat or new ways of breathing. When a baby is born it has a reptilian brain. That's what babies need to survive, but there's not a lot of logical thought going on.

The second is the limbic brain, which emerged in the first mammals. It is responsible for emotions, behavior, motivation, and long-term memory. The limbic brain records memories of things that produced good and bad experiences and it operates subconsciously. It is especially involved in emotions related to survival, such as fear, anger, and sexual behavior. It is also responsible for olfaction, the sense of smell, which is powerful and can (metaphorically) transport us back in time. The smell of coffee is a good example. Over 90% of Americans love the aroma of coffee which is 'imprinted' at a very early age and is associated with home, love, and family.

But only 47% like the taste of coffee.

The third part of the brain is the cerebral cortex, which is the thinking or rational part of the brain. It is responsible for language, abstract thought, imagination, and consciousness. It is more complex in humans than in any other species, probably in response to our complex social lives. It is the complexity of the brain rather than the size of the brain that determines how advanced a species is. For example, elephants have a massive brains but are not known for their mastery of rocket science.

What does this have to do with the stock market? Everything! Once we know that decisions are not made in the rational brain, but in the limbic brain or even the dinosaur brain then we can start to make sense of why markets react the way they do. Once we realize that the rational brain justifies decisions *after* they are made, we are able to think and see more clearly than most other traders.

If we think of the people in the last story, who lost all their money on the market, you realize that their decisions were based on emotion. *Fear* (of missing out) was the emotion that got them into the market, *hope* was why they stayed in, *fear* (that they were going to lose all their money) was what got them out, and *revenge* got them back in again. This happens with most traders, even professionals. They make gut decisions, then justify them afterwards with rationalizations.

That's why markets drop suddenly but climb more slowly. Remember *bulls take the stairs; bears jump out the window?* That is because fear is a much stronger emotion than greed. Greed can be a strong emotion, but it doesn't have the intensity of fear. If you see all your lovely money disappearing before your eyes you can't help it: your emotions react immediately.

It is really important to know this about the market. Mass psychology can help us understand what is happening. While you can never predict what one person is going to do, you can often predict what a crowd of people do. It's called 'Crowd Psychology' and it is a legitimate branch of social psychology. Wikipedia is a good place to start if you want to learn more about it.

Combining crowd psychology with looking at what has happened in the markets before (and everything has happened before - there's nothing new in the markets!) we can understand why there is so much 'noise'. Why so many people are trying to justify their decisions with rationalizations, and why so many experts are looking for more and more obscure charts and indicators and signs.

So, you must remember: the market is made up of people buying and selling stocks. People who make decisions on emotion, then justify them with rationalizations. If you remember this, then you are less likely to get caught up in the emotion and will be able to view dispassionately what is happening and take the emotion out of your decisions.

The Market Doesn't Care

Although you are the center of your universe, the market really doesn't care about you. Everyone is equal in its eyes. It doesn't care about who you are, what your qualifications are, your age, your looks, how hard you work, or your family situation.

It just doesn't care. It doesn't judge. It treats everyone the same. It is never nice to its friends and horrible to people it doesn't like. The market just IS. It does what it does.

I find that enormously exciting and freeing. I hope you do too!

In an essay, Warren Buffett, probably the world's most famous investor, explained how his mentor thought of the market:

He said that you should imagine market quotations as coming from a remarkably accommodating fellow named Mr. Market who is your partner in a private business. Without fail, Mr. Market appears daily and names a price at which he will either buy your interest or sell you his.

Even though the business that the two of you own may be stable, Mr. Market's quotations will be anything but. For, sad to say, the poor fellow has incurable emotional problems. At times he feels euphoric, and we can see only the favorable factors affecting the business. When in that mood, he names a very high buy-sell price because he fears that you will snap up his interest and rob him of imminent gains.

At other times he is depressed and can see nothing but trouble ahead for both the business and the world. On these occasions he will name a very low price, since he is terrified that you will unload your interest on him.

Mr. Market has another endearing characteristic: He doesn't mind being ignored. If his quotation is uninteresting to you today, he will back with a new one tomorrow. Transactions are strictly at your option. Under these conditions, the more manic-depressive his behavior, the better for you.

But, like Cinderella at the ball, you must heed one warning or everything will turn into pumpkins and mice: Mr. Market is there to serve you, not to guide you. It is his pocketbook, not his wisdom, that you will find useful. If he shows up someday in a particularly foolish mood, you are free to either ignore him or to take advantage of him, but it will be disastrous if you fall under his influence. Indeed, if you aren't certain that you understand and can value your business far better than Mr. Market you don't belong in the game. As they say in poker, "If you've been in the game 30 minutes and you don't know who the patsy is, you're the patsy."

Lots of investors invoke 'Mr. Market' but usually only after they have done something foolish, and the market has spanked them. While the Mr. Market character is amusing and we can learn from it, I don't think it is the best way to think of the market.

I think that the best way to think of the market is that it is like the ocean. It is huge. Any humans who venture into it are minuscule and don't affect it in any way. Even huge ships don't have any effect on it. The ocean does what it does. Some days it is stormy, some days it is calm. Some days it is grey, some days it is blue. The ocean doesn't care who is swimming or riding the waves. It will roll right over them without a second thought.

One thing we do know about the ocean is that some things it does are predictable. We can tell exactly what time the tide will come in and what time it will go out. We can tell how far it will come in and how far it will go out. But we can't tell if it is going to be calm and blue on our holiday next month.

The tides are predictable, but the waves are not. Although the tide is coming in, not every wave will go higher up the beach than the last wave. There may be a big wave that makes a new high, followed by several waves that don't even reach this new high. We do know that eventually a wave will make a new high, even if we don't know exactly when that will happen. We don't know if it will be the next wave or the one after, but we do know that in 10 minutes there will have been several higher waves. That will keep happening until the tide turns.

If we think of the tide as the market direction, the 'trend', and the waves as 'noise' we are coming closer to understanding how we can ride the markets safely. We are going to catch the tide and ignore the waves. We are going to ride the trend and shut out the noise. It can be hard to shut out the noise, but you have to do it otherwise you will be like our hapless people who lost their money.

It's A Short Life

Active traders tend to be in and out of trades, but just as surfers can't catch every wave on every beach, traders can't catch every fluctuation. That's why most traders have a limited life span as a trader.

I have known hundreds of traders (or people who fancied themselves as traders) and most have been 'temporary traders'. Only a handful have managed to survive in the markets for more than a few years. As the economist John Maynard Keynes said:

The market can stay irrational longer than you can stay solvent.

Investors ride the tides. Traders ride the waves. With the strategy that I am going to explain you will be riding the tide, not the waves. But you will do it in a boat with a very powerful motor!

There are many ways that people, say that you can stay safe in the market. Generally, they are unsuccessful traders who are trying to make money by selling you an education course or a system. One of the favorite 'safe' strategies is what is called a 'trailing stop'.

Let's say you bought a stock for $50 and being careful that you don't lose your money you put a stop in at $48. What this means is that you put in an order to sell if the price drops to $48. If it goes up to $52 then your stop 'trails' after the increased price and the sell order is moved up to $50. If the price increases again, then the sell order follows it, always $2 less than the current stock price. That sounds good, doesn't it? Nice and safe?

Actually, in practice, it is a good way of making sure that you always sell your stock at the worst possible time. Remember our ocean analogy? Well, it's useful here to understand why people crash and burn using trailing stops. Stock prices don't go up in a straight line, there is 'noise'. Even a stock that is rising strongly has down movements, sometimes quite large.

If you have a trailing stop, you will be likely to be stopped on one of these transitory down movements. Then when the stock rises again, you see that the trend is intact, so you buy your shares back, but at a higher price than you sold them.

The Problem with Trailing Stops

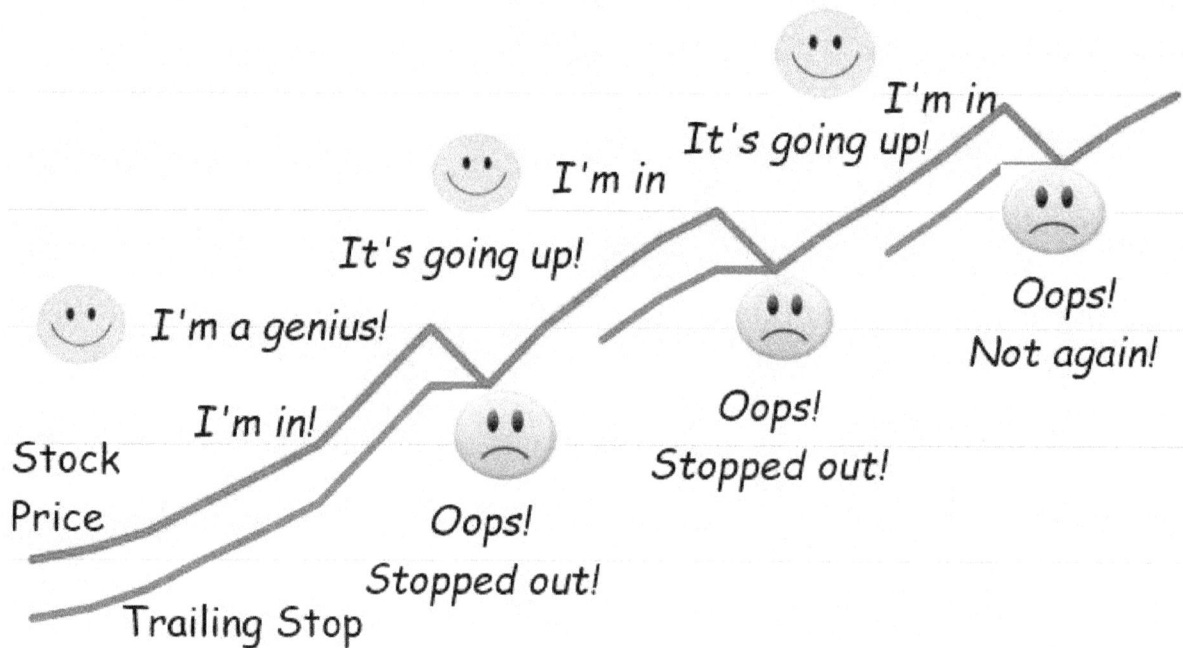

Let's say you buy 100 shares at $50, costing you a total of $5,000. The share price drops, but your trailing stop gets you out at $48. You've only lost $200 (plus brokerage, of course. Every trade costs you money, although now some brokers have commission-free trades, more of that later.) The stock starts to rise again. and you see it going up again so you buy back in at $52, but of course since you now have only $4,800 you can only buy 92 shares this time. It goes up to $53 and your trailing stop follows it, so that it is now $51. The stock then drops to $51, and your trailing stop does its job and gets you out. You've only lost $92; you still have $4,708.

The stock starts to rise again, and you get in again, but at a higher price than you sold so you can buy even fewer stocks . . .

Does this sound familiar? It's the same as the people we talked about earlier, just in reverse. Even though the stock is rising strongly your capital is being depleted. You are owning fewer and fewer stocks bought at higher and higher prices. Not a very safe strategy at all!

Other 'Safe Strategies'

Other strategies that supposedly keep you safe in the market perform just as badly. You may have heard of the advice that you can't go wrong buying 'blue-chip' stocks. By 'blue-chip' stocks we mean a very large company with a market capitalization in the billions. But just because they are huge doesn't mean that they can't go bust. Or just fade away. Think Lehman Brothers (which had $691 billion in assets in 2008), WorldCom, General Motors, Enron, Chrysler – all blue-chip stocks in their time.

'Dollar cost averaging' is another strategy to keep away from. This is where you buy the same dollar amount of a stock at regular intervals (e.g., every year or every 6 months), no matter what the cost of the stock is. This is as silly as it sounds. It is hard to believe anyone falls for it, but you would be surprised at how many people and institutions spruik it.

You'll Be In Good Company

So, what is the alternative? Firstly, I advise – strongly - that you do NOT buy individual stocks, unless it is with money you are prepared to lose. That's too risky, way too risky. I know, I have been there myself. There are few things as annoying as waking up to the news that the stock you bought yesterday is expected to plunge because the latest mining report shows that there wasn't any gold after all, or the surprise resignation of the CEO because he was having an affair with a staff member. What you paid $8,000 for yesterday is now worth $2,000. That quite wrecks your day.

This was one of my early 'lessons' from the stock market. I had just upped the amount I was investing in each stock from $5K to $8K – and the first stock I bought at the new level was suddenly worth practically nothing the next day. I remember walking around in a daze that day, in shock and wondering if it was even possible to make money on the markets. I was still working in my day job at the time, but I don't think I was terribly useful that day!

The stock market gives you lessons all the time. The difference between investors who last in the market and temporary traders is whether you listen to the lessons it is giving you. And losses? Hey, I have had heaps in my time, although (luckily) never enough to wipe me out completely. But all these losses have taught me valuable lessons, and I think that I have learned from them.

I think of the losses now as 'tuition fees.' I didn't make that up, although I wish I had. It comes from a book written almost 100 years ago by the original Wolf of Wall Street. It is called Reminiscences of a Stock Operator and it is written by Edwin LeFevre. It is my favorite book on the stock market, and I recommend it, it is definitely worth a read.

When I analyze why I lost money it was never the market's fault. It was mine. The market does what the market does. **I** made the bad decision, all by myself. No one was standing over me, forcing me to click on 'buy'. I did that, all by myself. It is important in the market, as in life, to take responsibility for your own decisions.

When I analyze *why* I made a bad decision it has practically always been through a lack of confidence in my own judgement and listening to someone else's advice. My gut feeling - or my heart, whichever you prefer - was saying *this person knows what he is talking about - after all he has a cool website and lots of followers. Do you think you know better than him? Who do you think you are? Go with his advice!*

My head was saying *come on, you know better than that! Remember what happened last time you listened to him! Don't do it!* If I went with my gut feeling instead of listening to my head, I usually lost money. And that's always painful.

Time and Tide

To sum up, you can predict the tide in the market but not the waves. You can't trade the market tide in an individual stock. That's why we are going to trade the SPY, the S&P 500 ETF (Exchange Traded Fund – this will be explained in the next chapter), the biggest ETF in the world. You will be in good company.

Warren Buffett recently revealed what is in his will about his children's inheritance. He has ordered it to be placed in an S&P 500 Index fund because in his words: *the long-term results from this policy will be superior to those attained by most investors – whether pension funds, institutions, or individuals – who employ high-fee managers.*

Which is what we are going to be doing – except we are going to be turbo-charging our results to get even better returns.

Chapter 2 Highlights

The major points in Chapter 2 are:

> ➢ The stock market is just a mass of people with emotions who make decisions based on these emotions.

> ➢ We can't predict what one person will do – but we can often predict what the market is going to do by looking at what has happened before.

> ➢ Most market traders have a short life because they don't know how to trade safely.

> ➢ Many of the touted safe ways to trade (dollar-cost averaging, blue chips, trailing stops etc.) are NOT safe.

> ➢ We are going to trade with the tide, using the biggest ETF in the world - with turbocharged results as an extra bonus.

And finally, some more words of wisdom this time from Warren Buffett:

Wide diversification is only required when investors do not understand what they are doing.

❖❖❖

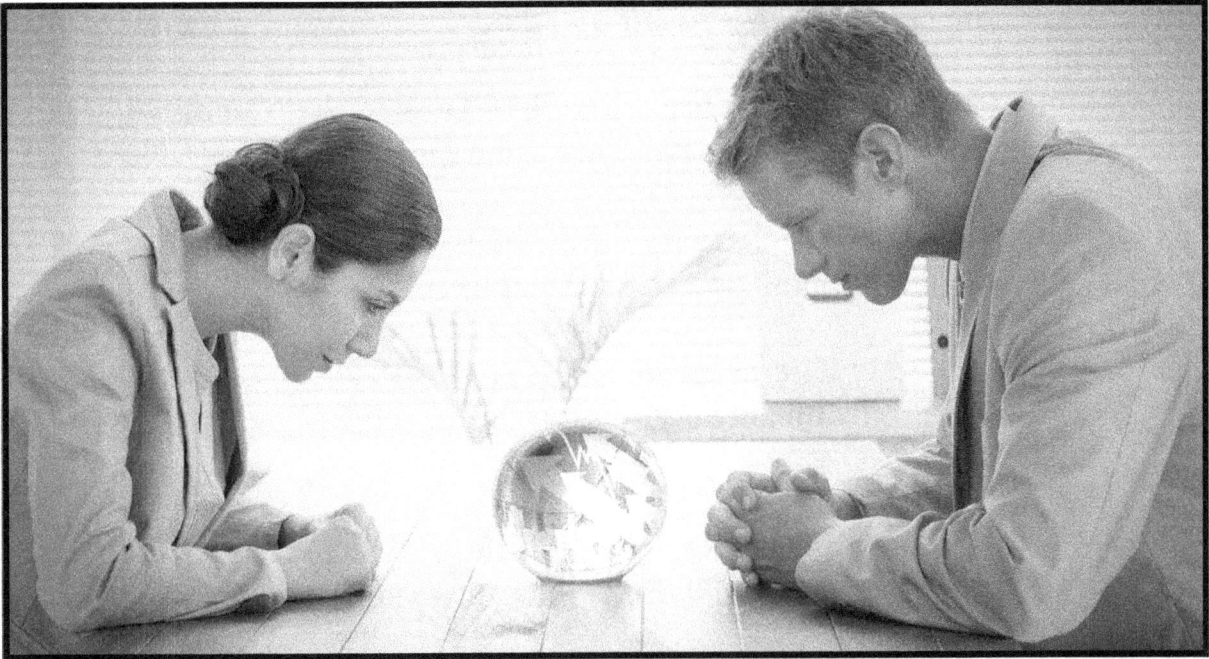

Chapter 3. Voodoo Science

What is the market going to do tomorrow? Next week? Next month? Next year? Ask the question and you will have hundreds of market experts lining up to give their opinion. And that is exactly what it is: just their opinion. Here is the correct answer:

We don't know.

That's right, *we don't know what the market is going to do*. And neither does anyone else! It is really important for your sanity and success to remember that. When you read the articles predicting a catastrophic drop or a wonderful rise remember that it is just someone's opinion. They don't have any special knowledge of the future or a crystal ball that works.

If you ever need to have the truth of this brought home to you (and want a laugh) read the previous opinions of experts. As a sample, look at these from some well-known pundits going back some years and in which time the SPY has more than tripled:

> ➤ 2018 November: **70% market crash in 2019** - Ted Bauman,

Economist. *The market went up 32%.*

> 2017 January: **Bubble bursting 2018 Dow to drop to 3,800** - Harry Dent, Financial Author. *The lowest the Dow went was 21,792.*

> 2016 January: **Sell everything, brace for A cataclysmic year** - Royal Bank of Scotland. *The market went up 12%.*

> 2015 March: **The crash of 2016 is really coming. Dead ahead** - Paul B Farrell, Financial columnist. *The market barely moved, up 1%.*

> 2014 July: **Stocks are in a bubble and will crash** - Ron Paul. *Stocks moved up slightly during the next year.*

> 2013 March: **60% stock market collapse in the next 3 months** - Chris Martensen, Economic Researcher. *The stock market went up 8%.*

> 2012 November: **The data is clear, 50% unemployment, a 90% stock market drop and 100% annual inflation starting in 2013** - Robert Wiedemer, Economist. *The market went up 33%.*

All these bearish predictions proved hopelessly wrong. You would think the experts who made them would be hideously embarrassed about how wrong they were, yet they don't seem to be. They just keep on making predictions! You would also think that people would stop listening to them. But no, these experts still predict that a crash is imminent. They still get publicity. And people still think they are worth listening to. Go figure!

It's not just the bears that get it wrong – the bulls have their share of shame. Some bullish books:

> Dow 30,000 by 2008. Why It's Different This Time (Robert Zucarro 2001)

> Dow 36,000 (James K. Glassman & Kevin A. Hassett 1999)
> Dow 40,000 (David Elias 1999)

➢ Dow 40,000 (Harry Dent, 2000)

The Dow is currently (December 2021) 34,500 more than 20 years after these predictions were made. It's obviously somewhat short of the bullish predictions! It's no coincidence that these books are published shortly before a market crash, in this case the 'tech wreck' of 2000.

Remember the end of the quote from chapter 1 'Bull markets die in euphoria'? These book titles all sound rather euphoric. As I mentioned before, if you hear the words 'This Time It's Different' (and that was even in one of the book titles) it should alert you to a coming market top, and you should be preparing to get out of the market.

It's not just the market that the experts get wrong. Experts on individual stocks also get it hopelessly wrong:

➢ **Netflix Overvalued** (2003, Paul La Monica)

- Netflix 2003: $11
- Netflix 2021: $602

➢ **Google's stock will be highly disappointing** (2004, Whitney Tilson)

- Google 2004: $50
- Google 2021 $2,893

➢ **NO! NO! NO! Bear Sterns is fine. Don't move your money from Bear, that's just being silly.** (Jim Cramer March 11, 2008)

- Bear Sterns March 11, 2008: $60
- Bear Sterns March 16, 2008: $2

Listening to market commentary by 'financial experts' is a sure-fire way of being wrong – so don't listen. Look for yourself.

Voodoo School

The question then is: if we don't know what the stock market is going to do how do **we** know what to do? This is where smart traders are separated from what I call temporary traders. We don't know what the stock market is going to do but we know what traders are likely to do. Not all traders of course, and certainly not individual traders, but we have indications of how the majority of traders behave under certain conditions and when faced with certain circumstances, and this gives us an edge.

When I first decided to get into the stock market many years ago, I did the 'smart' thing. I enrolled in an education course and paid a lot of money for the privilege. Nowadays there are hundreds of courses but 25 years ago this was quite unusual. Looking back, it was a pretty flaky course, but at the time I was very excited because I thought that these 'experts' were going to teach me how to get rich, preferably very quickly.

I knew that the founder and owner of the company owned a very big and very expensive catamaran which was berthed at a local yacht club. It was painted a rather questionable pink, with the name of the company on the side and on the sails. Clearly, he had a lot of money. What I didn't realize was that he didn't get rich from trading or investments. Oh no. The money came from idiots like me who paid to take his courses!

In one session the instructor was going through a long list of technical indicators which were supposed to predict what a stock is going to do. He talked knowledgeably about stochastics, bollinger bands, momentum, oscillators, fibonacci sequences, and many, many more. He explained how they were calculated and how to read them. But what he DIDN'T tell us was if any of them worked.

Which was my question. I asked politely *Which of the indicators are the most reliable in predicting future price movements?* To me, that seemed like the most obvious thing that we needed to know. My thought was what is the point of telling us all this stuff unless we know which indicators work and which don't?

I was sitting right at the back, and I can remember 19 pairs of eyes turning to look at me in disbelief. What I thought was a logical and reasonable question evidently wasn't logical or reasonable to anyone else.

But, I thought, I have paid a lot of money for this course and the least the instructor can do is to answer my question. Which he did, and I have never forgotten it: *You choose one or 2 that are your favorites and use them.*

That was it. Pick your favorites. It clearly didn't answer the question, so I clarified: *There are a lot of indicators – which ones work best? And in what circumstances?* This was met with: *I think that I have answered your question. Now can we move on?* There was a lot of murmuring and nodding in agreement from all the other guys in the audience (and guys they were - I was the only female) so we went on to look at yet more indicators.

If you think about the situation above, you get the reason there are so many temporary traders. *You pick your favorites.* But on what basis did you make your choice? Because you liked the name? Because you understood how it was calculated? (some of them are pretty complicated and not easy to understand). Because your friend said it was the best? Because it sounded cool?

It alerted me to the fact that most traders are not objective or logical, and that although they may use lots of complicated indicators they depend to some extent on feelings and superstition rather than quantifiable facts. I have talked with hundreds of traders over the years, and it has only confirmed that suspicion. I even heard of one trader who had spent hundreds of thousands of dollars developing a software system that was going to beat the market and this system had at its heart your birth date which had to be entered before it could do its stuff!

This probably explains why most traders are temporary traders. But we are not going to be temporary traders. The strategy we are going to use is quantifiable, and all our figures are replicable because they are based on the actual data.

To conclude the story, that particular Stock Market Education company is no more. They expanded, then actually listed on the stock exchange. Its price soared from 50 cents up to $2.10 before plummeting to 1.5 cents! Then they were delisted. I never saw him, or his pink boat, ever again.

Unpacking the Voodoo

Having spent years researching and back testing many indicators and combinations of indicators I can tell you some good news: *some of them work some of the time*. That's the best news I can give you. Indicators work some of the time, but not all, or even most of, the time.

The bad news is there is no way of telling which indicator is going to work when and in what situation. They are, necessarily, describing what has already happened not what is going to happen.

However, traders keep on using them, and this is something that gives us an advantage. If we know what people are going to do, based on the indicators, then we have a good indication of what the market is going to do.

For example, if we know that traders watch the 50-day moving average and we see the stock price fall through it then we know that further falls are likely as traders see this as an indication that it will continue to fall. In other words, it is a self-fulfilling prophecy.

To see how we can use this to our advantage we need to do a crash course in stock market charts so that we understand what they are telling us.

Candlestick Charts

If we want to summarize what a stock did on any day, then there are four measures that are important:
> The open price
> The close price
> The highest price
> The lowest price

The easiest way to think of these four figures is pictorially using a candlestick. Here are 2 typical candlesticks:

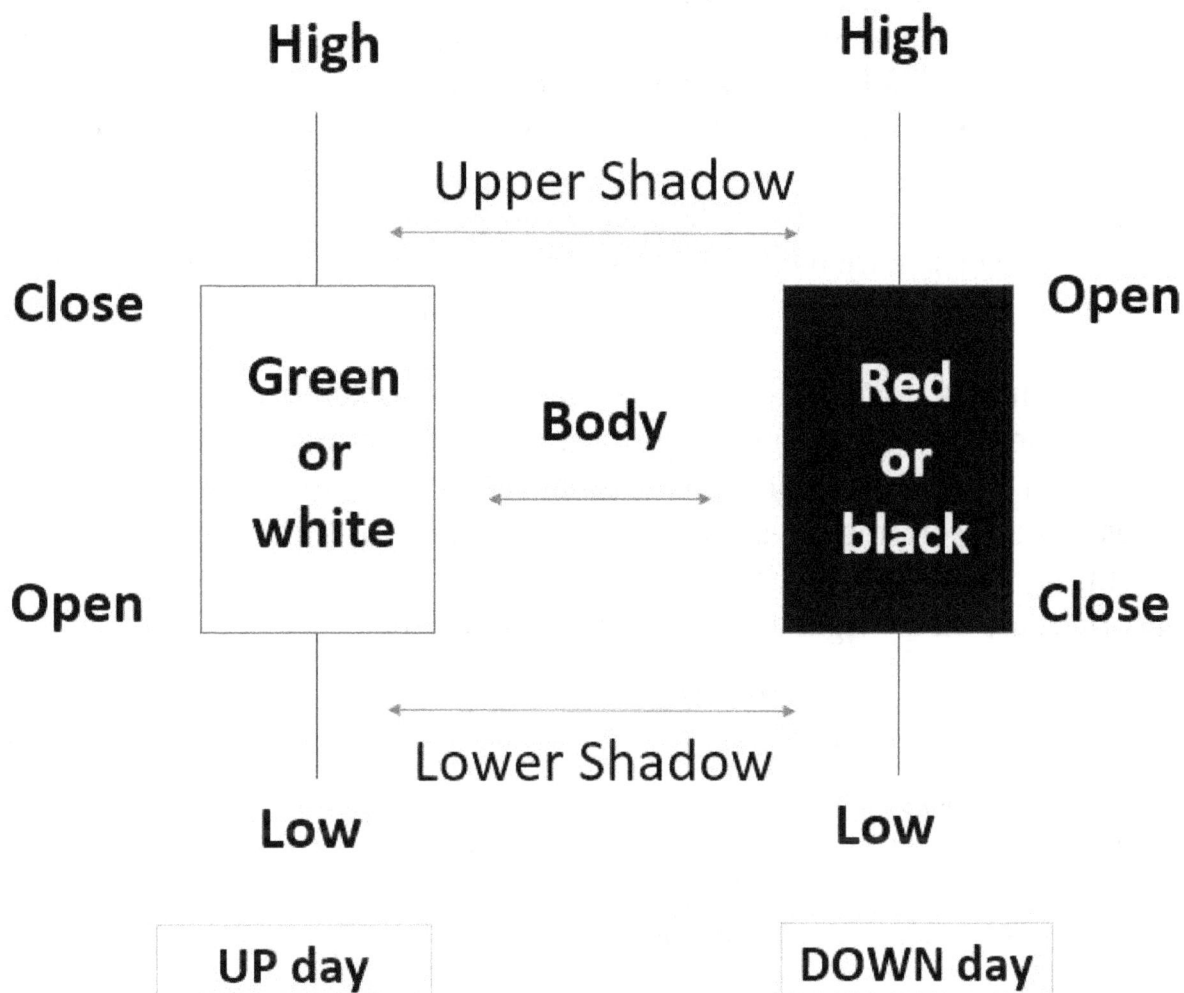

	High			High	
Close		Upper Shadow			Open
		Green or white	Body	Red or black	
Open					Close
	Low	Lower Shadow		Low	
	UP day			**DOWN day**	

Candlesticks are colored red or black if the close price is lower than the open price (a DOWN day) and green or white if the open price is higher than the close (an UP day). The colored part is called the **body** of the candle, and the lines at the top and the bottom are called the **shadows**. Normally in charting apps red and green are used, but if the chart is in black and white, up days are white and down days are black.

We are using a daily chart and will be throughout the book unless stated otherwise, but charts can be for any time period. They can be weekly, monthly, quarterly, or yearly. They can be hourly, every 15 minutes or every minute. The same candlesticks are used no matter what time period you are using. Traders choose the time period that most suits their way of trading, and in our case, this is the daily chart.

Day traders (temporary traders!) will use 5-minute or even 1-minute charts. Long-term investors may only look at weekly or monthly charts. We will be looking at daily charts and sometimes weekly charts just to check that we have the bigger picture.

Remember our analogy of the market and the ocean? Well, the 5-minute and 1-minute charts are the waves. The daily and weekly charts tell you about the tide.

To see how a stock performs over time we can look at a candlestick chart. We read the date on the bottom axis and the price on the side axis. On most charts, you have the option of changing your cursor to 'crosshairs' which makes reading off the axes easier. Here is the chart for Google in 2020 showing the big dip because of the coronavirus, and subsequent recovery. The prices are on the right and the date on the bottom.

A Day Trader's Day

I am not suggesting that you become a day trader. Perish the thought! That is the fastest way to the poorhouse. However, seeing how a day trader's day unfolds from market open to market close will give you an insight into how candles form.

If we look at the candle for an up day, it opens at the bottom of the body. Anyone buying at that time will be watching with their heart in their mouth as the price proceeds to drop.

Then, at some stage (the bottom of the lower shadow) the price has dropped sufficiently so that traders think 'that looks like good value' and start to buy, pushing the price up.

As more buyers join in the price gets pushed up, but then at some stage traders think 'Hey, this has gone up a bit too much', and stop buying. This is when we are at the top of the upper shadow.

Some traders start to sell, but there are no buyers at the top price, so they have to drop their price to get the sale. At the end of the day, we are at the top end of the body. It's been an up day but didn't finish at its highest point.

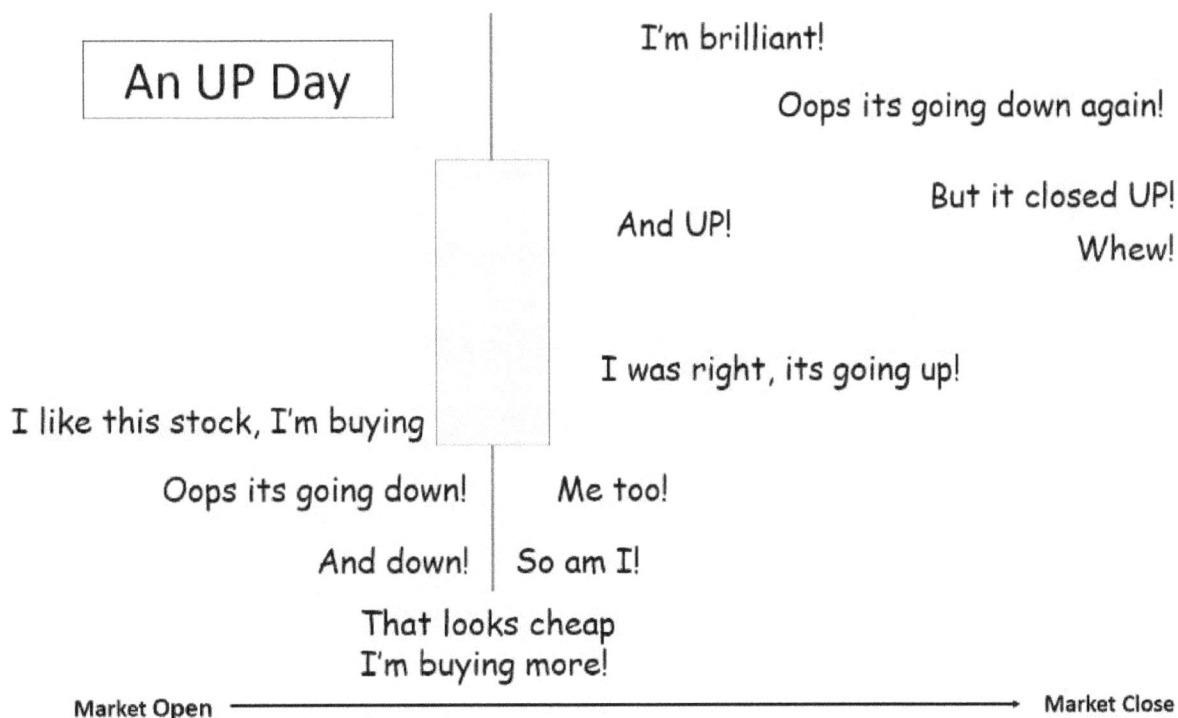

An UP Day

I'm brilliant!

Oops its going down again!

But it closed UP!
Whew!

And UP!

I was right, its going up!

I like this stock, I'm buying

Oops its going down!   Me too!

And down!   So am I!

That looks cheap
I'm buying more!

Market Open ⟶ Market Close

Of course, it does not always proceed in an orderly manner as I have described above. It can go up and down several times in a day, revisiting and changing the high and low prices. You can see this by looking at a 1 hour or

5-minute chart – but beware. It is addictive.

You can get fascinated and end up just watching for hours. I know, I have done it many times. And you know what's funny? It doesn't make any difference! The market does what the market does whether you watch it or not.

For a down day, typically the buyers start to buy driving the price up, then reach the point where traders start to think that they have driven the price up too high. They start to sell, but there is no one prepared to buy at the high price, so they have to lower their sell price and the price starts dropping.

The price keeps dropping, right through the open price and carries on south. Eventually, traders think that it has dropped enough, and the stock is good value at this price, so they start buying, driving the price up again. It doesn't reach the open price by market close, so it is a down day.

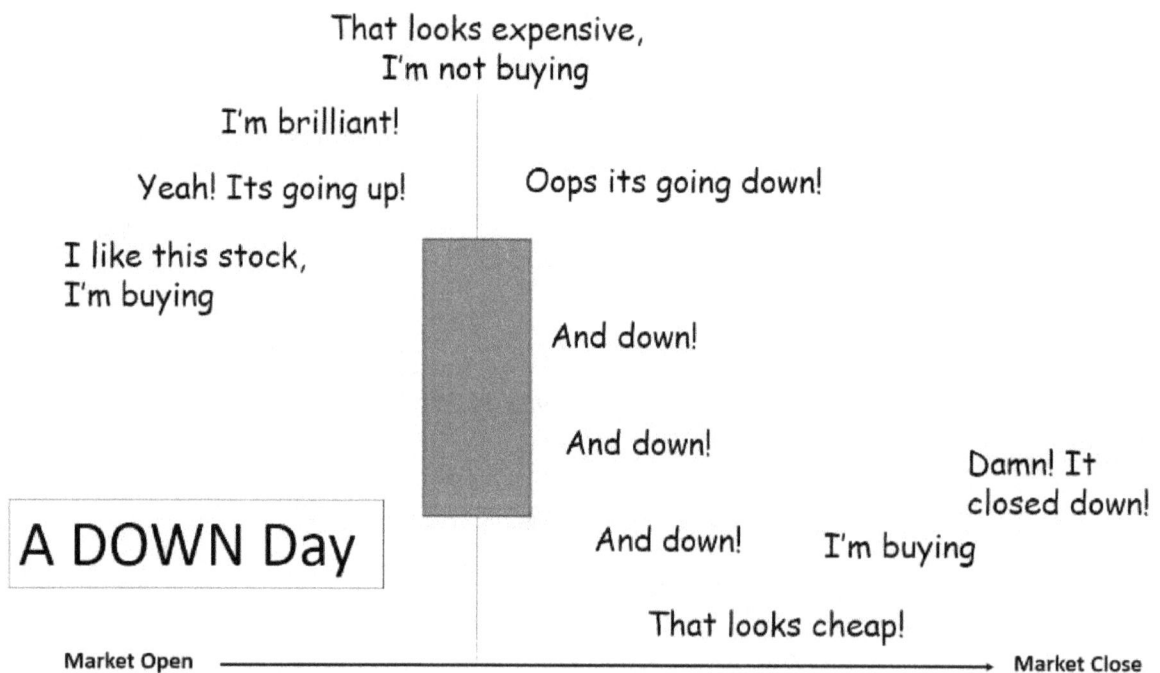

That looks expensive,
I'm not buying

I'm brilliant!

Yeah! Its going up!   Oops its going down!

I like this stock,
I'm buying

And down!

And down!
Damn! It
closed down!

A DOWN Day   And down!   I'm buying

That looks cheap!

Market Open ————————————————→ Market Close

Looks DO Count

Candlesticks can look wildly different. The body can be short or long, or even just a horizontal line which would mean that the open and close price was the same. The shadows may be short or long, there may be only one shadow, or there may be no shadows at all.

The different types of candlesticks mean different things, and this is a whole area of technical analysis, but all are describing the actions of traders and hence the mood of the market.

Individual candle types can have names, and some combinations of candles have names. However, all are a diagrammatical representation of traders' emotions in the market.

> Long body candles show that there is a lot of buying (green) or selling (red) pressure.

> Short body candles show that there is very little price movement because traders think that the stock is priced correctly.

> Short shadows show that most of the trading was near or between the open and close.

> Long upper shadows show that buyers (bulls) dominated for a while, bidding the price up, then the sellers (bears) forced the prices down.

> Long lower shadows show that sellers (bears) dominated for a while, driving the price down, then buyers (bulls) came back in and forced the prices up.

Let's look at some of the common candlesticks and their interpretations. Many of the candlestick and pattern names are Japanese because that is where candlesticks as a representation of prices originated.

The Marubozu

Long body candles are important, and perhaps the most important one is the Marubozu which has no shadows at all, either lower or upper. The name comes from the Japanese, and means close-cropped – i.e., bald or shaven.

The shadows have been shaved off.

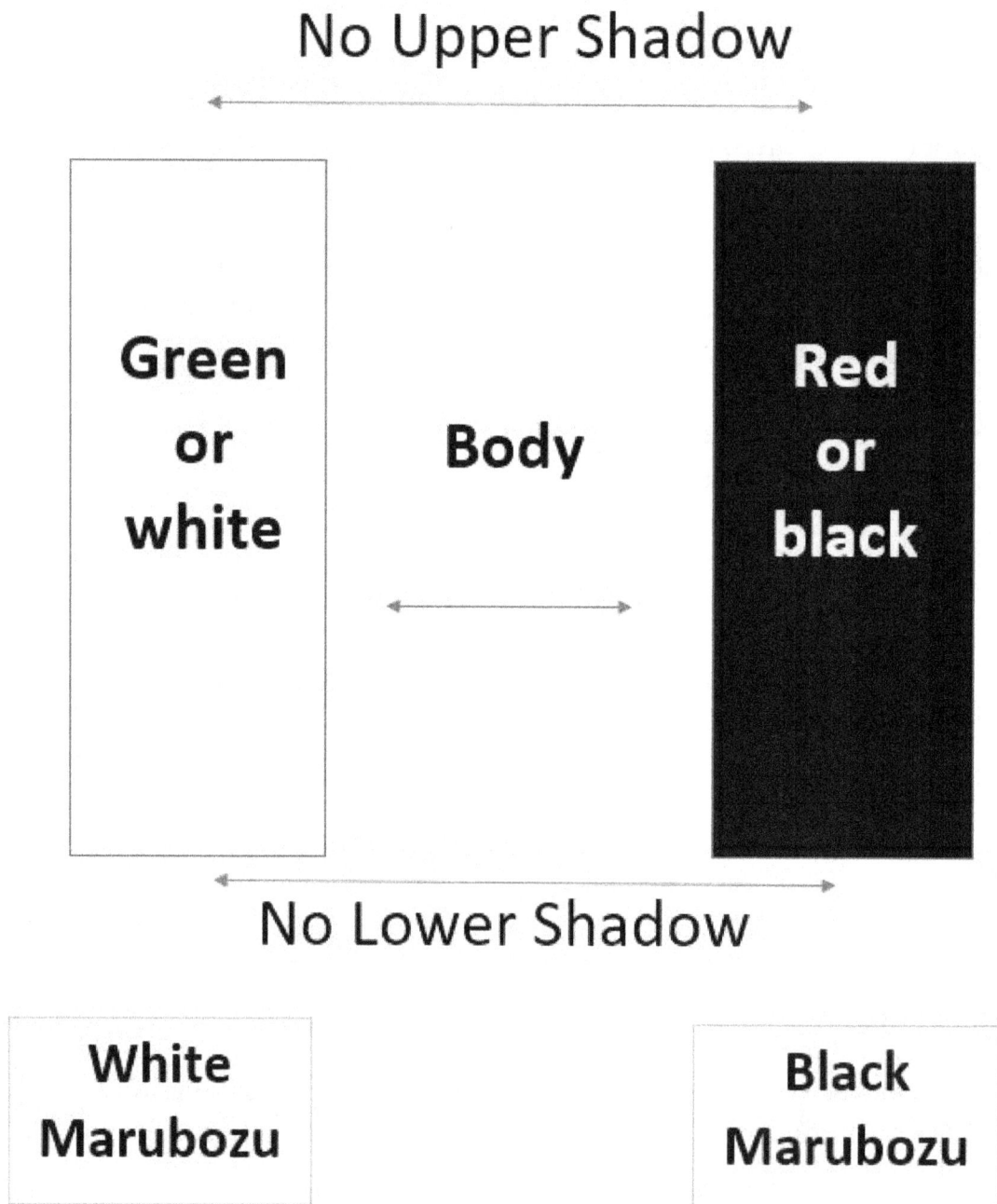

No Upper Shadow

Green or white	Body	Red or black

No Lower Shadow

White Marubozu	Black Marubozu

A Marubozu is significant as it shows that the stock has been trading strongly in one direction. All the trading took place between the open and the close price. Not having any shadows means that traders were generally in accordance with what the price was doing.

➢ The White Marubozu (normally green in colored charts) shows that there was strong buying. Traders forced the price up and the bulls (buyers) dominated for the whole day.

➢ The Black Marubozu (normally red in colored charts) shows that the bears (sellers) were in control for the whole day, and there were not enough bulls (buyers) to reverse the downward price action

A Marubozu is viewed as being a continuance pattern. If a white Marubozu occurs during an uptrend, then it signals that the uptrend will continue. If a black Marubozu occurs during a downtrend it signals that the downtrend is going to continue. However, as with all indicators sometimes they work and sometimes they don't. One of the confirming signals that you can look for is the volume. A Marubozu that happens on a day with a high volume is more significant than one on a day where the volume is low.

The Doji

The Doji is one of the most easily recognized and looked-for candles. It is formed when the open and close prices are the same, or very nearly the same, which means that it has a very small body. The appearance of a Doji shows that the market has not been able to decide if the stock should go to the upside or to the downside.

One explanation of the name Doji is that it comes from the Japanese word for a 'fool, or foolish thing'. In other words, traders can't make up their mind whether to push this stock up or down, so while it may move around during the trading day it ends up much the same. Another explanation is that it means a blunder, bungle, or clumsiness.

Types of Doji

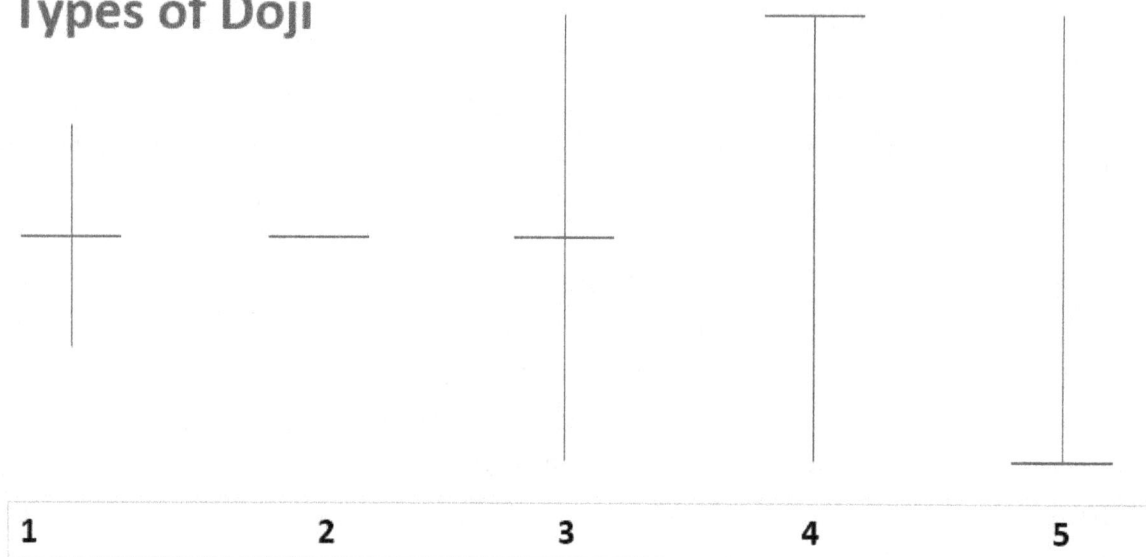

1	2	3	4	5

There are many different types of Doji, and they tend not to be hugely significant on their own, but as part of a larger candlestick pattern. However, you need to be able to recognize a Doji when you see one, so the diagram above gives the different types.

1.   Normal Doji (sometimes called a star Doji)
2.   Four-Price Doji (no shadows)
3.   Long legged Doji
4.   Dragonfly Doji
5.   Gravestone Doji.

Of course, the candles don't always look exactly like the diagrams, as in practice the open and close are rarely exactly the same, and the gravestone and dragonfly Dojis may not have the cross exactly at the top. The following would also classify as the 5 types above:

· Types of Doji

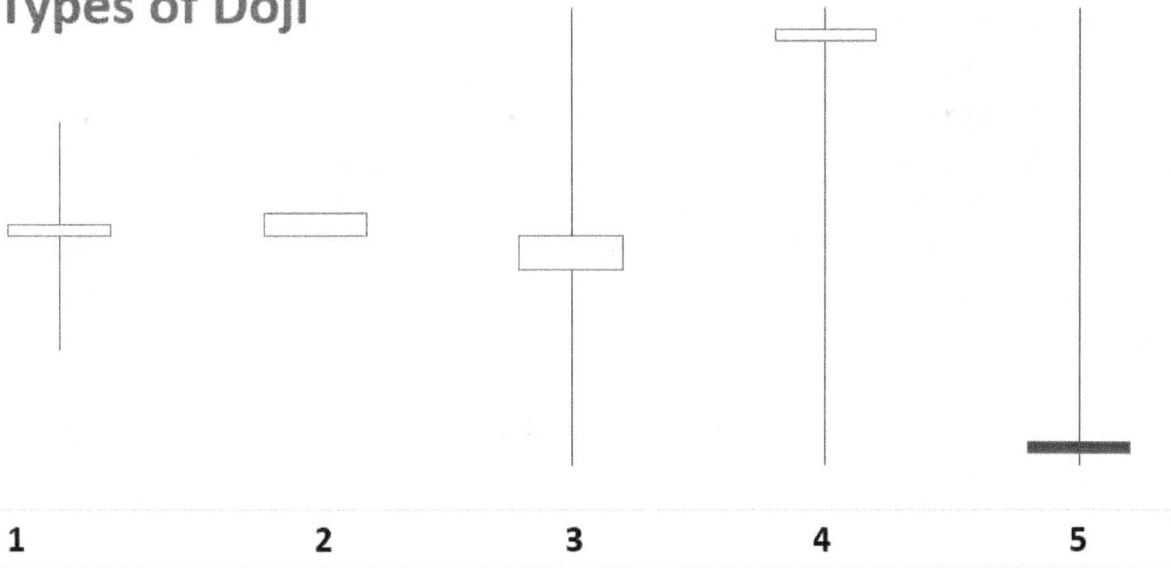

1	2	3	4	5

A related candle is a 'spinning top' which is a Doji with a larger body.

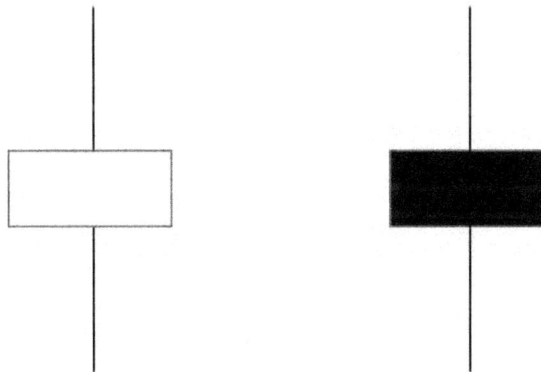

Spinning Tops

On its own, a Doji is not particularly significant, but it can be very significant when combined with other candles. The Doji in some combinations can signify the top or the bottom of a trend. Some of these combinations have very evocative names:

> Abandoned baby

> ➤ Evening star
> ➤ Hanging man
> ➤ Shooting star

To look at one example, the abandoned baby pattern can be either bullish or bearish, depending on which way the market has been trending. If the bullish abandoned baby puts in an appearance after the market, or stock, has been trending down, it signals that the trend is probably reversing and going up. The pattern is not complete until the candlestick after it is green and higher.

Conversely, the bearish abandoned baby appears at the top of an uptrend, and signals that the trend will probably reverse and start going down.

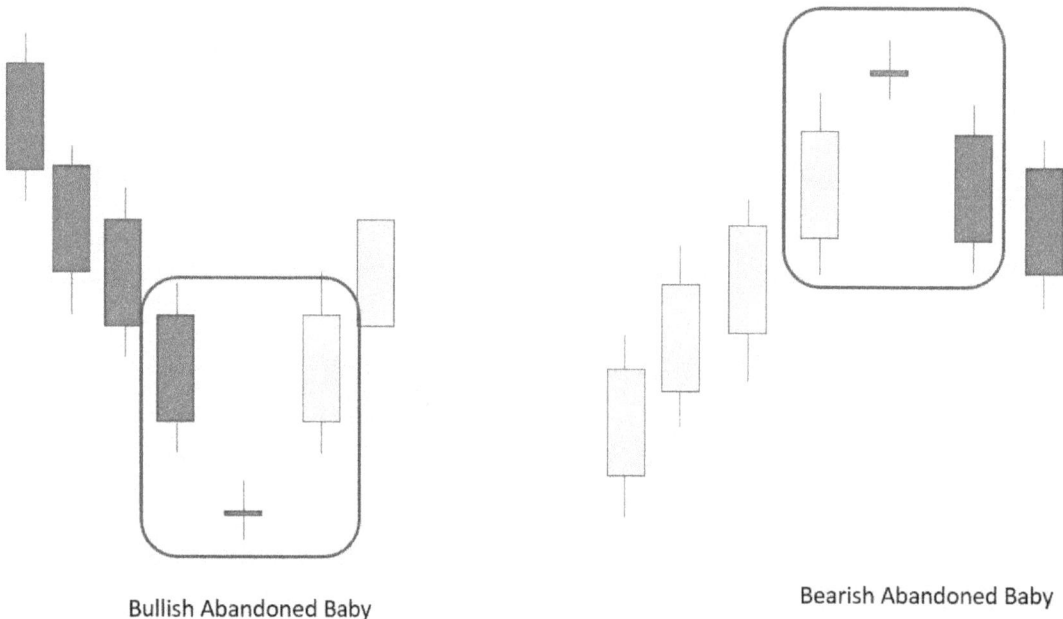

Bullish Abandoned Baby

Bearish Abandoned Baby

Other Combinations

There are many combinations that are significant but do not include the Doji, for example:

> ➤ Stick sandwich
> ➤ Three black crows

➢ Upside Tasuki gap
➢ Bearish engulfing

There are many more candlestick patterns. I could write a book just about candles! But we are going to leave it here. They are fascinating and very useful in some circumstances. If you want to read more about candlesticks, then just google 'candlesticks' or 'candlestick charts.' There are several (free) websites that give good overviews of the main patterns. We are going to leave it here because to do the ITM strategy you don't need to know candlestick patterns in detail.

All that is needed is a basic understanding of candles so that we can read stock charts. We need to understand that they are simply giving us a picture of the market's emotion (or rather the emotions of traders in the market) and using this we can work out what the market is doing and what it is most likely to do next.

Candlesticks are useful for reading the emotion of the market, but you don't need to know a lot of fancy names to be able to read what they are saying.

Technical Analysis and Indicators

Now that we know about candlestick charts, we know it gives us a picture us what traders are thinking and feeling. It tells us all about the behavior of a stock up until the present time. The next logical question would be **what is going to happen next? Where is the market going to go from here?**

If anyone knew the answer to that then they would be a trillionaire! The correct answer is that nobody **knows** what the market is going to do, but we can tell what the market is **likely** to do. We can do this by analyzing the charts and using indicators that often forecast market trends. These indicators are based on the data in the charts and try to predict whether the market is likely to go up and down from here.

This is another good news / bad news story. The bad news is that there are hundreds of indicators, most of them very complicated. The good news is that the simplest ones work better than the complicated ones. For our strategy, we are choosing the 2 most effective indicators. They are effective mainly because they are the ones that most other traders use, which is why they are better at predicting what those traders are likely to do. The indicators we are going to learn about are:

> Lines
> Moving averages

Compared with the 'DecisionPoint Intermediate-Term Breadth Momentum Oscillator' or the 'Pring's Diffusion Indicator' or the 'Klinger Volume Oscillator' they are a walk in the park. If you can draw a line and know what an average is, then you're already on top of it. Now what we have to do is work out where we are putting these lines and what they mean.

Support and Resistance

A Support Line is simply a horizontal line drawn on a chart that shows the price under which a stock is unlikely to fall. The stock price is 'supported' at this level, as every time it falls towards that level it bounces back up again What is happening is that as the price of the stock falls traders notice and start to think that the stock is getting 'cheap' and good value, so they start to buy. This forces the price up away from the support line.

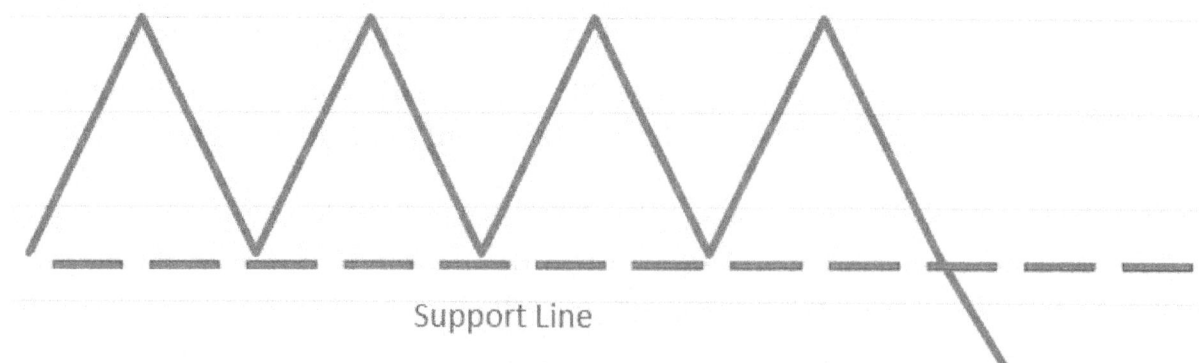

Support Line

This human behavior can be seen in any buying situation, whether real estate, cars, clothes, whatever. There is always a price where the potential buyer thinks *that's too good a bargain to miss* and moves in to buy it. If the support line is broken and the stock starts to trade under it, this is a bearish sign. Traders have no idea when the price may stop falling, so often they dump their stocks, accelerating the falls.

A Resistance line is exactly the opposite. It's where traders think that the stock looks 'expensive' and are not willing to buy if it is over that price. Traders who own the stock get nervous and start to sell their holdings, and as there are few buyers the price goes down. Every time the stock gets to that level it stops and the price starts falling back as buyers melt away.

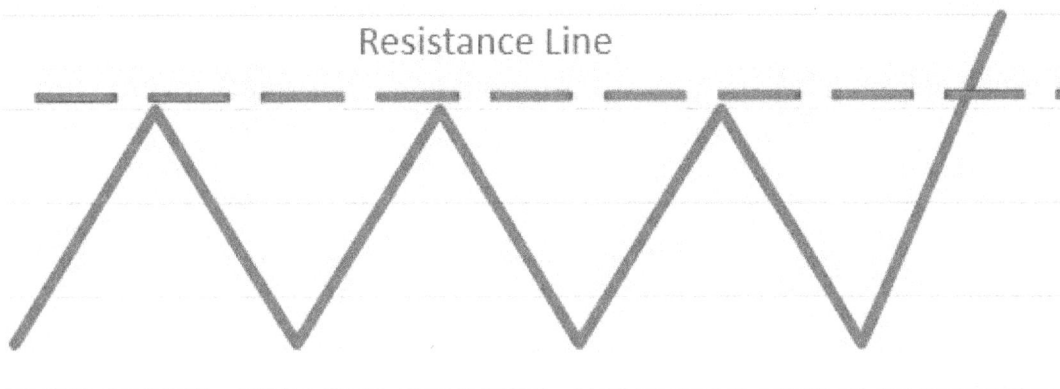

Resistance Line

Sooner or later (usually) it gets through this resistance line and that is a bullish sign that it now has enough momentum to keep going up for a while. This is one of the signals that traders use to enter a stock trade as it often continues to go up for some time. This is termed a 'breakout' and traders are always looking for these.

Often, the stock will retrace and 'test' the resistance line, which gives us another useful understanding. Previous resistance lines often become support lines.

It is normal behavior to bounce off support and resistance several times before breaking upwards (or downwards, that can happen too) and this is called a trading channel.

Trend lines

Trend lines are simply straight lines that are drawn on a chart to show which way the stock has been going. The 'has been' is significant. The reason we draw trend lines is that we are assuming or hoping that the stock will continue along the trend line so that we can trade accordingly. Now we know that **no one** can say what a stock is going to do tomorrow, next week, next month, or next year, but the good news is that they **often** follow the trend lines – that is, until they don't!

Up Trend

There are rules for drawing trend lines:

➢ Uptrend trend lines are drawn connecting 2 or more LOW points.

➢ Downtrend trend lines are drawn connecting 2 or more HIGH points

➢ At least 3 points must be connected for a trend line to be VALID

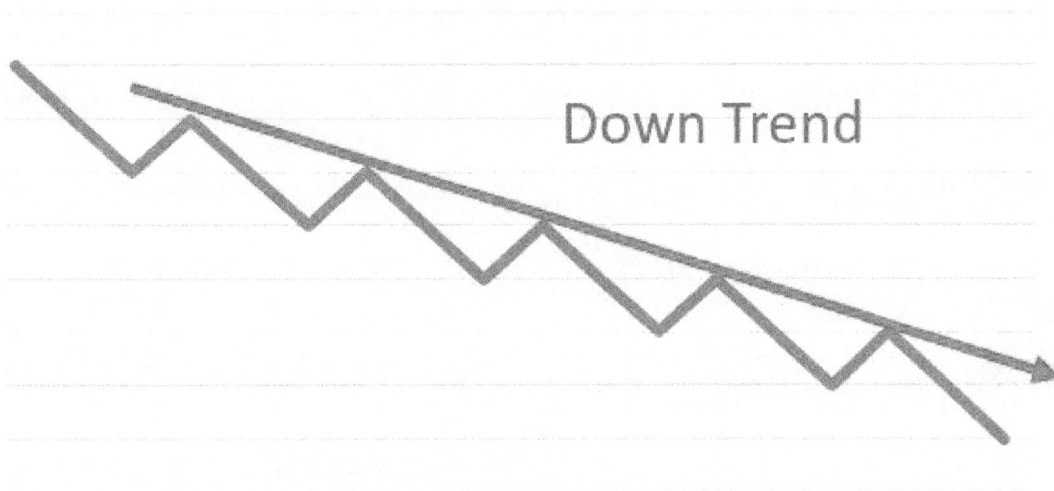

Down Trend

When you start to look at charts, drawing in the trend lines is good because it takes away all the noise, by which we mean the daily ups and downs that are part of normal stock movement. They also make you look at the chart and see what is actually there, not what you imagine is there because you have read it online that morning or someone has told you is there. As we mentioned before, keeping a clear head is absolutely vital to being successful. Listening to others is practically always guaranteed to bring you to a sticky end.

Trend lines are sometimes described as **lines of least resistance**. In other words, if a stock is going up then that is the easiest thing for that stock to keep on doing. To change the upward trend something must happen to change traders' point of view about the stock. That could be something that affects the whole market (like a recession, or inflation getting out of control) or it could be stock specific (all the executives were in the same plane, and it crashed. That actually happened once, just google Sundance Resources plane crash).

Trend lines often give us trading channels that are just like support and resistance lines except that they are not horizontal. Every time the stock gets to the bottom of the channel it looks 'cheap' or 'good value' and buyers step in, forcing the price up. When it gets to the top trend line then traders start to think that it is 'expensive' or 'toppy' and start to sell, moving the price down, away from the line. It will keep going in that channel until something changes the traders' minds about the stock.

When the stock breaks out of the trading channel that is significant, just like a breakout of the support and resistance lines we talked of earlier. If it breaks out of the top of the channel, then this is bullish, and it is likely to keep going up for a while at least.

It is also quite normal behavior to then retest by retracing to the top channel line and then bouncing off again. The top channel line then becomes the bottom channel line of the new channel. The same is true, in reverse, if it breaks out of the bottom of the trading channel.

Trading Channel Breakout

If you google to read more about this, you will see that the next thing they usually start talking about is putting the vertical axes on a logarithmic scale. Ignore this. It does not help. They are just trying to sound smart! The further you get away from the actual data the more you can persuade yourself that you see things that are not really there, and the more mistakes you will make. Usually costly mistakes. And we don't want that!

Moving Averages

To make sure that we are all on the same page with moving averages let's just start at the beginning. What we normally mean by 'the average' is correctly called 'the mean'. There are 2 other 'averages', the mode and the median, but they are usually referred to by name so we can ignore them. In this book, when we say 'average' we are talking about the mean.

An average is calculated by adding up all the numbers and dividing by the number of numbers. For example, the average of the numbers 3, 5, 4, and 8 is 5, calculated by adding them up (3 + 5 + 4 + 8 = 20) and then dividing them by 4 (there are 4 numbers). If we have a series of numbers, like stock prices over time, then we can use a moving average. We can have moving averages of different time periods, like 5-day moving averages, or 50-day moving averages.

Moving averages are usually referred to as 'MA'. They calculated by adding the new value (the latest one) and taking off an old value (the oldest one). Don't worry about doing the math. Any charting software will do it for you, all you have to give it is the time period that you want.

Remember we looked at the Google chart? Here it is with a 10-day (thin) and a 50-day (thick) moving average added. You can see that both MAs smooth out some of the noise so that you can see the trend more easily. Using a 10-day MA smooths a bit, but the 50-day MA smooths out even more. The disadvantage of the 50-day MA is that it takes longer to respond. You can see the 10-day MA starts to move down before the 50-day. Likewise, the 10-day shows that the uptrend started in April whereas the 50-day does not show it until May.

GOOG

| 2020 | February | March | April | May |

It is important that you get the concept of a moving average, and what it does. Essentially it smooths out the stock graph, eliminating the noise and enabling you to see the real movement. In other words, you can see the tide, not the waves!

The MA we have described above is often referred to as an **SMA – Simple Moving Average,** which of course implies that there is a more complex moving average. Of course, there is. Remember, this is trading – if they can make anything more complicated, they will. Exponentially!

The term **EMA** means **Exponential Moving Average**, and it gives more weight to the more recent prices which is logical. What happened yesterday should carry more weight than what happened 2 weeks ago, and this is what the EMA does for you. Again, you don't have to know how to calculate it, any charting package or website will do that for you. Just choose EMA and the time period that you want.

Which one should we use? Both have a place. If we are trying to predict what the market is going to do, then I suggest that you use the SMA as that is what most traders watch and act upon. However, I think that the EMA gives a truer picture of what is actually happening. So, which one do I use? I watch both.

So, to recap, the indicators that we need to know about are:

➢ Support and Resistance lines
➢ Trend lines
➢ Moving averages.

That's it. Ignore all the other complicated indicators. We don't need them, and they only work sometimes anyway.

Why are Indicators Important?

There is a very simple answer. ***They are important because traders think they are important and base their decisions on them.*** The price movements of a stock are simply the outcome of all the decisions that individual traders are making on buying and selling that stock.

Traders are watching the charts, often for hours and hours every day, and are making their decisions based on the chart behavior – or rather, what they 'see' in the chart. If you were to compare it with the ancient Romans telling the future by inspecting the entrails of sacrificed sheep, you could well be accurate! (They really did do that. Google 'haruspex').

> ***If we are going to predict what a stock is likely to do, we have to understand what traders are thinking and what they are likely to do based on the indicators.***

Three of the most widely used are the 50-day, 100-day, and 200-day simple moving averages. In fact, they are so widely followed you see them in news headlines, more often for bearish stories than bullish stories. **DOW drops through 50-Day Moving Average** is more commonly seen than **DOW bounces off 50-day Moving Average.** If a stock or index is approaching one of these moving averages, you can be sure that there are a lot of eyes watching it and holding off making decisions until they know what it is going to do when it reaches it.

While individual moving averages are watched, how they interact with each other is also watched closely and this is important for our strategy.

As we know, we can put the 50, 100 and 200-day moving average on a single chart. The 200-day one will be smoother than the 100-day SMA, which will be smoother than the 50-day. At some point, the SMAs will cross each other, and this is a trading signal that traders also watch.

The crossovers are very flamboyantly named:

> If the 50-day crosses to below the 200-day this is a very bearish sign called a **Death Cross** or a **Dead Cross**. When this happens, traders will start to behave in a bearish way by selling down their holdings, which will push the market down even further.

> If the 50-day crosses to above the 200-day this is a very bullish sign called a **Golden Cross**. Traders will start to behave in a bullish way by buying the stock, which will push the market up even further.

> If the 50-day is above the 100-day which is above the 200-day, then this is a bullish sign of a stock going up and continuing to go up. When traders see that they 'know' that all is OK and will continue to buy the stock, continuing its upward trend.

The following chart shows Google during the covid bear with 10-day and 50-day SMAs and the death and golden crosses.

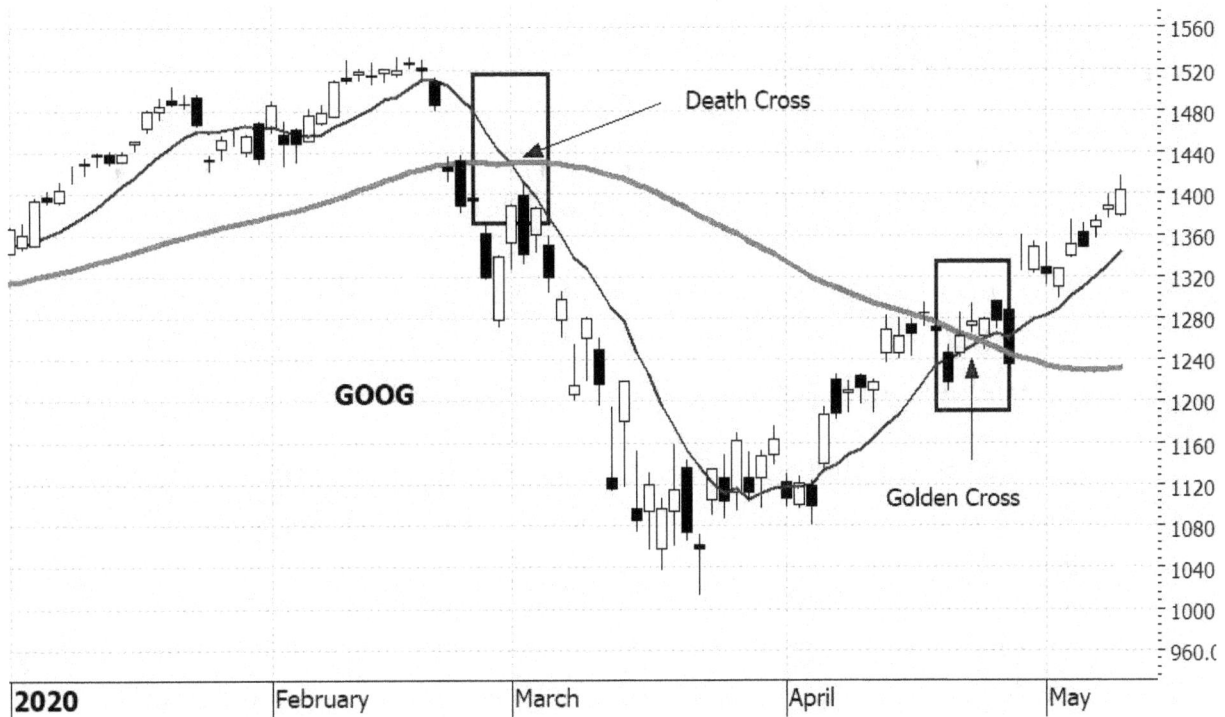

Remember, the stock market is only a mass of traders who are making decisions on what to buy or sell, and these decisions are based on emotions. If we know what traders are basing their emotions on, and what actions they have taken in the past when they have had those emotions, then we are able to understand what is happening now and make our decisions accordingly.

Chapter 3 Highlights

The major points in Chapter 3 Voodoo Science are:

➢ We don't know what the market is going to do. Nobody does. But we can make an educated guess about what is likely to happen based on what has happened before in similar situations.

➢ There is no such thing as a reliable indicator. Some of them work some of the time, but we don't know when they are going to work or not.

➢ Indicators are useful, but not in the way most traders think. They work because traders **think** that they work and act accordingly.

➢ When traders **think** that indicators are important, they make decisions based on them. Knowing the indicators most traders watch, use, and react to gives us an edge.

➢ The most widely followed indicators are trend lines, support / resistance lines and moving averages.

And finally, some more words of wisdom this time from Sir John Templeton:

The four most expensive words in the English language are "this time it's different."

❖❖❖

Chapter 4. All About Options

Right! This is where the rubber hits the road. We've done the background, got the basic concepts, dispelled a few myths and are now ready to actually start on our strategy, the ITM bull market strategy.

ITM stands for 'In The Money'. It's not just a catchy title, ITM means something in stock market terms. You can google 'in the money' and you'll find lots of definitions and information on it. I suggest that you leave the googling until later when you understand how the strategy works otherwise you might take fright as they can make it sound very complicated. Don't worry. It isn't. People just love to make things look complicated to show how smart they are.

The ITM strategy is incredibly simple, so simple that you will have a hard time believing that it produces the results it does. Many reviewers have said that it is too simple, it can't possibly work, and I must be cherry-picking the data (or worse!). My only answer is to say *look at the results.* The backtesting results are openly available and all trades for the last 30 years are listed with the ITM strategy reason for getting in and out. Nothing is hidden.

They say, there has got to be a catch. And how come, if it is so simple, that everyone isn't doing it? Why are people still borrowing to invest and buying on margin? There's a simple answer: I don't know WHY people aren't doing it. Presumably they haven't worked it out. Remember, I had been trading a good 16 years, using ever-more-complicated strategies before I worked out that they didn't work and ITM did.

Of course, it's not rocket science; I haven't created any wonderful new financial instrument, I have just used what is already available. People know about options; they are nothing new. Options have been around for a very long time. But using this simple strategy with this type of option more than doubles your returns and eliminates the threat of margin calls forever.

Using the ITM strategy you will beat the market – no ifs, no buts. It's guaranteed. You will double, treble (or even more) the market returns depending on which level of the strategy you choose. But when we say **beat the market** what do we really mean? Firstly, we have to know what we are trying to beat.

What Fund Managers Do

The market is made up of thousands of stocks, all being bought and sold, all going up or down or sideways. Naturally, people (fund managers or individual traders) want to buy a stock that is going to go up, not down. But how do they know? There are 3 main ways of determining whether a stock is going up or down.

> ➤ Know some inside information
> ➤ Look at the chart
> ➤ Look at the fundamentals

OK, the first was just a joke. It is illegal for a start, and most of us don't have contacts in high places who are going to give us advance warning of a takeover or unusual sales figures. Although it clearly happens - just look at the chart before and after a big announcement. You will often see that it rises *before* the announcement has been made. Someone is in the know and is using that knowledge to get in early and benefit from the rise. But as it is illegal, and as we probably don't know anyone to pass us the information, we will ignore that and look at the other ways.

The two legal methods that people use to decide what stocks they are going to buy are checking the stock chart and/or looking at the fundamentals, which is the publicly-available financial information on the company. Traders who make decisions based on the stock charts are called 'chart traders', or 'chartists.' Traders who base their decisions on fundamentals are called 'fundamental traders', or 'fundamentalists'. Both ways, they can look at a plethora of variables and then choose which stocks they think have the best market position and hence the best chance of going up. Then they buy them and hope that they are right.

And you know what? Most of the time they aren't right. Most don't even match the market as we saw in a previous chapter.

The Exclusive Club

What if there was a special, exclusive club for stocks, that only a limited number of the very best stocks could get into. To qualify for this exclusive, invitation-only membership the stock had to meet strict financial requirements.

In this club, there is no such thing as life membership. The membership is reviewed every quarter. When a stock fails to meet the requirements of this select club it is unceremoniously tossed out and replaced by a more deserving stock.

Well, there is such an exclusive club. It's called an index. This is how we measure market performance. The index we are going to be using for our ITM strategy is the S&P 500, SPX for short. It contains the 500 'biggest and best' stocks, the ones that have made the most money and have large capitalizations

All About Indexes

All markets have indexes, and there are all different types of indexes some more important than others. You will have heard of some of them but possibly not about others. The main ones in the US are:

➤ The Dow Jones Industrial Average (The 'Dow')
➤ The S&P 500 (The 'S&P')
➤ The Nasdaq 100 (The 'Naz')
➤ The Russell 2000 (The 'Russell')

In the UK the main one is the FTSE 100 (the 'footsie'), and in Europe, it's the Euro STOXX 50.

An index is simply a 'basket' of stocks. There are hundreds of indexes, and each is designed to track the performance of different markets, market sectors, or types of stock. There are industrial indexes, banking indexes, consumer goods, large-cap, small-cap indexes – practically anything that you can think of. The main one, and the one that we are going to use, is the S&P 500.

Most people have heard of the Dow - the Dow Jones Industrial Average. It is the oldest (it started in 1896) and is still most well-known index. The Dow is made up of 30 of the largest and most influential companies in the U.S. It represents about a quarter of the value of the entire U.S. stock market. So why are we not using the Dow? Because it isn't good enough for us! There are not enough stocks in it, plus the stocks have different weights depending on their market capitalization. (Just Google 'Dow weights' and you will get plenty of information about its components.) Currently, the five biggest stocks are:

➤ United Health Group 9.6%
➤ Goldman Sachs 6.5%
➤ Home Depot 6.5%
➤ Microsoft   5.7%
➤ McDonalds 4.5%

You can see that these 5 stocks alone make up almost 33% of the index, which is why it does not really represent the whole market. Instead of using the Dow, we are going to use the S&P 500.

Standard & Poor's 500 Index (the S&P 500) is made up of 500 of the most widely traded stocks in the U.S. And here's the good bit: it represents about 80% of the total value of the U.S. stock market. It has all kinds of stocks in it including energy, industrials, IT, healthcare, financials, and consumer staples. It's the biggest and the best for our purposes.

You're Fired!

Indexes, including the S&P 500, aren't static. The stocks that make up the index change frequently. The companies in an index aren't the same as they were last year or the year before and are considerably different from 20 years ago. If a stock starts to perform badly and it isn't big and important enough anymore it gets unceremoniously tossed out of the index, and a replacement is found right away.

This happens more and more frequently these days. On average, an S&P company is replaced every 2 weeks. Some of the big-name companies to exit are:

- ➢ The New York Times
- ➢ Sears
- ➢ Wendy's
- ➢ Kodak

Some of the big-name companies to come in are:

- ➢ eBay
- ➢ Netflix
- ➢ Amazon
- ➢ Google
- ➢ Twitter

Standard & Poors themselves reviewed the performance of managed funds over the last 15 years and found that almost 94% performed **worse** than the S&P 500. That means the odds are against anyone choosing to be in a managed fund: *there is only a 1 in 20 chance that you will beat the market.*

Remember, too, that this is the best of the funds. Only 34% of the funds actually survived the 15-year period. The rest were killed off. If they performed badly then they were merged or liquidated. This means that your chances of beating the market are in reality a lot less.

So, what are we paying fund managers for? To lose our money for us?

We could do that on our own! Although you have to feel sorry for fund managers, up to a point, of course. It's a short life. The average fund manager runs a portfolio for less than 5 years. This means that if you select a fund because of its record over a few years, then chances are that it's not the same fund manager that is still in charge.

Why Can't I Just Buy the Index?

OK, by now you will have thrown your hands up in frustration and said managed funds? No way! Why can't I just buy the index?

That's smart thinking. And the good news is that effectively you CAN. The even better news is that we can show you how to beat the index – guaranteed! With the ITM strategy:

➢ If the index goes up 5% you will go up 10% (or 15%).

➢ If the index goes up 10% you will go up 20% (or 30%).

➢ If the index goes up 15% you will go up 30% (or 45%).

The standard ITM strategy is to double the index returns. Later I will show you ways to triple and even quadruple the index return, but let's start with the plain vanilla ITM which doubles the market return.

Buying the index itself is becoming increasingly popular as more people are becoming aware that active fund managers perform worse than the index. When we say 'buying the index' we don't mean actually buying shares in an index. You can't do that. But you can invest in an index fund which is a fund that simply tracks the index. In other words, the index fund buys stocks in the index in the same proportion as they are in the actual index. You can buy shares in these index funds which is the same as buying shares in the index itself. These index funds are called ETFs – Exchange-Traded Funds. Remember the term 'ETF' as we will be using it quite a lot.

Investing in ETFs is becoming increasingly popular but by no means is it taking over from actively-managed funds. In October 2017, Black Rock estimated that less than 18% of the global stock market is owned by index-tracking investors

How Does An Index Fund Work?

An index fund is simply a 'basket of stocks' that mirrors the index they are trying to track. It can contain tens, hundreds, or even thousands of stocks depending on how many stocks are in the index they are based on.

- ➤ The Dow Jones Industrial Average ETF (DIA) has 30 stocks.
- ➤ The S&P 500 ETF (SPY) has 500 stocks.
- ➤ The Nasdaq 100 ETF (QQQ) has 100 stocks.
- ➤ The Russell 2000 ETF (RUT) has 2,000 stocks.

All stocks and indexes have short codes, usually 3 or 4 letters. The S&P 500 index has the code SPX, and the ETF that tracks it is the SPY. It is important to remember there is a difference between the index itself (which you *can't* invest in) and the ETF that tracks it (which you *can* invest in).

Warren Buffett, probably the world's most well-known investor, has consistently recommended S&P 500 index funds to his followers. He says:

> ***The trick is not to pick the right company. The trick is to essentially buy all the big companies through the S&P 500 and to do it consistently.***

In 2007, Buffett made a $1 million bet that the S&P 500 ETF would beat the active fund managers over the next 10 years. His opponents were able to select 5 actively managed funds, the ones they thought would outperform the rest of the funds.

Buffett won. In 2017, when the 10 years ended, the index fund had an average annual gain of 8.49% and the actively-managed funds ('hedge' funds) averaged an annual gain of 3%. If you had invested $10,000 in each strategy, today it would be worth:

- ➤ $22,500 in the index fund

➢ $13,600 in the actively-managed funds

That's a difference of $9,000! Or to put it another way, one has gone up 125% and the other 36%. Plus, if you look at the individual returns of the 5 selected managed funds their returns varied from 2.8% to 87.7%. Imagine investing $10,000 in one of these funds for 10 years and getting $10,280 at the end! You definitely would NOT be happy.

One of the reasons Buffett recommends throwing all your money into an index fund is that it is a form of 'passive investment'. You don't have to think about it or make any decisions. It's all done for you. You let the index do its thing, instead of buying and selling shares in particular companies.

Now that is probably good advice for someone who doesn't want to think and is happy to match the market. But that's not us! We want to **beat** the market. And we're not alone. What does Buffett do?

Do you think Buffett invests in index funds even though he recommends them? In 2008, right after his 2007 bet started, he (or rather his company, Berkshire Hathaway) invested $6 billion in General Electric (GE), and $5 billion in Goldman Sachs. His advice is a case of *this is good for you, but not for me!* To get rich, to be like Buffett, you need to have a better strategy.

Now, we don't have billions to invest in individual companies, so the kind of things that Buffett does are out of reach for us, as they are for most investors. But using index funds in a smart way gives us the ability to *leverage* our returns. In other words, we can increase the return on our investment.

And that is what the ITM strategy is all about.

Call Options

To beat the market, we are going to use an instrument called a 'call option'. They've been around for centuries, it's not something new that has just been thought up. Also, it doesn't just apply to the stock market. Call options are used in many different situations.

Let's look at the concept of call options in an area that most people find easy to understand: real estate. Your own home. Now, this book is not about real estate, we are just using it to explain about options. I promise that this is about as complicated as it gets!

The Option Seller

Emma is thinking of moving house. She would like something a little bigger, and a bit more upmarket. She decides to take action. But what is the first step?

First, get the money side of it sorted, of course. She has to work out what her current house is worth. Emma checks the real estate websites and sees that in the last year two houses in her street have been sold, and both were very similar to hers. One went for $102,000 and the other for $104,000. She has heard that the market has slipped a little recently, so she estimates that his house should be worth around $100,000. (Yes, I know that this is probably a bit low, but we are keeping all the figures nice and easy so that you can concentrate on the concept and not worry about the math.)

She has a mortgage on her house, and she still owes $40,000 on it. She works out that her equity in the house (the bit that she owns) is $60,000 (How? $100K house price - $40K owing on the mortgage). She checks with her bank, and because she is a good customer who has never missed any payments, they are quite happy to give her a loan of $110,000. Excellent! That means she can start looking at houses in the $170,000 range. (How? The $60,000 equity plus the $110,000 loan). But first, of course, she has to sell her current house.

Now you'll have to work with me here and use your imagination. Imagine that just then Emma's doorbell rings. It's a well-dressed woman who says that she is interested in her house and hands her a business card which says Prestige Property Investments. Goodness! What a coincidence!

Emma asks the woman how much she is prepared to pay for her house. The woman explains that she is not buying today, but that her company options properties. Emma has never heard of this and has no idea what she is talking about, so she asks her to clarify what she means.

'How it works,' the woman explains, 'is that we option properties. We offer above the market rate and as well we pay you a premium. Your house, for example. We would be willing to option it for one year at $120,000. And we would pay you a premium of $10,000.'

Emma doesn't really understand what the woman is talking about. The explanation is not exactly helpful, but Emma hears the figures and thinks they sound good. Is she interested? Not interested? Is it a good deal? A bad deal? What should Emma do?

OK, let's unpack the Prestige Property offer to see whether Emma should be interested or not.

➤ Emma is being offered a selling price of $120,000. She knows that this is quite a bit over the market price of $100,000.

➤ The period of the option is one year, which means that anytime within the year they have the right to buy it from Emma at $120,000.

➤ Emma is getting a $10,000 premium, which is an upfront payment. This means that if she agrees to the option contract, she will get $10,000 when she signs it, and that is on top of the $120,000.

Do Prestige Property Investments **have** to buy the house from Emma? No, they don't. They have the **right** to buy it but not the **obligation** to buy it. But if they do decide to buy it then the selling price is $120,000.

What about the $10,000 premium? Emma gets to keep that whether they buy the house or not. That's hers, right now, and she never has to pay it back whether the house is sold or not. In other words, the premium is a payment for entering into the contract. Let's look at the pros and cons to see whether Emma should be interested or not.

The Pros:

> ➤ Emma is thinking of moving anyway and getting $120,000 is a lot better than the $100,000 she was expecting.

> ➤ The $10,000 premium makes the deal really worth $130,000. This means Emma could start looking in the $200,000 range. (How? $120,000 sale price + $10,000 premium + $110,000 loan - $40,000 mortgage)

> ➤ Even if they don't end up buying the house, Emma gets to keep the $10,000 – and she still has her house of course.

The Cons:

> ➤ For a year Emma loses control of whether her house is sold or not. Prestige Property has the right to buy her house at any time during that year, but they do not **have** to buy it.

> ➤ They can choose NOT to exercise their right to buy her house, in which case the option simply expires.

Should Emma be interested? Or not?

That all depends on her plans and priorities. If the sale goes through, she is making a lot more money than she would otherwise. If the sale doesn't go through, she has got $10K in her pocket, but for 1 year the decision about whether the house is sold or not is theirs, not hers.

Why Would They Do It?

There are lots of reasons people option properties rather than buy them outright. In fact, in commercial property it is extremely common, although less so in residential properties.

Perhaps the company is trying to buy several properties in the street so that they can amalgamate the land and build a multi-unit dwelling. If they can get all the neighbors to agree to option their properties, they will go ahead and buy all the houses and build the apartment block. If one or more of the neighbors don't want to move, they will not be able to go ahead with the apartment block, so they will not buy any of the houses. They will just let the options expire. That is *their* risk. And, of course, they will have blown all their premium money.

There are other reasons that they could want a property as well. Perhaps there is a large garden, and they think that they could subdivide it and build an additional dwelling and make a profit that way. Perhaps they think that property prices in the area are going to increase. Perhaps there is a new train station going to be built nearby.

There are many reasons they could want it. The point is, that they are using options to *reduce their risk*, but that reduced risk comes at a cost. Rather than buy the house outright they are offering a 'sweetener' up front in order to have a year to decide whether or not they are going to buy the house.

If Emma chooses to take the deal, she is not actually selling her house, but **selling an option** on her house. The property company is not actually buying her house but **buying an option** on it.

Now for the terminology.

- ➢ This is a **call option** – in other words, Emma's house can be 'called away' from her.

- ➢ $120 K is the **strike price** – the price they have agreed will be paid for the house.

- ➢ $10 K is the **premium** – the money Emma gets for entering the contract

- ➢ 1 Year is the **time period** during which the option is valid

- ➢ If the sale goes through the option is **exercised**. If it doesn't then the option **expires**.

The Option Buyer

Let's look from the other side, another 'let's pretend'. Imagine Rachel is at a friend's place for lunch. She's always loved their house, and the terrace with a view over the river is just what she has always wanted. During lunch, they mention that their next-door neighbor, whose view is even better, is thinking of selling. They suggest: Why doesn't Rachel buy her house?

Rachel thinks. She can't afford it right now, but she knows that Great Aunt Harriet turned 101 last week, and she knows that as she is the favorite (well, only) niece, Aunt Harriet, who is very wealthy, is leaving everything to her. A very tidy sum. More than enough to buy the house next door, and still have lots to spare. She reflects that Aunt Harriet has been looking a little peaky lately and sadly can't last much longer.

Is there a way Rachel could buy the house?

Absolutely there is.

Rachel could buy an option on the next-door house. Let's say that the house is worth $1 million (it's a VERY nice house, and we are keeping the math simple). She could offer the current owner a 2-year option for $1.1 million with a premium of $20,000.

Let's unpack how that is going to work:

➢ Rachel is **buying a call** option on the house - she can call it away from the current owner any time within the next 2 years.

➢ The **strike** (the agreed price) is $1.1M - which is over the current market price of $1 million, but she thinks prices are on the way up so it may well end up as a bargain.

➢ The **time period** is 2 years - by which time poor Aunt Harriet will, no doubt, have shuffled off this mortal coil.

➢ The **premium** is $20K – which is all her savings, but she has it in the bank so can pay it right away.

This means that Rachel has the right, anytime in the next 2 years, to buy the house at the strike price of $1.1 million. As a 'reward' for entering the contract she is paying the current owner $20K up front, in addition to the strike price.

Why would the seller agree? Well, if she sells, she is getting over the market price plus she gets the $20K premium right away and she never has to give that back whether the house is sold or not.

The Risks

Now, suppose Aunt Harriet suddenly changes her will. She finds she has a long-lost sister and decides to leave everything to her instead. Where does this leave Rachel? (apart from being extremely disappointed!)

Rachel is protected by the call option. It gives her the **right** to buy the house, but not the **obligation**. She doesn't **have** to buy the house; she can just walk away from the deal. Of course, she loses the premium she has already paid but apart from that she has no obligations.

And what about the seller if the sale doesn't go ahead? Well, she gets to keep the $20K premium and she still has her house.

Buyers? Or Sellers?

With options, people sometimes get confused about who is the buyer and who is the seller. In our examples:

Emma's $100k house

Ø Emma is the SELLER – she is *SELLING an option* on her house

Ø Prestige Properties is the BUYER – they are *BUYING an option* on Emma's house.

The $1m house next door

Ø Rachel is the BUYER – she is *BUYING an option* on the next-door house

Ø The next-door neighbor is the SELLER – she *is SELLING an option* on her house.

Where Options Started

Options and futures are not new sophisticated financial instruments, some diabolical invention designed to trap the unwary and unsophisticated. They weren't dreamed up by Wall Street in an attempt to fleece the unsuspecting investor. In fact, they didn't start on Wall Street at all. They started a long, long time ago and far, far away. Many thousands of years ago on the other side of the world.

For futures, we have to go right back to Sumer in ancient Babylon in 8,000 BC. They used clay tokens as a promise for a farmer to deliver a quantity of goods (for example the grain harvest) by a certain date. This was a 'forward' or 'futures' contract because the actual transaction would take place in the future. The farmer could then go ahead and plant his crop knowing that at harvest time there was an agreed price and quantity.

It was a few thousand years later in 500 BC when options as we know them today were first used. There was a Greek philosopher, astronomer and mathematician called Thales. As well as philosophizing, he grew olive trees and he studied astronomy as a way of predicting olive harvests. One year the stars told him to expect a bumper crop of olives. Good news indeed! But of course, in farming, as in life, nothing is certain, so he wanted to be able to deal with the massive harvest if it happened. That is, **if** it was going to be a massive harvest. He just didn't know.

Not being rich, he did not own his own olive press. Instead, he paid a fee to use another farmer's olive press at harvest time. This time, instead of the usual arrangement, he negotiated a different type of contract. This contract gave him the ***right but not the obligation*** (sound familiar?) to use the presses, and he paid a sum of money for the contract.

Now he was covered whatever happened. If it was a great season, he could be sure of getting all his olives pressed. If it was a bad season, then he hadn't paid for time on the olive presses that he didn't need. Of course, he had paid for the contract itself and wouldn't get that money back whatever happened. Options work just like insurance. You pay the premium, but you don't get it refunded if you don't make a claim.

Thales' contract had all the facets of a call option today:

- ➢ The **underlying asset** (use of the olive press)
- ➢ The **strike** (the contract specified how much he would pay for use of the press)
- ➢ The **premium** (how much he paid for the contract)
- ➢ The **expiry date** (valid for the next harvest)

The story has a happy ending: Thales was right, it was a great season, and he was able to press his olives! And he also invented options as we know them today.

During the middle ages various forms of forward contracts were used, and the first 'stock market' as we know it started in the 1500s in Antwerp in Belgium. They built a huge market building, called the Bourse, where buyers and sellers from all over Europe sold their wares. But there was one big difference between the Bourse and all the other markets. In the Bourse they didn't buy and sell the *actual* goods. They bought and sold *the right* to buy and sell *goods*. Instead of real, physical goods, they traded bills of exchange. This was the first real European financial market. The beautiful building has recently been renovated, and to see it Google 'Bourse Antwerp'.

On the other side of the world, in the late 1600s, things were happening there too. Japan had an elite class called the 'Samurai'. They were the ruling military class that became the highest-ranking social cast. Strangely they were not paid in yen, currency or even gold. They were paid in rice. Naturally, they wanted to be in control of the rice markets, so they established the Dojima Rice Exchange which was the first real centralized futures market. It introduced paper money, and with it trading in futures.

Options Today

In 1791 the New York Stock Exchange (NYSE) opened. Stock options started to be used but there was no centralized marketplace for them. It was 'over-the-counter'. You had to rely on broker-dealers who would try to match option sellers and option buyers. There were two problems with this. Firstly, liquidity. Once you had bought the option it was hard to sell it as there was no marketplace, so you probably had to hold it until expiration. Secondly, there was a risk that the seller might not honor the obligation.

After the stock market crashed in 1929, Congress set up the Securities and Exchange Commission (SEC), and they started to regulate the over-the-counter options market. Nothing much happened until 1968 when the Chicago Board Options Exchange (CBOE) was created, and they standardized contract size, strike prices, and expiration dates.

In the 1970s computers changed everything as there could now be a central clearinghouse and prices could be listed. In 1992, surprisingly late I always think, trading became electronic so there was a worldwide upsurge in trading stocks, commodities, and derivatives.

Call Options In The Stock Market

The stock market also has call options, which work in exactly the way our call options for houses work. Often, people shy away from options and claim they are too complicated, and they can't understand them. This isn't right. They are no more complicated than our 2 examples of the houses. So, before we move back to the stock market make sure that you understand the two situations above.

Options are called derivatives because when people trade options, they are not trading the actual underlying asset, but a contract **derived** from the underlying asset. Complicated? Not really. Remember the houses in our example? The houses themselves were not sold. It was the call options, the derivatives, that were sold.

Now you know all about call options. There are put options as well, which give you the right to sell to someone at an agreed price. In other words, rather than 'calling' something away, you are 'putting' something to them.

But you don't need to know about puts for the ITM bull strategy, so we are going to leave them out.

I'm operating on a 'need to know' basis! If something isn't necessary for you to be able to do the ITM bull strategy, then we won't include it here.

Chapter 4 Highlights

The major points in Chapter 4. All About Options are:

➢ We learned about indexes, in particular, the S&P 500 (SPX) and the exchange-traded fund (ETF) that mirrors it, the SPY.

➢ Call options give the right (but not the obligation) to buy an asset (e.g., a house or a stock) at an agreed price (the strike price) any time before a nominated date (expiry).

➢ If the sale goes ahead then the option is said to be exercised. If the sale does not go ahead then the option expires at the nominated date.

➢ Call option buyers pay a premium to the seller, which is kept whether the option is exercised or not.

➢ Options are derivatives, in that they are not trading the underlying asset, but a contract **derived** from the asset.

And finally, some more words of wisdom this time from Warren Buffett again:

Wall Street is the only place that people ride to in a Rolls Royce to get advice from those who take the subway

◆◆◆

Chapter 5. In and Out the Money

We now know that SPY is an ETF (Exchange Traded Fund) that mirrors the S&P 500 index (SPX). If SPX goes up 1% then SPY goes up 1%, if SPX goes up 5% then SPY goes up 5%, and so on. If we put it on a chart it would look like this:

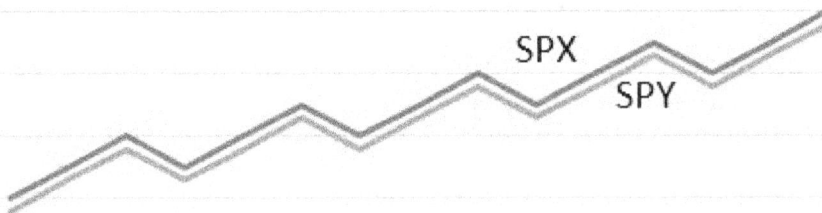

Indexes can go down as well as up. If SPX goes down 1% then SPY goes down 1%, if SPX goes down 2% then SPY goes down 2%, and so on. It moves in lock step. Over time indexes tend to go up, but it is quite normal to have a down day, maybe even several in a row. Remember, we are looking at the tide (the trend) not the individual waves (the noise).

With the basic ITM strategy we double the rate of return so that:
- ➤ If SPX goes up 1% ITM goes up 2%
- ➤ If SPX goes up 5% ITM goes up 10%
- ➤ If SPX goes up 10% ITM goes up 20%

In this case the graph would look like this:

ITM doubles the SPX increase

Of course, the SPX can go down as well as up, in which case you still have the same ratio of return. If SPX goes down 1% then ITM goes down

2%, and so on. But overwhelmingly indexes go up even if they have down years. Over the last 50 years, the SPX has gone up 80% of the time. The average return of positive years is 19% and the average return of the down years is -14%. If you want to check, just google 'SPY Total Returns' for the actual figures. Note that this is including all the really bad years, like the 'Tech Wreck' of 2000 and the GFC (Great Financial Crisis) of 2008.

So, you can see that by doubling your return you are going to get to your goal much more quickly. How much more quickly? The average return for S&P 500 over the last 100 years is 6.7%, or 10.8% with dividends reinvested. That may not sound a lot, but let's see what it means in real life.

So, imagine. If you had invested $1,000 in the stock market 100 years ago and just left it there it would be worth an eye-watering $28 million today. That's not a typo. This is assuming that you just put the money into the market in 1921 and then ignored it. Any dividends and distributions were just added to your balance, but you didn't put any more funds in or take any out. It's hard to believe that that figure is right, but it is.

Without adding any extra money, by just leaving the index to do its thing, this is what you would be worth. Hard to get your head around, isn't it? But go and check for yourself. Those are the real figures.

The average return for the S&P over the last 100 years is 10.8%. We must understand, however, that the 10.8% increase is not like bank interest where the capital always goes up. If that were the case and you had put your money in the bank at a 10.8% interest rate then your $1k would now be worth $19.8 million, and you wouldn't have had any down years. But good luck in trying to get 10.8% interest nowadays!

In the stock market, things go up and things go down so returns can be quite unpredictable, and a couple of bad years can have a huge effect on returns. There have been a few quite horrible years in the market. The worst one was almost 100 years ago during the Great Depression when the market went down over 50%. Really bad years like that take a long time to recover from.

To illustrate: if you started with $1,000 and the market went down 50%

then you only have $500 left. When the market recovers, let's say it went up 50%, then you are still not back to where you started. Your account would be worth $750. The market must go up 100% for you to get back where you started at $1,000.

What Were My Grandparents Thinking?

About this time, you are probably thinking ***Why on earth did my great grandparents not do that? Were they dim? I could be worth an extra $28 million!*** That was my thought when I first did the calculations, then I had some wonderful daydreams about spending the $28 million. Helicopters, islands, and chateaux figured very strongly. But back to reality.

Don't be too hard on your grandparents. The figures above don't take inflation into account. $1,000 was worth a whole lot more in 1921 and they probably didn't have a lazy $1K just sitting there. For a start, the average wage was $1,407 a year according to U.S. Government Statistics.

The average price of a house in the US in 1921 was $6,300. Today, the average price of a house is just over $375,000 over 60 times more. A big increase – but not as big as the stock market increase. If you had bought one-sixth of a house for $1,000 in 1919 it would be worth roughly $63,000 today. Of course, it's not that simple. Location makes a difference. Some houses, for example, those in New York, would have gone up much more than 60 times, but in other, less populated areas, they may not have gone up by even that much. It varies, and that's not including the cost of holding the house. Houses have to have money spent on them in upkeep, rates, and taxes, so once these costs are deducted the figures look even less appealing.

So, property doesn't measure up. Let's check the effects of inflation on things other than houses. The US Inflation Calculator shows that $1,000 in December 1921 is the same as $16,116 today (December 2021). That's a big increase, but still dwarfed by the stock market figures above. Plus, things change in their affordability. Some things get cheaper, others more expensive. In 1926 a Frigidaire 'Electrical Refrigerator' cost $285. Translated into today's figures that means that a refrigerator would cost $4,593 if you bought it today. Definitely a luxury item! The first Model T was made in

1915, and cost $850 , $13,699 in today's dollars which is roughly comparable.

You can see that the stock market has performed extremely well over a long time period which included the great depression, the great recession, 13 recessions, 2 world wars, and several regional wars. This doesn't mean that there aren't years where the stock market goes down. There are. Over the last 100 years there have been 32 years when it went down – but 68 years when it went up. And we have already seen that the down years tend on average to go down less than the up years go up. The good years far exceed the bad.

It also explains why a lot of people get burned on the market. Bad years tend to come after a string of good years – remember optimism turning into euphoria? It is in the euphoric stage that people who have never actually traded before are lured into the market by the easy profits they see other people making. They tend to get in at the top of the market, then never recover because they have lost a great chunk of their initial capital.

The ideal situation is, of course, if you can add to your capital as you go. If you had invested an additional $10 per month, then over the years this would have more than doubled your money and your account would now be worth almost $62 million. Now that's worth another daydream!

You probably don't want to wait 100 years to become rich, so let's see about getting you wealthy within 10 years. Some of you will get to financial freedom before that. It depends a lot on how much you can invest, both at the start and on the way.

How Much Do I Need To Get Started?

When the first edition of **In The Money: Bull Market Strategy** came out in September 2020 the SPY was $325. Today (mid December 2021) it is worth $470. That's a massive increase of 45% in just 15 months. In the original edition I wrote: *To do the standard ITM strategy it is best to start with around USD10,000 (US Dollars).*

With the SPY at $325 it was easy to do the ITM strategy with $10K;

today it is a harder simply because the market has become so much more expensive. The starting account value to do the original ITM strategy is now bigger, at the time of writing around $13 - 14K.

I was being contacted by readers who were asking very specific questions about what options they should buy if they had an account value of $10K or less. This prompted me to issue this second edition, which takes into account the current level of the market and people with smaller accounts.

It is recommended that if you have an account of $14K or more that you do the original ITM strategy as laid out in this book. If your account hasn't reached that level yet, then there is a new strategy in **Chapter 11. ITM for Smaller Accounts** that is for you.

However, the new strategy, which I will call ITMS (for ITM Small) works in almost exactly the same way just on a different underlying ETF so everything in this book is relevant to you. Hopefully, your account will soon reach the level at which you can start using ITM on SPY.

What Does the ITM Strategy Do?

What the ITM strategy does is buy deep-in-the-money (ITM) SPY call options at least one year to expiry with a delta close to one. OK, that got technical pretty quickly, didn't it? If you didn't understand a word of that don't worry. It's not your problem, it's mine. I have to explain it to you so that you understand. And you will be surprised that it is not as hard or complicated as many people (usually option traders!) would have you believe.

We will look at what the words actually mean and how the strategy works because you need to understand what you are doing and why. You have to know how much money you will make, and how much money you could lose. Playing with the stock market always has risks, but the ITM strategy minimizes these risks so that you will always stay within your comfort zone.

Let's take it bit by bit.

ITM uses call options. We have already looked at call options in the context of buying or selling a house. Let's do a refresher on the situations and introduce the right terminology.

In both cases, the house itself (the underlying asset) was not sold. That would not happen until later, IF and WHEN the option was exercised. To be clear: the call option did not involve actually selling the house. The call option was a contract to sell the house at a later date, anytime in the next year. ***This contract was the call option or derivative.***

Example 1

Emma wanted to sell her house which was worth $100K. She was offered $10K if she would agree to sell her house for $120K any time within the next year.

> *Emma is **SELLING a CALL** option on her house*
> *She receives a **PREMIUM** of $10K*
> *The **STRIKE** price is $120K*
> *The **EXPIRY** Date is 1 year from today*

Example 2

Rachel wanted to buy the riverside house worth $1M but didn't have the money right then. She offered the house owner $20K if she would agree to sell her house to Rachel for $1.1M at any time in the next 2 years

> Rachel *is **BUYING a CALL** option*
> *She pays a **PREMIUM** of $20K*
> *The **STRIKE** price is $1.1M*
> *The **EXPIRY** is 2 years from today*

Two important things to remember about options are:

> The person who owns the option has the **right,** but not the **obligation** to exercise the option. If Rachel decides not to buy the house, then she doesn't have to. She can walk away from the deal.

➢ The Premium is always kept whether the sale goes through or not. ***The premium is not included in the strike price, they are two different things.*** The premium can be thought of as the payment to the seller for entering into the deal.

The essential information that we need to know about a call option is:

➢ The ***underlying asset*** (a house, a shopping mall, a diamond, an ETF, a stock)
➢ Whether you are ***buying*** or ***selling***
➢ The ***Premium***
➢ The ***Strike Price***
➢ The ***Expiry Date***

If we know all these things, then we have a complete picture of what the call option contract is about. Of course, every call option has 2 sides: the buyer and the seller. To make sure that we are clear who is the buyer and who is the seller let's go back to Rachel who is expecting to be left a lot of money in her great aunt's will and buys a call option on the riverside house.

Let's say the riverside house that Rachel wants to buy is owned by Jane. Jane is happy to enter into the option deal because:

➢ If Rachel decides to go ahead with the purchase (i.e., she ***exercises her option***) she (Jane) will be selling the house at a higher price than she thinks is the market value.

➢ If Rachel decides not to go ahead with the purchase (i.e., her ***option expires***) then Jane will get to keep the premium ($20K) and she still has her house.

So, who is the buyer and who is the seller?

➢ Rachel is **BUYING** the option

➢ Jane is **SELLING** the option

Selling an option is often called ***writing*** an option. In this case, Jane is writing the option which did not exist until she wrote it. Yes, people buy and sell options, but you can also create one from nothing, that's why it is called 'writing'. Rachel created the option; it did not exist before she wrote it.

Of course, with ITM we are not going to be buying and selling houses. We are going to be buying and selling options on an ETF. We have already met SPX and SPY earlier in the book, but let's look at them in more detail.

The Biggest ETF in the World

As we know SPY is an ETF (Exchange Traded Fund). It is the world's largest ETF, with net assets of over $400 billion (that's right, billion with a 'b'). It started in January 1993 so there is a good long record of prices to analyze. It also has a huge options market, with around 2 million options being bought and sold every day. It has a huge number of strike prices to choose from and has expiry dates going out 2 years.

It has also the most liquid options market of any ETF or stock. By a liquid market we mean one where there is a lot of buying and selling going on, so it is easy to do a trade quickly as there are many buyers and sellers. With 2 million SPY options being bought and sold every day you won't get stuck with a position that you can't sell. As well, there are market makers, who we will touch on later in the book, who ensure that there is a bid / ask for every strike with a mandated low spread. If you don't understand that right now don't worry. It will become clear later, and we don't need it for the next bit.

What Are We Really Buying?

When we buy a SPY call option, we are buying the right to buy 100 shares of the underlying ETF at the strike price. Let's say that SPY is currently trading at $320. If we bought 100 shares of SPY, then that would cost us $32,000 which is rather a lot and would be too expensive for many people with smaller accounts. Instead, we are going to buy a call option for a lesser outlay.

How much less? That depends on the Strike and Expiry date. Options cost varying amounts of money, and you get the prices of all the different options in an 'options chain'. Here are two general rules:

➤ The closer the expiry date the cheaper the option

➤ The higher the strike price the cheaper the option

Expiry: If you buy an option that has only 1 week to expiry then it will be cheaper than one with the same strike but has 3 months to expiry, which, in turn, will be cheaper than one with 2 years to expiry. If you are effectively controlling the underlying stocks for a longer time you have to pay a higher premium.

We are going to use options that are around 1 year to expiry – we are giving the market time to move up and make money for us. We are not jumping in an out of trades. We don't want to do that. That is a way to lose money quickly. *An aside: technically these are not LEAPS (Long term equity anticipation securities). LEAPS have an expiration date of more than one year and up to three years from issue and we are going to be using up to a year for ITM and 6 months for ITMS (the smaller account strategy).*

Strike: If you buy a strike price much higher than the current price then the options are cheaper, and for a good reason: the high strike price is likely never be hit. For example, let's say that SPY is trading at $320. If we bought a 1-year to expiry $400 option, then SPY would have to increase by over 25% in a year to hit the strike price. That isn't impossible, but it is unlikely. Looking at the performance of Spy in the 29 years since inception:

SPY Returns	Years	% of Years
Over 10%	16	55%
Over 20%	9	31%
Over 30%	2	7%

Please don't read this table as meaning that in 27 out of 29 years SPY made a profit of more than 10%. It didn't. Think about it. If the return is, say, 32%, then it is in all 3 boxes as it is over 10% and 20% and 30%. There were thirteen years when SPY didn't make over 10%, and 8 of those were years where it made a loss.

Expiring Worthless

If at the expiry date the underlying stock or index (in our case the S&P 500) has not reached the strike price, then the option would not be exercised. Holding the option means that you have the right to buy the stock at a higher price than is it currently trading – but why would you do that? Would you buy the SPY for $400 when it is trading at, say, $360? No, of course you wouldn't. Effectively your option is worthless, and you have lost all your money. In stock market parlance your option has ***expired worthless.***

This situation is why people who don't know what they are doing lose money, and often lose their money big time. Sadly, it is sometimes their entire capital. And this is why options have a reputation of being 'bad' and 'dangerous.' You'll see them described as 'notoriously risky' and 'complex' and a 'dangerous lure'. Just google 'options bad dangerous' and you'll see what I mean.

It is a widespread misconception. Options are not inherently risky. People just use them in risky (and very stupid) ways. It is like someone getting behind the wheel of a car when they don't know how to drive, and don't know any road rules. That's dangerous. Yet most of us drive cars safely every day *because we understand what we are doing.* It is the same with options. We are going to understand what we are doing and do it safely.

A Bit More Terminology

To understand the ITM strategy we have to know a few more technical terms. They're not hard. People love to make them sound hard and complicated so that they seem terribly clever, but it's seriously not at all hard.

Options can be classified by their strike price relative to the current price:

> ➢ A strike price ABOVE the current price means the option is **OTM**

(Out of The Money)

> ➤ A strike price the SAME as the current price means the option is **ATM** (At The Money)

> ➤ A strike price BELOW the current price means the option is **ITM** (In The Money)

These are the general classifications. We are going to add one more that is not usually used. It is **DITM** – Deep in the Money Options. It's a subset of ITM options where the strike price is well below the current price.

Let's look at a practical example: if SPY is trading at $319 then a strike price of:

> ➤ $350 is OTM
> ➤ $320 is ATM
> ➤ $300 is ITM
> ➤ $220 is DITM

Looking at the relevant pricing of a 1 year to expiry SPY option. With the SPY at $319 the options are priced as follows:

> ➤ OTM: a $350 strike costs $6.15
> ➤ ATM: a $320 strike costs $19.85
> ➤ ITM: a $300 strike costs $33.17
> ➤ DITM: a $220 strike costs $99.98

You can see that the further OTM we go the cheaper options become. Why? Because there is a good chance that SPY will never get to the strike, and they will expire worthless. So why do people buy them? They buy them because they are cheap. If the market goes your way, then you can clean up big time. I know. I've done it, but it is far from the norm.

There is a real thrill when you have bought a cheap stock option for $200 and then the company is the subject of a takeover, and you suddenly find your $200 is worth $18,000. That actually happened to me once, and it's very nice when it happens. You think you are really smart, but actually you're not; it was pure luck. It is certainly not what usually happens. I have had a **lot** more options expire worthless, and I can tell you **that** isn't fun. It certainly doesn't improve your day knowing that (a) you were wrong and (b) you have lost money.

To reiterate: ***buying OTM is risky because there is a high chance that you will lose your entire stake***. There is a place for doing this strategy in conjunction with others and we will cover it later in this book, plus another of my books, **Compare Option Strategies,** enables you to practice with different options. But we will NEVER buy OTM options other than with money that we don't mind losing. OK, maybe we will mind a bit because losing money is always painful, but we will only use a very small part of our portfolio. If the trade goes against us and it expires worthless then the loss, while annoying, is not significant. We are still in the game, which is the most important thing.

So, why the enormous price difference between ITM and OTM options? Let's recap exactly what we are buying when we buy the option, using the actual figures above. It gives us the *right* but not the *obligation* to:

- ➢ OTM: buy 100 SPY at $350
- ➢ ATM: buy 100 SPY at $320
- ➢ ITM: buy 100 SPY at $300
- ➢ DITM: buy 100 SPY at $220

Now let's look at what we are really doing based on the prices above. Let's see exactly how much we will be paying if we exercise our options. Let's assume that SPY is trading at $319.13. If we exercise (use our options) we are buying SPY at:

- ➢ OTM: $356.15($350 + $6.15)
- ➢ ATM: $339.85($320 + $19.85)
- ➢ ITM: $333.17($300 + $33.17)
- ➢ DITM: $319.98($220 + $99.98)

We are going to call this the **Effective Price** because that is what we are effectively paying if we exercise our options. So, which offers us the best value? Clearly, the DITM option because it is closest to the actual price, so effectively we are not really paying for the option at all. But - and it is a big but - it is going to cost us more. A lot more. $99.98 for a single DITM option, compared with $6.15 for a single OTM option. That means it will cost $9,998 for one DITM option compared with $615 for an OTM option.

If we choose OTM 350 strike, then we are paying $37.02 more than SPY is currently worth. Why would anyone buy above market price? No one in their right mind! But, as we mentioned before, people buy OTM options because:

➤ They are cheap.
➤ They may provide a higher return.

In this example the price for a single OTM 350 option is $6.15, which is a LOT less than $99.98 for a DITM option. Remembering that each option is a contract for 100 shares the actual cost to us of the DITM option is $9,998 and the OTM option is $615, so you can see the OTM option requires less cash up front, which increases its attractiveness to people with smaller accounts.

Right! Decision time. What option shall we buy?

We need some practical examples. Let's look at the actual effects of buying each type of option on your account and be aware that we are rounding so figures will not add up exactly. I want to make the math easy so that you can concentrate on the concepts.

We could not totally invest the $10,000 because you can't buy a fraction of an option or a fraction of a SPY contract. Part of the account would have stayed in cash, and to make everything accurate that should be added to the totals. I chose not to do this as it would complicate things and readers might not be able to easily see how I got the figures in the table. But to be completely accurate we should be adding into the totals:

➤ OTM: $160
➤ ATM: $75
➤ ITM: $49
➤ DITM: $2
➤ SPY: $111

So, you can see that the SPY returns are underestimated a little. The figures also exclude brokerage costs, but with many brokers now offering no commission trades then this is a reasonable thing to leave out nowadays. More about commission-free brokerage later in the book.

Your First Account.

Let's say that you have opened your first account with $10,000 that you've saved. This is a good figure to start with. More is better, of course, because your profit will be bigger, but you can add to it as you go. Even adding $1,000 a year to your account can have a huge effect on the bottom line.

So, we have an account value of $10,000. How many options could we buy? And which ones should we choose? Looking at the options with 1 year to expiry we get the following numbers:

Option	Strike	Option Price	Cost of option	Number of options
OTM	$350	$6.15	$615	16
ATM	$320	$19.85	$1,985	5
ITM	$300	$33.17	$3,317	3
DITM	$220	$99.98	$9,998	1

You can see that we can buy a lot more OTM options than we can DITM options. In fact, we can only afford one DITM option. That makes a difference. How do we work out how much our options are worth at expiry? Let's start by looking at shares.

If you bought 31 shares of SPY, then you would pay $9,889 for them (31 * $319). If at the end of the year SPY had gone up, what would they be worth? You calculate by multiplying the number of shares by the end of year price. So, if at the end of year:

> ➢ SPY was $400, then your shares would be worth $12,400 (How? 31 * $400)
> ➢ SPY was $350, then your shares would be worth $10,850 (How? 31 * $350)
> ➢ SPY was $320, then your shares would be worth $12,400 (How? 31 * $320)

➢ SPY was $300, then your shares would be worth $9,300 (How? 31* $300)

Remember that the $111 that was left after your purchase of SPY shares needs to be added on to get your exact account value. And let's face it, that is what we are really interested in: how much our account is going to be worth at the end of the year if we use options instead of simply buying the stock.

Of course, this will depend on where the market is at the end of the year. Let's look at the different scenarios, and to make the math easy we are going to ignore the cash in the account and concentrate on the value of the options.

A Really Good Year

Let's imagine it has been a bumper year for the market and it has gone up 25% (it has 11 times over the last 40 years) and SPY is now worth $400.

If we had bought $10,000 of SPY shares then they would be worth $12,400 and our account would now be worth $12,511, a 25% increase (How? $12,400 + $111 cash). Very nice.

But let's look at our options. How much would our account be worth?

Option	Strike	No. of Options	Start of Year	End of Year	Return
OTM	$350	16	$10,000	$80,000	700%
ATM	$320	5	$10,000	$40,000	300%
ITM	$300	3	$10,000	$30,000	200%
DITM	$220	1	$10,000	$18,000	80%
Shares		31	$10,000	$12,400	25%

You can see that the OTM options have WAY outperformed everything else. You've made a profit of $70,000 from your $10,000 starting account – that's huge! That's 700%! And those poor bunnies who just followed the market have only made $2,400. Brilliant! You're a genius!

But don't give up your day job just yet. Unfortunately, this is how new traders become temporary traders. They are dazzled by the returns that are possible. And traders *can* get lucky and make these returns. Trades like these are fun to do with a small part of your account. Just make sure that you can afford to lose the money because most likely that is what is going to happen. But let's see how this works.

A Good Year

Let's assume now that we had a good year, not great but quite solid. Let's say the market went up by 12.5% and the SPY is now trading at $360. If you had just bought shares, then you would be up $1,160. Nice, but nothing to write home about. If we were using options how would our account look now?

Option	Strike	No. of Options	Start of Year	End of Year	Return
OTM	$350	16	$10,000	$16,000	60%
ATM	$320	5	$10,000	$20,000	100%
ITM	$300	3	$10,000	$18,000	80%
DITM	$220	1	$10,000	$14,000	40%
Shares		31	$10,000	$11,160	12%

Nice! All the options have beaten the market but notice that the OTM has not had such a stellar increase as it did in the previous example. It still had a very healthy return. Who wouldn't be pleased about making 60% when the market only made 12%?

But if you look closely, you will see something interesting. *The ATM option has overtaken the OTM*. What is going on? If you think about it is entirely logical.

The OTM option was effectively bought at $356.15 (How? $350 strike +

$6.15 premium) so was only making a profit of $3.85 per option (How? $360 price - $356.15 effective price). There were 16 options, so the profit was 16 * 100 * $3.85, or $6,160.

The ATM option was effectively bought at $339.85 (How? $320 strike + $19.85 premium) so was making a profit of $20.15 per option (How? $360 price -$339.85 effective price). Since there were 5 options and each option controls 100 shares the total profit is 5 * 100 * $20.15, or $10,075. So, the ATM option has made a significantly bigger profit than the OTM option. Interesting.

Let's try another scenario. Let's check this out further.

A Slow Year

Let's assume that it has been a very ordinary year. The market has only gone up by 6%, and SPY is now trading at $340. What does our account look like now?

Option	Strike	No. of Options	Start of Year	End of Year	Return
OTM	$350	16	$10,000	$0	-100%
ATM	$320	5	$10,000	$10,000	0%
ITM	$300	3	$10,000	$12,000	20%
DITM	$220	1	$10,000	$12,000	20%
Shares		31	$10,000	$10,540	5%

Whoa! What has happened to your OTM options? You have lost 100%? Your account is worth ZERO? ZIP? ZILCH? NADA?

Unfortunately, that's correct. You used all your money buying options that gave you the right to buy SPY at $350. But at the end of the time period it is trading at $340. So, you **don't exercise** your options. Why would you buy SPY for more than it is worth? If you can buy it for $340 on the market, why would you want to buy it for $350 just because you have an option? You wouldn't, right? You have just lost all your money. It's called *expiring worthless.*

And, yes, it is painful when it happens, and that's why there are so many temporary traders. Dazzled by the possible returns they splurge on OTM options hoping to get a huge return, and more often than not they get wiped out. That's why people think that options are dangerous. They are, but only in the hands of people who don't understand the risks and don't manage those risks.

That's why you only use a small part of your account if you want to dabble in OTM options. I am not saying that you shouldn't. It's great fun but remember that it is dangerous. Best not to play there until you are really sure that:

> ➢ you know what you are doing and
> ➢ you can afford to lose money.

It's definitely not part of the vanilla ITM strategy.

Let's look at how the other options have performed. The ATM $320 option has only made $75, even though technically it expired in the money. This is because while you will definitely exercise your option to buy SPY at $320 when it is currently trading at $340, the amount you paid for that privilege cost you $19.98 so effectively you paid $339.85 for something you could buy for $340.

Definitely disappointing. Especially if you had just bought the straight SPY shares you would have made 6%.

But look – our ITM and our DITM options are still performing better than the market. Let's try another scenario. Both made 20% even though the market only made 6%. Let's check another scenario.

A Disappointing Year

Let's assume it was a really disappointing year. Nothing much happened, and the market only went up 3%, to $330. What has that done to our account?

Option	Strike	No. of Options	Start of Year	End of Year	Return
OTM	$350	16	$10,000	$0	-100%
ATM	$320	5	$10,000	$5,000	-50%
ITM	$300	3	$10,000	$9,000	-10%
DITM	$220	1	$10,000	$11,000	10%
Shares		31	$10,000	$10,230	2%

Oh dear. Now the ATM option has joined the OTM at the no-fun party. It's not completely wiped out, but it has lost half of its value. Let's see why.

The ATM bought the right to buy SPY at $320 and it is currently trading at $330. That's good, technically it is in the money, and you will exercise the option. But, because the option cost $19.85 were effectively buying SPY at $339.85.

Oops. Sorry, you just lost half your money.
The ITM option has also lost money to now be worth only $9,000. Why? It bought the right to buy SPY at $300 when it is trading at $330. That's good, it will be exercised, you paid $33.17 for the privilege, so you are down on the deal. That's $3.17 per option and you had 3 of them so you are around 10% down. Not good.

You may have noticed that the DITM options are still chugging away, more than doubling the market return. Not a stellar performance, but still more than double the market.

Now, let's look at what happens if the market doesn't move at all. Unlikely, but it could happen.

A Completely Flat Market

Let's say that the market doesn't move at all. That is, it is absolutely flat, and finishes the year the same as it started, at $320. Let's see what would happen.

Option	Strike	No. of Options	Start of Year	End of Year	Return
OTM	$350	16	$10,000	$0	-100%
ATM	$320	5	$10,000	$0	-100%
ITM	$300	3	$10,000	$6,000	-40%
DITM	$220	1	$10,000	$10,000	0%
Shares		31	$10,000	$10,000	0%

It's not good news. If you had bought either OTM or ATM options, then you are now completely wiped out. The ITM options are not looking very healthy either having lost almost half of their value, but the DITM options haven't lost anything and are still close to the market. Now you will be starting to see the importance of choosing the right strike.

If the market doesn't move, then nothing moves. Not shares, not options. It is extremely unlikely but so that we have the complete picture I am including it.

A Losing Year

Now we get into what happens if the market makes a loss, which it does from time to time. In the last 50 years it has happened 10 times, which means that statistically 20% of the time there is going to be a loss. We have to consider the possibility that it could happen. If we follow the guidance from Chapter 1 then we will know the signs of a downturn. In **Chapter 9: Stay in or Sell?** I will show you what to do to avoid the worst of these.

If we have an advance warning that the market is going to dip then we need a signal to get out of our bullish positions and get ready to change to a different strategy, one that works in a bear market.

*The bear strategy is detailed in **In The Money: Bear Market Strategy** but not covered in this book.*

But let's look at what happens using the ITM strategy if we decide to ride out the downturn. Let's say the market drops to $300. What happens to our account?

Option	Strike	No. of Options	Start of Year	End of Year	Return
OTM	$350	16	$10,000	$0	-100%
ATM	$320	5	$10,000	$0	-100%
ITM	$300	3	$10,000	$0	-100%
DITM	$220	1	$10,000	$8,000	-20%
Shares		31	$10,000	$9,300	-7%

It's not pretty. If you were holding SPY shares, then you would be down 7% and have lost $700. You can see that the DITM options are the only options with any value left as all the others are completely wiped out. Using the DITM option you would lose 20%.

This is what ITM does for you: it always more than doubles the market return, both positive and negative.

The ITM strategy does not guarantee that you won't lose money. If the market drops then your account will drop too, but unlike using other types of options it is unlikely that you will be wiped out. The market would have to drop around 50% for that to happen.

This can happen, but markets recover and if you have time on your side (as in having an option with months left to expiry) then you are giving the market time to recover.

SPY Chart 2020

Above is a snapshot of SPY during and after the COVID crisis. You can see that although the drop was swift and sudden the recovery was also fast and by the end of August it was starting to make new highs. If you had decided to ride it out – and your options had enough time on them – you would not have been wiped out and would have recovered all your losses within 5 months.

But they would have been a pretty harrowing 5 months, which is why in a later chapter we are going to go through the pros and cons of staying in the market and riding out market downturns.

To reiterate: ***you can still lose money doing the ITM strategy. Just as ITM enhances your profits it can also enhance your losses.***

There are also ways that we can turbo charge our returns in good years. But the basic ITM strategy is to at least double the market returns. Mathematically, that is what happens. It has to. It always works.

A Temporary Trader's Tale

As I discuss later in the book, I rarely talk about what I do or how I do it. A couple of years ago I broke this rule, and it did not end well.

I had a friend (notice the past tense!), let's call him Tom. Tom asked me to show him what I did on the stock market, so being a nice friend, I did. I explained the ITM strategy, and he wanted to try it, so I helped him get started in the market. He started trading and started making money as it was a bull market.

I asked him from time to time how it was going, and he was always very positive and said he was making a profit. Then one day he mentioned how much profit, and I just about fell off my chair. He had started with $10,000 and now his account was worth $100,000. Yes, a ten-bagger!

I knew that by using ITM he could not possibly have done that in a few months, so I asked him to show me his positions. Yes, you guessed it. Every one of them was OTM, most of them by a fair bit. Even worse, they were all short-dated options, with only a few days or a couple of weeks to expiry.

It looked incredibly dangerous, so I offered to help him close his positions and more to a safer strategy. His answer? *'No, leave me alone, I know what I am doing!'*

Well, you guessed it. The market turned against him, nothing major just a mild correction, but because he did not have time on his side all his lovely profits started to disappear. Instead of selling when he was a little down and preserving his capital, he kept on buying more positions as they got cheaper.

He was determined to win back his profits, but alas. It didn't work, and he exited when his account was down to where it started - $10,000. Sad, but true. Technically, he didn't lose any money as he ended where he started, but it definitely shook his confidence, and he exited the market.

It is easy to get dazzled by the profits you can make with OTM options, and it is easy to get wiped out. That's why there are so many temporary traders.

Chapter 5 Highlights

The major points in Chapter 5. In and Out the Money are:

➢ The stock market over the long term gives better returns than any other kind of investment. Over the last hundred years, it has averaged 10.8% per year.

➢ Options have value at expiry only if they are in the money (ITM). Otherwise, they expire worthless.

➢ Options become cheaper the more out of the money they are and the nearer the expiry date. The cheapest options are near-dated, out of the money (OTM) options. They are also the most likely to expire worthless.

➢ Deep in the money (DITM) options with around a year to expiry are the most expensive but are the least likely to expire worthless. They can still deliver more than double the market return depending on the strike price.

And finally, some more words of wisdom this time from Mark Twain. Note the word 'speculate' – that's what temporary traders do. It's not what we are doing.

October is one of the peculiarly dangerous months to speculate in stocks. The others are July, January, September, April, November, May, March, June, December, August, and February.

◆◆◆

Chapter 6. Spiders and Witches

Let's recap on some terminology just so that we are clear before we introduce the next part of the strategy. Options can be:

> **OTM** (Out of The Money) - their strike price is ABOVE the current market price

> **ATM** (At The Money) – The strike price is AT the current market price

> **ITM** (In The Money) – The strike price is UNDER the current market price

> **DITM** (Deep In The Money) – The strike price is well below the current market price.

You will probably have noticed that options can change their classification when the market moves. If SPY was trading at $320 then a

$330 option (an option with a strike price of $330) would be classified as OTM. If the SPY moved up to $330 then it would be ATM. If the SPY moved up more, to $340 then it would be ITM. It is the same option, but the classification changes with the market price.

Exercising an option means that you exercise your right to buy the SPY at your strike price. If your option has expired ITM then you will exercise. For example, if your strike is $300 and the SPY is trading at $340 then you would definitely want to buy at a $40 'discount'.

If it is OTM then you would not exercise. Why? Because you would be buying something for more than it was currently worth. For example, if your strike was $350 and SPY was trading at $340 why would you want to buy it at a higher price? Obviously, you wouldn't want to do that, so you let it **expire worthless**.

We also saw the situation where an ITM option was exercised, and it still lost money. This happens if the amount that we paid for the option (the premium) is bigger than the gap between the strike and the current market price. We also looked at the **Effective Price** which is what we are actually paying for the stock / ETF. The formula is:

Effective Price = Strike + Premium

As we move deeper in the money the effective price reduces. OTM options will have a higher effective price than ATM options who will in turn be higher than ITM options. DITM options will have the lowest effective price of them all.

We saw that the DITM options we were looking at always more than doubled the market returns, whether positive or negative. The DITM options outperformed the others and enabled you to make more than double whatever the SPY makes (depending on the strike you choose) and with much less risk.

Why did we choose a DITM strike of $220 and not some other DITM option? Great question. To answer that we first need to look at types of options and introduce another concept.

Types of Options

Let's look at the various options and work out what are we really buying. There are two main types of options: American and European. The name does not refer to where the stock is, but to how you can exercise them. When we say 'exercise' we mean acting on our right to buy, and actually going ahead and purchasing the underlying stock or ETF.

The two types of options are:

> **American** options can be exercised at any time up to and including the expiry date. We are going to be using American options to trade SPY.

> **European** options can only be exercised on their expiry date, but we don't have to worry about them as we are not going to be using them in the ITM strategy.

While SPY options can be exercised anytime within the time period, they are never exercised before their time has expired. Why not? Because you would be losing the time value. Options give you the right to buy something – a house, a boat, a stock, an ETF – for a specified time. You are paying for that time. Why would you give it away?

The next question is *what do we do instead?* Easy. If we no longer want the option, we simply sell it, just like we bought it. That's what the options market is. People buying and selling options, not usually exercising them. That only happens on particular dates – the option expiry date.

The Witching Hour

Every option has an expiry date, and the most common option expiry date is on the third Friday of the month. On those days there is usually heavy volume as traders close out option contracts before expiry. It is particularly heavy during the last hour of trading, just before the closing bell, and it is called, rather charmingly I always think, the **Witching Hour**.

Witching hour originally meant the hour between midnight and 1 AM, when witches, demons and ghosts were thought to be at their most powerful and when supernatural events happened. It was thought that black magic was most effective in that hour. Witches, demons, goblins, and ghosts would appear, and they brought havoc and bad luck to anyone unfortunate enough to chance upon them.

While SPY options can expire on a Monday, Wednesday, or Friday (or the day after if there is a public holiday) most of these tend to be 'weekly' options, which are more lightly traded. Witching for stock options and index options is on the third Friday of every month, but on the third Friday of March, June, September, and December there is what is called 'quadruple witching' when they are joined by index futures and stock futures.

It is usually referred to as 'triple witching' because before 2002 there were only 3 classes of options. The term 'quadruple witching' never really caught on, possibly because three is a more 'magic' number.

Why is there increased trading? Because as the expiration hour approaches, traders have to decide whether to close out their positions or to 'roll' them to a future date. Traders also find out if their options are in the money or not. If they are in the money at expiration, they automatically get exercised, in other words, they actually buy the stock (or rather their broker does it for them).

Most traders don't want the hassle of being exercised. That means that you actually buy the stock and then, unless you have a LOT of money in your account, you probably have to sell it again right away. If you do it within 3 days (called T+3) then brokers don't require that you actually come up with the cash to buy it, but they may charge you brokerage.

In other words, when you buy SPY (or any other stock or index) you have 3 days to actually pay for it, hence T+3 (trade date plus three days). What usually happens is that you sell SPY 'at market' as soon as you can, and no money actually has to be deposited.

It is best to unload (sell your options) or roll (sell your short-term position and buy a longer-term one) some days before expiry, if possible, just to avoid any hassle. This may sound complicated, but it isn't really, and we will look at how to do it later in the book. Before we get to that, we have to work out what options we want to buy.

The Options Chain

For SPY (or any other index or stock with options) there is an *options chain.* This is a list of all options and the possible expiration dates, strikes and prices. Two prices are given:

> ➢ The **BID** – the price that a buyer is offering
> ➢ The **ASK** – the price that a seller will sell.

The difference between the bid and the ask is called the **spread.** In thinly traded options the spread can be quite large which is annoying as you may have to buy at a higher price or sell at a lower price than you would like. With SPY, because of its high liquidity, the spread is quite small and guaranteed by market makers, but more of that later.

Here we have an example of a call options chain for SPY with just over a year, 386 days, to expiry. This table is just a small part of the full SPY options chain, which has many expiry dates, and strikes of $25 right through to $420. We are looking at the chain for SPY options expiring in January 2021, or just over a year away when this snapshot was taken.

Options chains may look slightly different depending on your website or broker, but they will all have the same elements.

SPDR S&P 500 ETF
322.94 +1.71 (0.53%)

Last Trade 8:00:00 PM ET ↻ Refresh

Bid	Ask
323.37	323.40
High	Low
322.95	321.64

Collapse All   **Calls**

Action	Build		Volume	OI	Last	Change	Bid	Ask	Strike

SPY Jan 15, 2021 (Fri: 386 days)

Action	Build		Volume	OI	Last	Change	Bid	Ask	Strike
Trade	Select	ⓘ	11	7,517	28.81	+0.28	29.41	29.70	310.00
Trade	Select	ⓘ	0	847	27.43	0	28.71	29.05	311.00
Trade	Select	ⓘ	0	965	27.20	0	28.02	28.35	312.00
Trade	Select	ⓘ	0	552	25.02	0	27.34	27.66	313.00
Trade	Select	ⓘ	0	569	25.14	0	26.65	26.97	314.00
Trade	Select	ⓘ	9	4,305	25.71	+0.79	25.98	26.29	315.00
Trade	Select	ⓘ	0	701	22.35	0	25.31	25.61	316.00
Trade	Select	ⓘ	0	472	23.60	0	24.64	24.94	317.00
Trade	Select	ⓘ	0	456	21.20	0	23.97	24.27	318.00
Trade	Select	ⓘ	0	437	20.81	0	23.32	23.61	319.00
Trade	Select	ⓘ	144	3,940	22.60	+1.07	22.67	22.80	320.00
Trade	Select	ⓘ	8	458	22.00	+0.93	22.02	22.31	321.00
Trade	Select	ⓘ	126	597	21.13	+0.70	21.45	21.67	322.00
Trade	Select	ⓘ	30	332	20.48	+0.54	20.74	21.03	323.00
Trade	Select	ⓘ	0	305	19.19	0	20.12	20.40	324.00
Trade	Select	ⓘ	82	5,385	18.92	+0.38	19.49	19.78	325.00
Trade	Select	ⓘ	0	221	17.90	0	18.88	19.16	326.00
Trade	Select	ⓘ	5	218	17.80	+0.51	18.27	18.56	327.00
Trade	Select	ⓘ	0	270	16.75	0	17.67	17.95	328.00
Trade	Select	ⓘ	5	323	16.66	+0.34	17.08	17.36	329.00
Trade	Select	ⓘ	81	1,958	16.37	+0.74	16.51	16.78	330.00

First, you will notice that the SPY is referred to as a SPDR, commonly called a **'spider'.** It stands for Standard & Poor's Depository Receipts. A spider (SPDR) is simply an ETF (Exchange Traded Fund), and SPY is a SPDR that tracks the S&P 500 index. We will keep on using the terminology SPY as it is quicker and easier, and it is how people generally refer to it.

The table may look complicated but once you know what everything means it will make sense and you will be quite at home looking at options chains. Let's just run through what everything means.

Going along the top line:

> **Volume** – the number of options that were bought and sold in the last trading day.
> **OI** – Open Interest – the number of options that exist for this strike.
> **Last** – the last price at which the option traded.
> **Change** – the change in price from the close of the day before.
> **Bid** – the price a trader is offering to buy this option.
> **Ask** – the price a trader is offering to sell this option.
> **Strike** – the strike price of the option.

You can see that some lines in the table are colored pale blue, others white. The pale blue means that the option is ITM and the white means that it is OTM. On this day, the SPY was trading at $322.94 so technically a strike of $322 is ITM and a strike of $323 is OTM.

There is no option actually ATM, which is normal as SPY options usually go up in $1 increments. SPY would have to be exactly $322.00 to have a technically ATM option. Having the SPY finish on a 'nice' number like $300, $320 or $350 rarely happens; statistically only about 1% of the time.

It is standard practice to refer to ones *near* the current price as ATM, so both $322 and $323 would be classified as ATM.

Analyzing the Chain

It looks like there are lots of numbers, but when you are doing the ITM strategy you will only have to worry about a very few of them, so don't take fright! Once you know what everything is it will all make sense and seem quite simple.

Looking at this option chain you can see that there was not much activity, and the volumes were low. In other words, not many options were bought and sold on this day. This is because the snapshot was taken between Xmas and New Year, typically a very slow period on the market.

You can also see that the open interest (the number of options at this strike price) is highest on 'nice' numbers like 315, 320 and 325. This is normal; humans tend to do this. Just like you do when you book a restaurant for 7 PM, not 7:08 PM.

The difference between the bid and the ask price is called the **spread**. Usually, the actual price at which the option will be sold is somewhere midway between the bid and the ask.

Small spreads (in other words, the bid and the ask are close together) are considered good because you know with more certainty what the option will trade at. In some of the smaller, less traded stocks, the option spread can be alarmingly big, but on SPY it is always small, so we don't have to worry about that.

Open Interest (OI) is not a worry either. Often, I get emails from readers querying whether they should only buy options with a high open interest. With SPY it doesn't matter; you will see that there is a bid and an ask for each strike, and the spread on the strikes with lower OI are almost exactly the same as the spreads with high OI.

This means that we can choose the option with the exact strike that we want without worrying about being able to buy it or to later sell it again.

Just to reiterate, the blue background indicates which options are ITM (In The Money). The white background indicates that it is an OTM (Out of The Money) option.

You will notice that options get cheaper as they get further OTM, and more expensive as they get deeper ITM. You may be wondering why this happens. Let's take some examples from a cut-down option chain and figure it out. We will only look at the 'nice' even-numbered options like 200 and 250 to make the math easier.

Volume	OI	Last	Change	Bid	Ask	Strike
0	318	120.37	0	123.62	125.42	200
0	1,090	75.81	0	77.18	78.40	250
26	6,032	36.05	0.54	36.62	37.03	300
144	3,940	22.60	1.07	22.67	22.80	320
422	1,560	7.06	0.51	7.03	7.23	350
85	931	0.52	0.05	0.49	0.52	400

You can see that the Ask price of the options varies from $125.42 through to $0.52. The deeper in the money we go, the higher the price. The further OTM, the cheaper the price. And so that we are clear let's check what each option gives you the right to do.:

You have the RIGHT but not the OBLIGATION to buy SPY at the strike price at any time up until the expiration date.

You will effectively be buying SPY at the strike price + the premium. That means that if you exercised your option then the **effective price** (what you would actually be paying for SPY) is:

Strike	Bid	Effective Price
200	123.62	$323.62
250	77.18	$327.18
300	36.62	$336.62
320	22.67	$342.67
350	7.03	$357.03
400	0.49	$400.49

The SPY was trading at $322.94 at the time of this snapshot. Let's say you bought the $300 strike option, for $36.62 (the bid price). This means you have the right to buy SPY at $300, but you have effectively paid $336.62 which is $13.68 more than it is currently worth. If you bought the $400 option, then you are paying $77.55 extra. That's almost 25% extra! Why are you doing this?

Time Value

This is where we introduce the concept of **Time Value** and **Intrinsic Value**.

> **Intrinsic Value** is the difference between the strike and the current price, or what you would get if you exercised the option right now.

> **Time Value** is the extra you are willing to pay for the option, over and above the intrinsic value.

The easy way to remember it is:

Option Price = Intrinsic Value + Time Value.

Why do people pay for time value? Because they are hoping that the underlying SPY will move up before expiry and make them a nice profit. We saw how that worked in the last chapter when we were looking at the effect on our account of the different levels of options.

If we remember our real estate examples, in both cases the buyer of the option was paying for time value hoping that an event would happen to make the purchase desirable (the developer) or even possible (the inheritance).

Let's go back to our practical example and make sure that you understand it. We will use the bid price so that you can see exactly where the figures come from.

Example 1: ITM

At the time of these examples, SPY was trading just below $323. If we look at the $300 option, which is ITM, then:

- ➢ $36.62 is the price of the option
- ❖ $22.94 is the Intrinsic Value
- ❖ $13.68 is the Time Value

ITM $300 Option

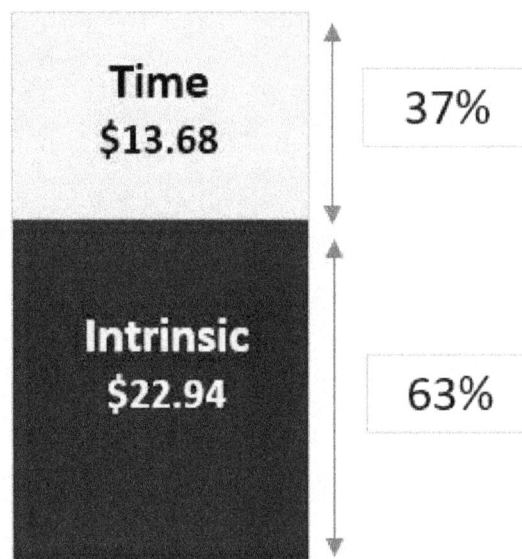

Time $13.68	37%
Intrinsic $22.94	63%

Option Price = Intrinsic Value (63%) + Time Value (37%)

Even though the $300 option is clearly ITM, there is still a considerable time value component.

Example 2: ATM

Let's go a little closer to an ATM option. Let's choose a $320 strike and see what happens.

- ➢ $22.67 is the price of the option
- ❖ $2.94 is the Intrinsic Value
- ❖ $19.73 is the Time Value

ATM $320 Option

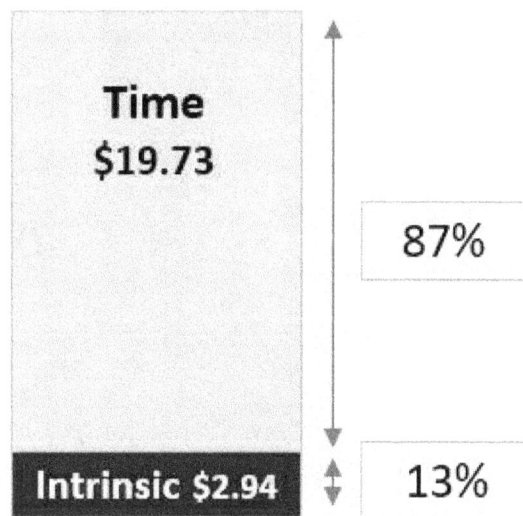

Option Price = Intrinsic Value (13%) + Time Value (87%)

What is happening here? Although the option is cheaper it has *less intrinsic value*, and a lot *more time value.* Intrinsic value makes up only 13% of the option price, with the remaining 87% being time value. The rule is, that as we move the strike higher, the intrinsic value gets smaller, and the time value gets bigger.

Example 3: OTM

Let's look at what happens with a $350 strike OTM option:

➢ $7.03 is the price of the option
❖ $0.00 is the Intrinsic Value
❖ $7.03 is the Time Value

OTM $350 Option

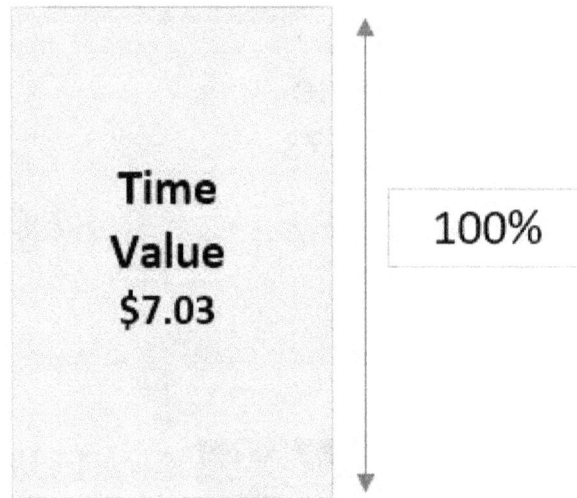

Time
Value
$7.03

100%

Option Price = Intrinsic Value (0%) + Time Value (100%)

OK, what just happened? *Why is there no intrinsic value?*

Easy. Because the Strike is higher than the current trading price it is all time value. Any option with a strike higher than the current trading price (which is **any** OTM option) is ALL time value – there is no intrinsic value whatsoever.

So here we see what happens when you buy an OTM option. You are **only** buying time value as it has no intrinsic value. You are hoping that the SPY will move up so that your OTM option becomes ITM and has some intrinsic value, otherwise you are going to lose all your money as it will expire worthless. Not a pretty thought.

Example 4: DITM

Let's look at what happens when you move down into deeper ITM options. Let's choose the $250 strike and see what is different.

- $77.18 is the price of the option
- $72.94 is the Intrinsic Value
- $4. 24 is the Time Value

DITM $250 Option

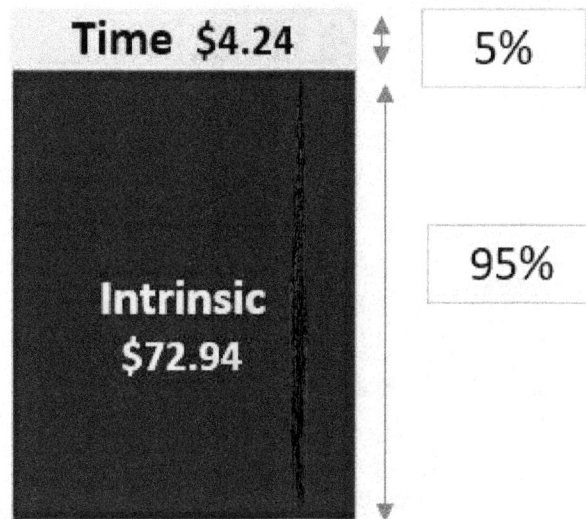

You can see that as we go deeper in the money the intrinsic value is getting bigger, and the time value is getting less. Our option price looks like this:

Option Price = Intrinsic Value (95%) + Time Value (5%)

Example 5: Deeper DITM

What happens if we go even further deep in the money? Let's look at the $200 strike option.

- ➢ $123.62 is the price of the option
- ❖ $122.94 is the Intrinsic Value
- ❖ $0.68 is the Time Value

DITM $200 Option

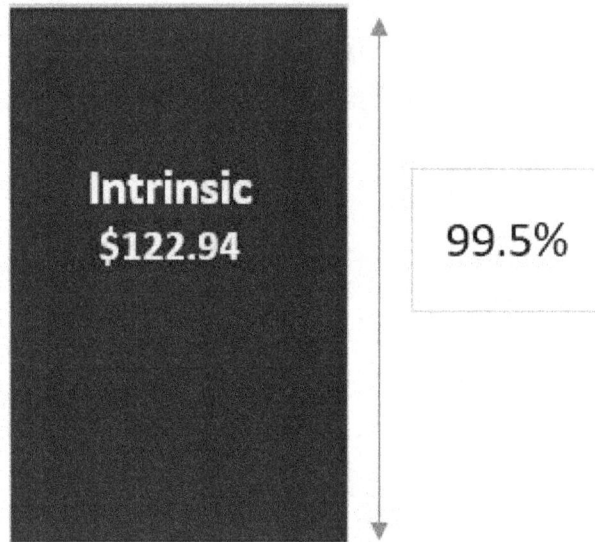

The intrinsic value has increased, and the time value has decreased. Our option price looks like this:

Option Price = Intrinsic Value (99.5%) + Time Value (0.5%)

That is starting to look good. We are actually getting a high proportion of real (intrinsic) value for our money. Our time value is becoming negligible (less than 1%), so we don't have to worry about the option losing value as the time progresses. This happens. ***Time value always reduces to zero at expiry.*** More of that shortly, let's keep on with our examples.

Example 6: Really Deep DITM

If we go really DITM, to the halfway point of $160, what happens then?

- ➢ $162.96 is the price of the option
- ❖ $162.94 is the Intrinsic Value
- ❖ $0.02 is the Time Value

In other words, the time value is negligible. Our option price looks like this:

Option Price = Intrinsic Value (100%) + Time Value (0%)

Since our option price has only intrinsic (real) value we don't have to worry about it losing money over time. We are actually buying real (intrinsic) value.

This is the essence of the ITM strategy.

We buy DITM options with little or no time value and then hold them until near expiry, then 'roll' them which means buying another option with more time to expiry.

Later chapters will show you exactly how to roll your options, but right now we want to concentrate on how time value affects option prices.

Why would we buy DITM options rather than just buying shares? Because you are getting at least twice as much 'bang for your buck' so that you get to your goal quicker.

Each option controls one hundred shares and even DITM options will give you much more leverage than simply buying the shares.

TIME VALUE AND INTRINSIC VALUE

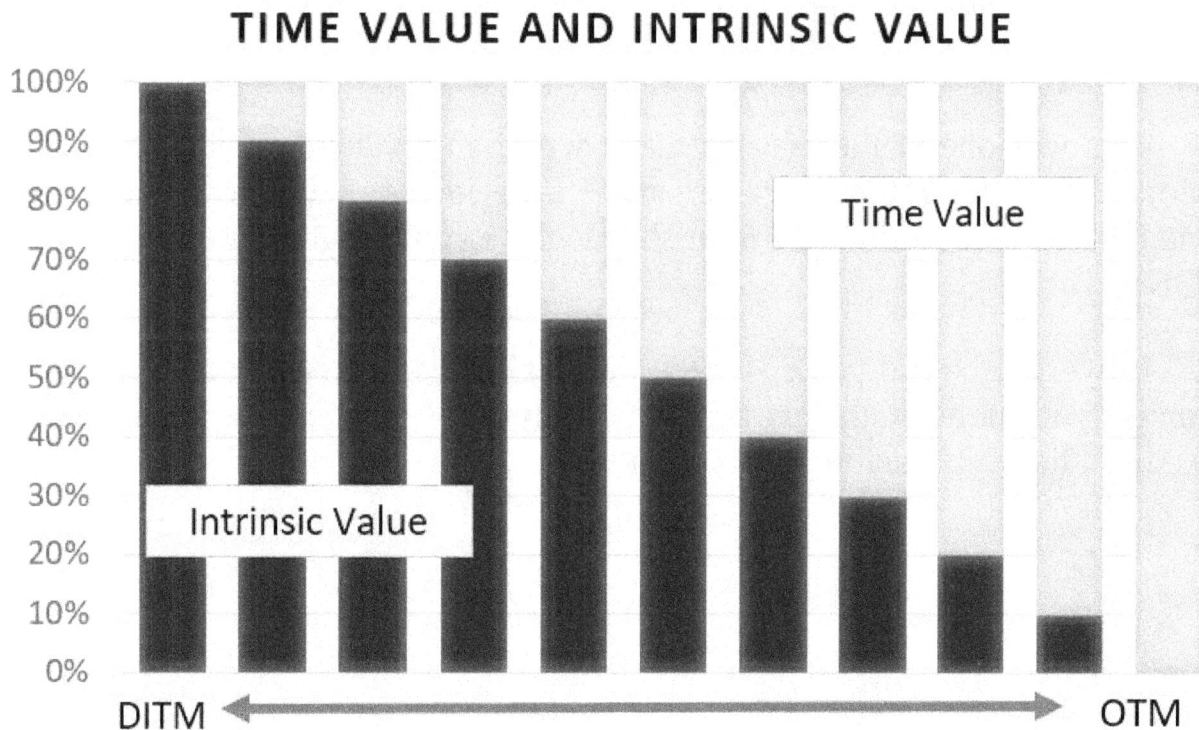

How Much Extra?

The 'vanilla' ITM strategy is to go for double the SPY returns. That is the basic strategy. To do this you would buy options with a **strike price exactly half what SPY is currently trading at**. This will give you exactly double the SPY returns. No ifs, no buts. That's what happens mathematically.

If you buy an option with a strike price more than half the current price you will get more than double the returns. However, using the ITM strategy we have to buy options with little or no time value which means that we can't have a strike that is too close to the current price. In a later chapter, we will look at exactly how to choose your options.

There is one problem, of course: **how much money do we need to get started?** If we choose an option with a strike of $160 then we need $16,000 to buy it. Each option controls 100 shares, remember, so the option price has to be multiplied by 100.

Originally when I wrote the book, I was aiming to make ITM accessible to accounts of $10K or more. At that time, it was possible to find options that met the ITM criteria, but today it is harder because SPY has increased so much in the last year.

This was one of the reasons that I wrote an updated version of In The Money: Bull Market Strategy because I have included an ITM strategy for smaller accounts (called ITMS for short) where you can get started for around $3K.

However, the end game is to do the 'real' ITM strategy. However ITMS can get you started in the market, and hopefully your account will soon reach the level that you need to transition to ITM.

Chapter 6 Highlights

The major points in Chapter 6. Spiders and Witches are:

➤ Options prices are made up of 2 components: Intrinsic Value and Time Value.

➤ Intrinsic Value is 'real' value and is the difference between the strike and the current price.

➤ ITM and DITM are the only options with Intrinsic Value.

➤ OTM options have no Intrinsic Value and are all Time Value.

➤ If an option is OTM at expiry, then it expires worthless.

➤ The ITM strategy involves buying DITM options on SPY with a very little Time Value.

➤ The ITMS strategy is a new strategy that enables people with smaller accounts to get started in the market.

And finally, two rules of investing from Warren Buffett:

Rule No. 1: Never lose money

Rule No 2. Never forget Rule No. 1

❖❖❖

Chapter 7. Never Go Naked

Option prices change all the time, minute to minute, day to day. When the underlying asset (SPY) moves the option prices move also. As the SPY goes up so do the call option prices, if SPY goes down then so do the call options.

In the examples in the last chapter, we were taking the bid price, which is what someone is prepared to pay for the option. However, no one may be prepared to sell it for that. The ask price is always higher than the bid price. From experience, I have found that if you put your order in halfway between the bid/ask plus one cent (or whatever the minimum is) it is almost always filled, presumably because that is the algorithm that is used for determining option pricing and sales.

Brokers differ in how they fill your trades. If you put in a limit price some brokers will fill at exactly that price; others will try to improve the price. One of the brokers I use has what is called 'price improvement', which means that your trade can be executed at better prices than the best-quoted market price which is called the National Best Bid and Offer (NBBO). I have found that if I put in a buy at the ask price, then I am usually filled right at, or very near to, the bottom of the spread. If you want to find out more about this then google *'price improvement NBBI'*.

Volatility

Another factor in option pricing is volatility. If a stock has a price that is stable (i.e., its price stays roughly the same over a time period) then it is said to have **low volatility**. If the price jumps around a lot, then that stock has **high volatility**. Low volatility stocks are less risky because, based on recent history, it is unlikely that the price will change dramatically. High volatility stocks have a higher risk because they are more erratic, with faster increases and dramatic falls, making it more likely that you will either make profits or losses.

Options on stocks with high volatility are more expensive than options on stocks with low volatility. As we are trading SPY, because it is based on 80% of the market it is considered relatively stable. However, the market as a whole can change from a period of low volatility to high volatility, and back again. If the SPY moves from a period of low volatility into a period of high volatility the option prices will increase even though the SPY itself hasn't changed in actual value.

Volatility

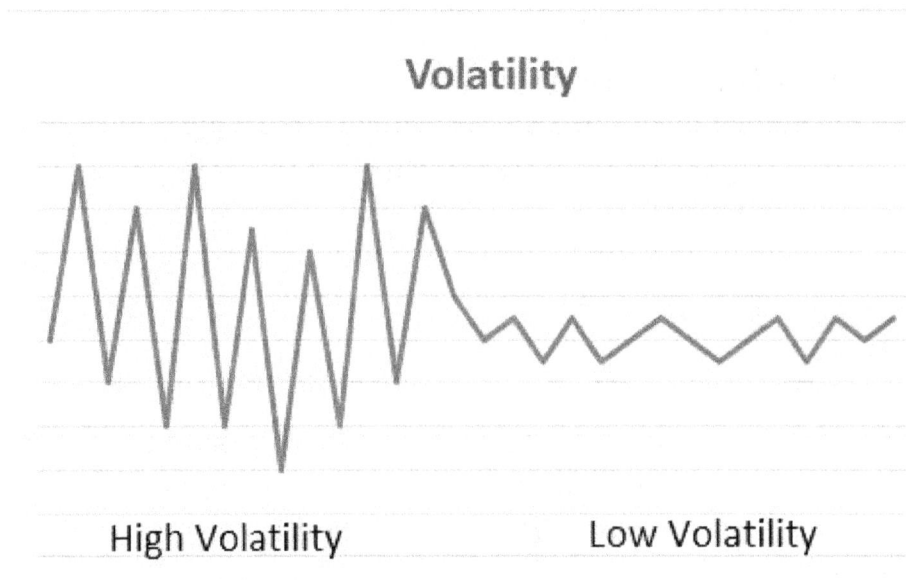

High Volatility   Low Volatility

There is even an index that tracks the volatility of SPX. Its commonly called the VIX, the CBOE Volatility Index. It's also called the 'Fear Index'. When the VIX is high it is generally because trader sentiment is fearful. People are wary and jumpy, worried about their investments, and tend to do things impulsively.

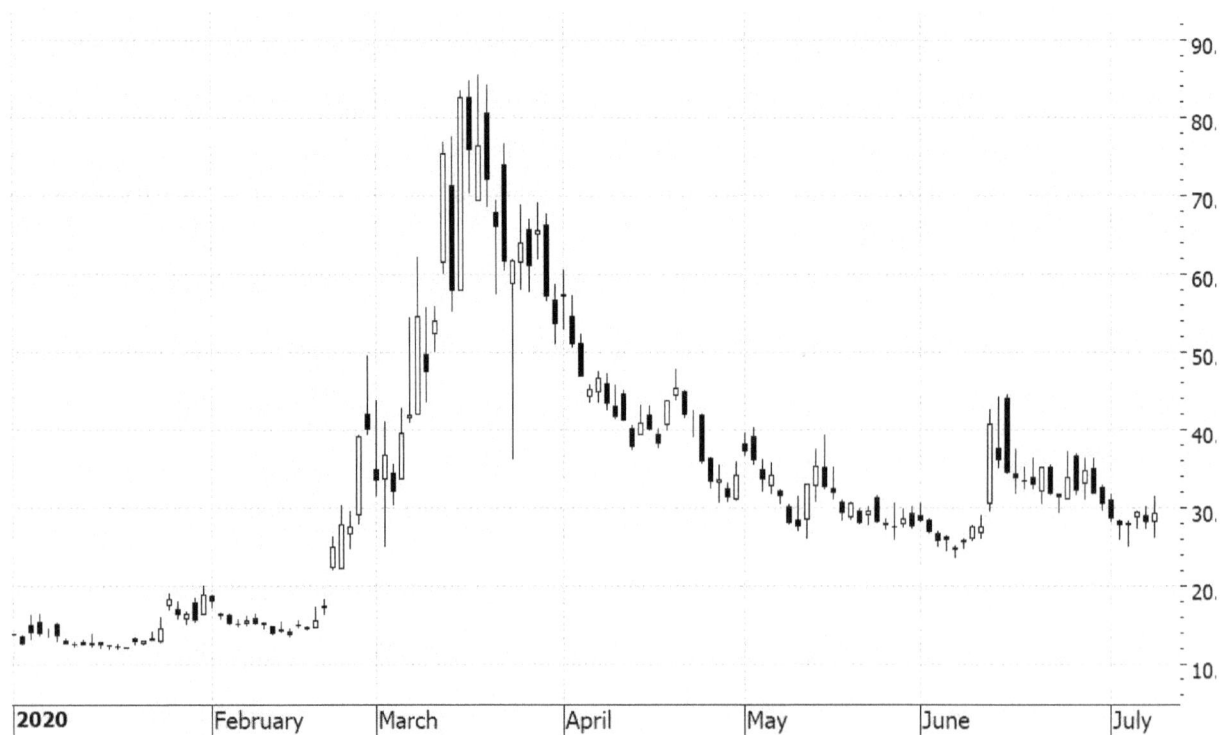

Here is the VIX during the Covid crisis in 2020. Until late February it was very low (anything less than 20 is considered low) and relatively stable. You can see it started to increase in late February, reached extreme levels during March, and then started to taper off with a bit of a bump in June. After that, although the market was booming, the VIX stayed elevated when compared with before Covid. It didn't get below 20 until a year later, in March 2021.

If there is a sudden, sharp drop in volatility this can bring about what is called a 'volatility crush'. Even though the share price may not have dropped, your option price can drop because the volatility has dropped.

This generally happens after events take place that affects the market, like quarterly earnings reports, or a new regulation. And, speaking from experience, it is really annoying when the underlying stock has not changed in price, but your options have dropped in value.

But there is good news: It is ***only the time value that changes***. If we have options with little or no time value, then we don't have to worry about it. It's not a problem for us!

Who wants to be Cheap?

OTM options are cheap for a reason: the higher OTM you get the less likely they are to make you any money. It's all about probability and whether, at expiry time, the strike price has been reached by the underlying asset. Even when it has, we have seen that we can still lose money when we take the cost of the option into account.

We have also seen that as the strike price increases the cost of the option comes down, but the time value goes up. You may be wondering if OTM options have only time value why don't we buy the cheaper ones and buy more of them. This is the mistake that many new traders make. Just get on any stock chat site and people will be raving about how cheap the OTM options are and bragging about the price they got them for. Beware. Do not listen to them. They are 'temporary traders', prime for being forced out of the market – that is if they are even in the market at all!

There is a widely-quoted statistic that 80% of options expire worthless, which sounds alarming. You may have heard it used as a reason why you can't win with options because the odds are against you. Personally, I have had it quoted to me so many times I can't count them, usually by people who have themselves crashed and burned and are now telling me that what **I** am doing is dangerous.

They are close, however. Most options **do** expire worthless. The actual figure is 76.5% but it is not a scary statistic. It simply means that *there are more OTM options than ITM options.* Around 3 times more. It is that simple. If an option is ITM then it has Intrinsic Value and is not worthless. If it is OTM then it only has Time Value, and when the time runs out it has no value left and is **worthless.** Therefore if 76.5% of options expire worthless it is because 76.5% of options are OTM at the expiry date.

I find it very hard to understand why people don't get that, but most people don't. And that includes traders, which may be the reason why so many of them go bust or at least part of the reason. It shows a basic misunderstanding of what an option is and how it comes into being.

Don't Trade Naked!

Why are there more OTM options than ITM? That is an easy question to answer, but one that most traders fail to grasp. Options are written by people. Options are not made up by the stock exchange. If you write a call option and you do not hold the stock you are writing against it is called a 'naked' option. It's also called an 'uncovered' option. It is dangerous. Very dangerous. You definitely don't want to do that!

How it works is this: if I decide that I want to live dangerously, I could go and write 100 options for the SPY $350 strike. These 100 options have just been created out of thin air. They didn't exist until I wrote them, and if you looked at the options chain you would see that it adds to the number of options for that stock. If, for example, the Open Interest (the number of options at a particular strike) was 1,560 and I wrote 100 options, then you would see that the OI would change to 1,660. I have just increased the number of options by writing 100 options.

Once an option is written it can't be unwritten. It can be sold, exercised, or expire worthless, but it can't cease to exist. It's there until expiry.

So why do around three-quarters of all options expire worthless?
Because more people write OTM options than write ITM options!

Why do people write more OTM options?

Because they hope that they won't be exercised and that they can get to keep the premium.

In our case, if we wrote 100 SPY options with a strike of $350, we would be hoping that the SPY would finish below the $350 at the expiry date. If it did, we would keep our premium. If we use the example from the last chapter, we could sell the option for $7.03.

Of course, it is not just $7.03. We would actually make a lot more than that because selling each option at $7.03 would bring us a total of $703 per option, as each option is a contract for 100 shares of SPY.

And if we sold 100 options then we would have made $70,300. A nice, tidy little sum! You can see why people want to write OTM options.

But there is a MAJOR downside

Let's say the SPY shot up to $380 at expiry. To fulfill our contract, we would have to buy them at market ($380) and sell them at the strike ($350), so we would be losing $30 per SPY share. But there are 100 SPY shares for each option contract, so on each option we would be losing $3,000. And we sold 100 of them! That's a loss of $300,000! Of course, we would get to keep our premium of $70,300, but we would still make a loss of $229,700. That would hurt. A lot.

That's one of the ways people lose their shirts on the market. Writing naked is bad news. It is far too risky. Don't do it. Remember that trader from an earlier chapter who lost her entire stake and was afraid to tell her husband? Well, that was what she was doing, writing naked options on gold.

Suddenly writing OTM options doesn't seem quite so attractive, does it?

Running out of Time

The main thing to remember is that at expiry the time value is zero for ANY option, whether ITM or OTM. Why? Because there is no time left so there is no time value. Only intrinsic value is left which means that only options that are ITM have any value at all.

➤ An OTM option, which has only time value, will **expire worthless**.

➤ An ITM option will be **exercised**, which means the holder of the option can buy the underlying stock or ETF at the strike price, realizing the intrinsic value.

Options traders tend not to take delivery of the underlying shares. In practice, most traders exercise then sell right away 'at market', which means at the current trading price. They don't want to have to come up with the money to buy the underlying 100s of shares. This is absolutely fine, and quite normal.

If you buy and sell on the same day the trades cancel each other out and brokers don't require you to stump up the money. They may, however, charge you brokerage.

Brokers are very used to this, and even if you forget to exercise and sell, if there is not enough money in your account to take delivery of the underlying stocks then your broker will automatically exercise and then sell it for you.

As we know, option prices depend not only on the strike but also on the time to expiry. If we look at the same strike with different expiry dates, we see that the longer the time to expiry the more the option costs.

As an example, here are the bid prices for options expiring on 17 Jan 2020 (in 15 days) and 15 Jan 2021 (379 days) taken when the SPY is trading at $324.87.

Strike	Days to Expiry	
	15	379
160	$164.87	$164.82
200	$124.91	$125.34
250	$74.97	$78.50
300	$25.21	$37.59
320	$6.25	$23.40
350	$0.00	$7.21
400	$0.00	$0.39

The first thing you will probably notice is that the DITM option prices for the 160 strike are almost the same whether they are long-dated or short-dated. Because DITM options are almost all intrinsic value, with no time value at all, the price reflects this. This is why, using the ITM strategy, we don't have to worry about our options losing value over time. The other DITM options (250 and 300 strikes) also have similar prices.

When we look at the 300 strike, we start to notice a difference. It is ITM by almost $25 but the time value is still significant, with the 2021 option costing almost 50% more. When we get to the 320 strike (technically ITM, but so close to the current price it would normally be classed as ATM) the 2021 option costs 274% more.

When we get to OTM options the difference is stark; nobody wants the 350 or 400 strike if it is expiring in 15 days. No one is offering to buy. Why? Because the chances of the SPY jumping 8% or 23% in 2 weeks is remote. Not impossible, but extremely unlikely.

You will notice, though, that there are buyers for them with 379 days to go. This is because buyers are willing to pay for time value as the SPY may then move up past the strikes. It would only take a move of 14% over the year for the 350 strike to make a profit, and that is a quite reasonable expectation. A move of 23% over the year is not unheard of but less likely. That's why the 400 strike is priced more cheaply.

An interesting observation is the difference in the number of options for each expiry date. The number of strikes is similar (214 for 2020 compared to 204 for 2021) but look at the number of options:

> ➤ 1,487,827 (2020)
> ➤ 149,403(2021)

Why are there more options for the near term? Because if you remember options are created out of nothing. Someone decides to write an option and so creates it at that moment. Partly it's because near-term options have had a longer time for people to write them because you can only write options for around 2 years in advance. But mainly, it's because option writers like to write options with a short time to expiry as there is less chance that they will be exercised, and then they get to keep the premium without having to provide anything in return.

Falling off a cliff

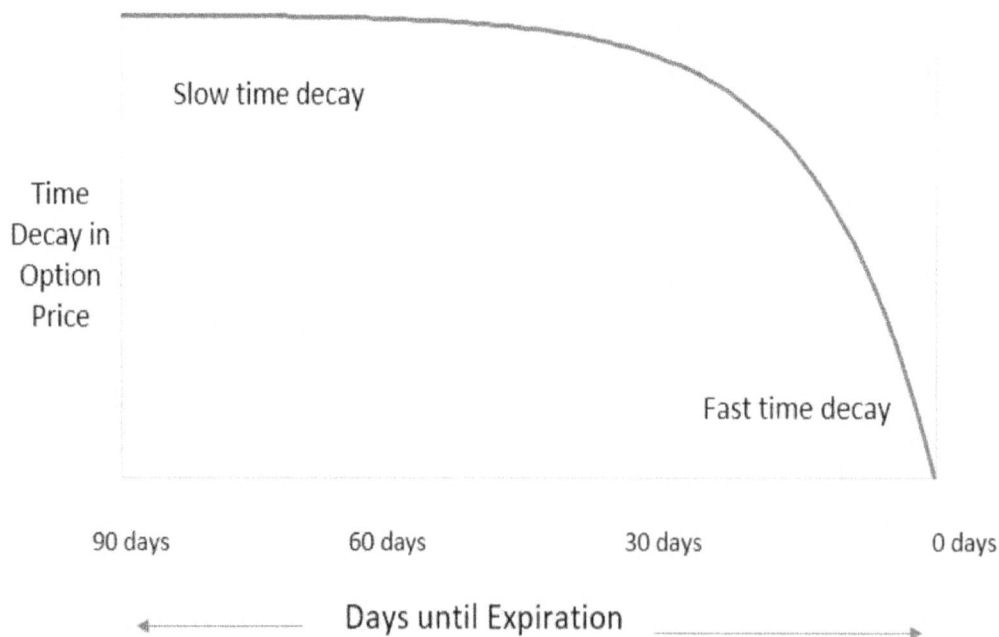

Time value decreases the closer we get to the expiry date. This is called **time decay** and it is really quite dramatic. The chart below shows the drop in time value over the last 90 days. It starts slowly and then picks up speed, eventually dropping off a cliff.

The most dramatic fall is in the last 30 days which is why you do not ever want to be holding an option with any time value until expiry. You've paid for that time value –so don't let it decay away. Someone else can buy it and it can be their worry!

Most savvy option buyers make sure they exit or 'roll' (sell the near-dated option and buy a longer-dated one) at least 30 days before expiry.

Of course, the last 30 days are the ideal time to be *writing* options, because you are selling time and it is decaying all the time, like an iceberg that is slowly melting away. You *want* to be left having sold an option that has expired worthless, because you get to keep the premium. That's what you were hoping would happen.

Writing options can be dangerous, although there are ways of managing that risk. But that is a different strategy for a different book.

Greeks Bearing Gifts

If you have ever talked to an options trader, chances are they loved to make it sound complicated. They probably used a lot of jargon some of which you now know and can't be impressed by (strikes, expiry, ITM, intrinsic value, time decay, and so on). They may then try to establish their superiority by bringing out the big guns: *The Greeks!*

They start banging on about delta-neutral strategies, gamma trading or something equally as nasty-sounding. Fear not, I am going to make it simple.

The funny thing is that most options traders don't really understand what the Greeks are, what they do, and where they are important. And the good news is that there is really only one that you need to know about to do the ITM strategy. However, we will have a quick look at all of them just so that you know what they mean and won't be intimidated if someone tries to impress you with their cleverness. We will use SPY as the example, but the Greeks apply to any stock or index that has options.

There are 5 Greeks: delta, gamma, vega, theta and rho. They are all letters from the Greek alphabet. If you are interested just Google 'Greek Alphabet' to see their symbols. The five Greeks are all measures of how option pricing can change. We already know that the price of an option depends on:

> The strike price (Greeks: delta and gamma)
> The time to expiry (Greeks: vega and theta)

Delta is the only Greek that we really have to understand for ITM, and even there we use it is more as a descriptor than something we use to select our option.

Delta is how the option price will move relative to the underlying stock or ETF.

Which, in our case, is the SPY price. Deltas vary from -1 through to +1. The negative numbers are for puts which we are not going to trade in this book so we will ignore them and assume that delta is a value between 0 and 1. A delta of:

> 1 means that for every 1 cent move in SPY the option moves 1 cent.
> 0.5 means that for every 1 cent move in SPY the option moves 0.5 cents.
> 0 means that for every 1 cent move in SPY the option moves 0 cents.

That seems pretty easy, doesn't it? Nothing to be afraid of! But how do we know practically, what this means?

> DITM options have a high delta, close to 1.
> ATM options have a medium delta, around 0.5
> OTM options have a low delta, close to 0

That's all we need to know. Simple really, isn't it? To make sure that you can hold your own in any discussion we will quickly look at the other Greeks:

> **Gamma is the rate of change of Delta.** We don't need to know about this as we are not going to be jumping in and out of trades.

> **Theta is a measure of time decay**. We already know about this and are going to be buying options with very little time value, so it does

not affect us.

> ➤ **Vega is a measure of the sensitivity to volatility** of the underlying. Again, we don't need this for the ITM strategy.

> ➤ **Rho is a measure of sensitivity to interest rates** and so is not at all relevant to us.

So, the Greeks *are* bearing gifts that tell us how much we should be paying for an option, but as in real life, some gifts are more useful than others. And delta is the only Greek gift we need to do the ITM strategy – the other Greeks can be regifted!

If you want to read more about option pricing, then google 'Black Scholes' and you will find numerous websites that will tell you about it at great length. It is very mathematical and if you are into that it is really quite interesting. But if you're not, don't worry, you don't need to know. To be clear:

You don't need to know how to calculate the option prices to use options.

Especially the way we are going to use them in the ITM strategy. Just as you don't need to know how an internal combustion engine works to be able to drive a car.

He Said, She Said

You may be wondering why I don't use TV and IV instead of writing 'Time Value' and 'Intrinsic Value' all the time. This is for clarity because IV also means Implied Volatility and it could confuse. It is best to be absolutely clear as it avoids misunderstandings.

I remember one time when I was discussing a trading strategy with another trader and we both used the term 'vol' and we were getting nowhere. He thought I was nuts, I thought he was off the planet. Then we worked out what was going on.

When I said 'vol' I meant 'volume'; when he said 'vol' he meant 'volatility'. Naturally, the discussion didn't make any sense until we worked out what each other was talking about. That's why it's better to use the full terms, then no one misunderstands.

Chapter 7 Highlights

The major points in Chapter 7. Never Go Naked are:

➢   Volatility has an effect on option prices. High volatility means higher option prices.

➢   Almost 80% of options expire worthless. This is because they are OTM at expiry.

➢   More people write OTM options so that's why there are more of them.

➢ Selling naked is dangerous and NOT recommended.

➢ Time value decays over the life of the option and is zero at expiry. The last 30 days are when time value decreases the most.

➢ Delta (a Greek) is the amount an option is expected to move if there is a $1 change in the underlying stock / ETF.

And finally, some perspective from Howards Marks:

The most dangerous time to buy anything is at the peak of its popularity. At this point, all favorable facts and opinions are already factored into its price and no new buyers are left to emerge.

◆◆◆

Chapter 8. Don't Trade Angry!

Now it's time for the practicalities of what options to pick. As we said in the last chapter, what the ITM strategy does is buy deep-in-the-money SPY options around one year to expiry with practically no time value (i.e., a delta close to one). When you read that before you probably went 'huh?' but now you should understand what we mean.

When I originally wrote this book, I was aiming to make the ITM strategy accessible for people to be able to start with $10,000 in their account. At the time it was quite easy to find options within that budget. Now, just over a year later, it is much harder. Circumstances have changed dramatically.

SPY has increased so much that starting with $10,000 is becoming increasingly difficult. That has been wonderful for many people following the ITM strategy since 2020, as many have doubled their money, but it is proving a barrier to entry for people with lower account balances. I have been contacted by lots of readers who wanted to start doing the ITM strategy but as they had smaller accounts they couldn't, and they wanted to know what they should do instead.

Chapter 11 is devoted to doing ITM with a smaller account, but it still requires that you know how to do ITM so everything in this chapter is relevant to you. The hope is that soon your smaller trading account will be healthy enough to start doing the full ITM strategy and trading SPY options.

SPY Options

We know that the SPY price changes from day to day, and from minute to minute when the market is open. The SPY options pricing changes with the SPY, which makes it quite hard when showing examples. What we have to do is to take a snapshot in time and explore that, knowing that it will be similar, but not the same, as it is today.

For this chapter, we are going to look at the SPY option chain for expiry in January 2021 which, at the time of the snapshot, was one year to expiry. At that time, SPY was trading at $322.41.

We are going to look through the options chain for DITM (Deep In The Money) options that meet both the ITM requirements and our budget.

Basically, we want to look for options that have very little time value. We can find out which ones have very little time value in 2 ways:

➢ We can look at the effective price (remember? The strike plus the cost of the option) and see how close it is to the current value; or
➢ We can use a Greek, Delta.

I recommend using the effective price. It's the easiest and the most accurate. I find that delta is more of a descriptor rather than being a useful parameter to select our option. By looking at the effective price we are getting a much more precise picture of what we are actually paying for our option. So, let's do a recap:

Effective Price = Strike + Premium (the cost of the option)

Now let's use this to find the option(s) we are going to buy.

Choosing your Options

For this example, let's start looking at the option chain at the halfway mark, say $160 (half of the current SPY price of $322). Here is a summary of some of the DITM options in the chain with the delta, the bid / ask and the strike:

Delta	Mid Bid/Ask	Strike	Effective Price	% from Current Price
0.93	163.18	160	$323.18	0.24%
0.92	123.70	200	$323.70	0.40%
0.87	85.94	240	$325.94	1.09%
0.76	51.65	280	$331.65	2.87%

You can see that the deltas get closer to 1 as the strike decreases. You may be wondering how you get the deltas for a particular option? Most charting packages and online charts give them, and also online brokers usually include them as a choice in the option chains.

I rarely use delta because using the effective price is a much easier way of working things out.

Looking at the effective price you are paying is much simpler, and you can do it in your head.

The effective price - the strike price plus the cost of the option - is what we are buying SPY for if we exercise the option. The $160 option gives us the right to buy at $160. If we pay $163.18 for the option (The halfway point of the spread – see the extra bit below on market makers to explain this) then we are buying SPY for $323.18 only very slightly ($0.77 or 0.24%) over the current trading price of $322.41.

In other words, the option is practically all intrinsic value. That seems like a good deal, but what we are interested in is:

➢ How much will this cost us?
➢ How much profit will we make?

The price of the 160 option is $163.18. This means that it will cost $16,318 for one option (remember an option controls 100 SPY shares). This may seem like a lot of money, and it may be out of many peoples' budgets, but bear with me because if we understand the payback and leverage in this example, then the next one (which shows you how to do it with $10K) will be so much easier.

Let's look at the effect on our accounts for the different outcomes. If we have $16,318 in our account, then we can buy:

➢ 50 SPY shares; OR
➢ 1 SPY 160 Option (which controls 100 shares)

Buying SPY Shares

Let's look at the outcomes of buying the straight ETF. For an account starting with $16,318, we can buy 50 SPY contracts, so at the end of the year our account will be worth:

SPY at end of year	% increase	Account End of Year	Profit	Profit %
390	21%	$19,698	$3,380	21%
370	15%	$18,698	$2,380	15%
350	9%	$17,698	$1,380	9%
330	2%	$16,698	$380	2%
310	-4%	$15,698	($621)	-4%
290	-10%	$14,698	($1,621)	-10%

The profit is calculated by multiplying the number of contracts (50) by the end of year SPY price ($390, $370, $350, etc.), and then subtracting the account value at the start of the year ($16,318). The cash left over after the purchase of the shares ($197.50) has to be added to the account value at the end of the year.

Buying SPY Options

Now let's look at what happens if we buy the 160 strike option instead. For our account of $16,318 we can buy 1 contract with a strike of 160. Each contract enables us to buy 100 SPY at $160. If we look at our account value at the end of the year for the different SPY prices we have:

SPY at end of year	% increase	Account End of Year	Profit	Profit %
390	21%	$23,000	$6,682	41%
370	15%	$21,000	$4,682	29%
350	9%	$19,000	$2,682	16%
330	2%	$17,000	$682	4%
310	-4%	$15,000	($1,318)	-8%
290	-10%	$13,000	($3,318)	-20%

You can see that DITM $160 option returns are exactly double the market. Rather nice. Most professional fund managers would give their eyeteeth to have a performance like that!

Whatever percentage SPY goes up, if you choose options with a strike one-half the current SPY price then the ITM strategy exactly doubles the market return. This is **leverage.** Of course, if SPY goes down, we lose double as well, which is why this is a bull market strategy. In a bear market, we can do a different strategy, using puts instead of calls, and this is in the book _In The Money: Bear Market Strategy._ Right now, at the time of writing, we are still in a bull market.

But you said that we only needed $10,000!

When ITM came out you did only need $10K to start with. Options were much cheaper then! We are going to look at how we do that, and the outcomes are even better. Let's see take an example to see how it works. Of course, SPY has gone up since these snapshots were taken, but that doesn't matter as it is the concept we are going through here.

Let's go back to the option chain and see what options we can buy for $10,000. We scroll down and see that the $225 has a bid / ask of $99.75 / $100.42. Perfect. We can get it for a smidge over $100, probably $100.08, but let's assume that we can get it for $100 to keep the math easy. We can buy 1 contract for $10,000, which gives us control over 100 shares, instead of the 31 shares we would buy if we weren't using options.

So just checking our choice of the $225 option. Does it conform to the ITM rules?

> **Is it DITM?** Yes, $225 is well below the current price of $322.41.

> **Is the effective price less than 1% away from the current price?** Yes, we are effectively buying SPY for $325.00, which is only $2.59 or 0.8% (less than 1%) away.

> **Is it long dated?** Yes, it has 1 year to expiry.

So, all good. The option we have picked out follows all the rules. But what will it do to our results? We want to double the market return! Will that do it? Let's check what our returns would be, remembering that this time we are starting with an account value of $10K:

SPY at end of year	% Increase	Account Shares EoY	Account Option EoY	Option Profit	Options Profit %
390	21%	$12,096	$16,500	$6,500	65%
370	15%	$11,476	$14,500	$4,500	45%
350	9%	$10,856	$12,500	$2,500	25%
330	2%	$10,235	$10,500	$500	5%
310	-4%	$9,615	$8,500	($1,500)	-15%
290	-10%	$8,995	$6,500	($3,500)	-35%

You can see that we now are getting triple the market returns! Even better returns than with the $160 option.

Now, a note of caution. This is great while we are in a bull market. As long as the market goes up year to year, we can make triple the returns. But you can see that if we were in a bear market then we would be still making triple the market returns but in the wrong direction. If the SPY has a negative year, then we would now be making 3 times the loss. Which is **not w**hat we want to happen.

That's why it is important to keep an eye on the market and the economy in general. In January 2020 when I was writing the first draft of this chapter I wrote:

> *At some stage, the bull market will end, and we will go into a bear market. Then this strategy will not work, but a mirror-image strategy will work. But that's for another book. Right now, we are in a bull market.*

Prescient words. A few weeks later we entered a very sharp and sudden bear market, due to the COVID 19 virus. Since that time, we have had a very sharp, V-shaped recovery. All the losses from that bear market were made up, and soon the market was hitting new highs.

That did not make the bear market any more enjoyable, but the ITM strategy can protect you. Using the ITM signal (the 10/200 death cross), I got out before the major falls happened, protecting my capital.

We have already looked at how to tell the end of a bull market, and when we see the signs, we wait for the signal and then simply sell our positions and move to cash.

In the next chapter, **Stay In Or Sell?** we will revisit how to tell the end of a bull market and look at whether you should sell and get out of the market or whether you should try to ride out the downturn.

Double? Triple? You Choose!

What we need to take from this chapter is the knowledge that with we can

- ➢ Double or triple the market returns depending on which options we choose.
- ➢ Choose an option that fits within the rules AND our budget.
- ➢ Know exactly how much money we will make for the various market outcomes.

Now it may be that you can't choose an option that fits the size of your account. As we mentioned, there is a strategy (ITMS) coming up for smaller accounts to use until their balance grows to enable them to do the full ITM strategy.

Borrowing to Invest

You may have heard of people borrowing to invest in the stock market. You may even know someone who has done this. There is a word of advice that I want to give you:

DON'T!
And two more:

NOT EVER!

I can't reiterate this enough. Don't borrow money for investing. Apart from doing your head in and affecting your clear thinking, you can get into deep water very easily, and you don't control the outcome. Once you have borrowed, then the company you have borrowed from calls the shots.

The Dreaded Margin Call

Not being in control leads to bad thinking and bad decisions. You don't want either of those. You need a clear head. If you are not intending ever to borrow to invest then you can skip the next section, although it would probably be good if you understood how margin calls work.

You may have heard of a 'margin call'. You don't ever want to have one because they are nasty. Very painful. How they work is this: let's say that you have $5,000 that you want to invest, and your broker offers you a further $5,000 as a margin loan, on which, of course, you have to pay interest. This is called 'buying on margin'. In this case, it gives you $10,000 to invest (How? $5K of your own money, and the borrowed $5K) so you can get to your goal more quickly. Sounds good? Yes, it does. But there is a risk. A **major** risk.

Let's say that you invested the whole $10,000 buying shares in a stock that is trading at $100. Let's call the stock XYZ, and you now have 100 shares.

As you and the broker have equal shares in your account, your equity (the bit that you own) is 50%. But you will get all the profit because you will only have to pay the broker back the original $5K, plus interest of course.

Then, disaster strikes!

The market suddenly goes against you. Perhaps there was some rumor of coming bad news, like the CEO suddenly died or the earnings were below what was expected. It happens with individual stocks. Suppose it was a really serious incident, and XYZ dropped suddenly from $100 to $50.

Written into your margin contract would be a little thing called an MMR – a maintenance margin requirement, typically 30%. You may have overlooked it, or simply didn't know what it meant. ***This tricky little MMR now comes into play. And it's not fun***.

What an MMR of 30% means that you have to keep your level of equity over 30%. When you started it was at 50%, well over that requirement so everybody was happy. But not anymore. Your broker is not happy about it. And I guarantee you are not going to be happy about it.

Let's work out what it actually means in practice. In your $10K account, $5K was yours and $5K was borrowed money so it was a 50-50 split. If the account value goes down, then your equity also goes down. The following table shows how:

Account Value	Your Equity	Borrowed Funds	% Equity
$10,000	$5,000	$5,000	50%
$9,000	$4,000	$5,000	44%
$8,000	$3,000	$5,000	38%
$7,000	$2,000	$5,000	29%
$6,000	$1,000	$5,000	17%
$5,000	$0	$5,000	0%

You can see that if the account drops to $7K or below then you are below the 30% Margin Maintenance level. What happens then? Your broker will require that you fix it. The two ways to fix it are:

➤ Deposit cash into your account to bring it over the required level
➤ Liquidate (sell) stock to pay back the margin loan.

The **margin call** occurs when your broker calls or emails to let you know that you are below your margin level and asks what you are going to do about it. If you don't respond, then your broker has the right to close out any open positions without consulting you or gaining your approval. She doesn't even have to let you know! To add insult to injury, you may get charged commission for them doing this, and, of course, you are responsible for any losses.

Basically, once you have a margin loan you lose control over your account. You can't decide to hold on and ride it out. They will sell your shares from under you – quite legally – to pay themselves back. Apart from messing with your thinking, and stopping you seeing clearly, you could end up *owing* money.

A Real World Example

So back to our 'real life' disaster. You read that the XYZ CEO and his executive board were all on a private plane which has been reported as missing. They have no idea where it is. That's pretty serious; how can the company survive? The market reacts to the bad news. XYZ drops suddenly from $100 to $50.

Your account also drops in value. It's now worth $5,000 instead of your initial $10,000. But guess what? You still owe the broker the $5,000 she loaned you, so actually your share of the account is now $0. Not good news. Not good news at all. You are way below the margin requirement, so the broker can sell all your stocks to cover the loan. Which she does. You don't end up owing them money, but your money is all gone. Now that IS a disaster, because that means you are out of the game.

If it had dropped more than 50%, then you would have ended up OWING the broker money. That's why it is dangerous to borrow for investing. You could end up in debt.

If you didn't have the margin loan you would still have $2,500 of your original $5,000 left – not good, but a whole lot better than nothing.

Of course, things may not be as bad as they seem. Let's imagine that two days later the plane has been located. Great news! Even better, there was no crash, and everyone is alive and well. They just decided on a quick stopover in Vegas, and somehow the flight didn't get recorded (OK, unlikely I know, but just work with me here!). The entire executive team is just fine, and back at work. The share price shoots back up to $100.

But it's too late for you. You don't have any shares left. Your broker has sold them all. You've lost all your capital. And, probably, your confidence which is even worse.

Very Expensive Tuition Fees

I have had 2 margin calls in my life as a trader, and both cost me money. That hurt, but not as much as watching the stock come right back up again after the margin call had been triggered and the stock was sold from under me. If I hadn't done it on margin then I would have been quite OK, as the stock recovered quickly.

What was I doing playing with margin calls? Confession and disclosure here. I am not trying to hide that I have done some really stupid things in my time as a trader. This was probably one of the most stupid. It was January 2016 and the market had just had a drop, and I had lost some profits. I was angry. I was out for revenge. I was going to MAKE the market give back what it had taken from me.

Silly. Very silly. I should have known that the market didn't care about me, it was nothing personal. The market just does what the market does. But humans (including me) have a tendency to take it personally and want to hit back. It's not a good idea. If you trade angry you usually end up getting hurt. As Keynes said:

The market can stay irrational longer than you can stay solvent!

What was I doing was writing naked puts on some European indices? I would never stay in the positions overnight, instead getting in and out within the day, often within the hour. It's called day trading but should be more correctly called temporary trading.

It was my sister's birthday. We were all going to an outdoor theatre where people brought picnics and I had cooked a surprise birthday cake (although the surprise was probably that the cake turned out well!). I was due there at 7 PM.

Around 4 PM I was happily trading, selling naked puts, and intending to sell them all before I left for the party. But then: disaster! There was a sudden drop. It does happen, and when it does it can do it so quickly it takes your breath away. I sat there glued to the screen like a rabbit in the headlights. It went down and down, and my positions went deeper and deeper into the red. I got that cold, sick, shaky feeling, and sat there desperately waiting and hoping for it to come up again. I scanned the news headlines, but there was nothing that I could see that would explain it. It was just one of these dips that happen – a big wave, but not the tide.

I waited. I started panicking. The market stopped going down, but it didn't start climbing. I knew that I had triggered the margin call, but that it wouldn't come into effect until after the market close, so I had time for it to recover. Six hours, in fact. BUT – I was due at the birthday party in 1 hour!

I hung on as long as I could and left it to the last minute but there was nothing for it but to buy back my positions at a loss as I would not be back before the market closed. I closed all the positions. I took the loss. It was big. It hurt.

I went off to the birthday party knowing that I had just lost almost $20,000 because of my own stupidity. I shouldn't have been writing naked puts, and I certainly shouldn't have been doing it when I had a limited time available. Of course, I didn't tell anyone although I probably wasn't the life and soul of the party. In a later chapter, we look at managing yourself and what you tell people. Kipling's poem IF has some good advice:

> *And lose, and start again at your beginnings*
> *And never breathe a word about your loss.*

So, I smiled and laughed and tried to enjoy the party, although it's hard when you realize you have been an idiot. And of course – you've guessed it – when I got home after market close, I saw that it had come right back up again. I would have been absolutely fine if I had just been there. Talk about adding insult to injury. There was a lot of angry walking around, cursing myself for my stupidity.

But you know what the really funny thing is? I did it again! Just a couple of weeks later, and the really strange thing was that I was going to the same theatre that night. Almost exactly the same situation and I lost around the same amount of money. You wouldn't believe anyone could be so stupid. But I was. What a slow learner!

Again, I was seeking revenge. I wanted my $20K back and I wanted the market to give it to me. It didn't, of course. But it shows how if you don't master your emotions, you can get hurt. Trying to wreak revenge on the market simply doesn't work. The market had to 'spank' me twice before I learned that lesson, and it was a very expensive tuition fee.

So, no more writing naked puts for me. There are ways that you can write puts but limit your downside, which is much more sensible. You can still have the thrill, and make money, just not quite as much. But, on the upside, you won't end up losing your shirt.

Of course, the sensible thing to do is not to do risky strategies. I learned that the hard way. Eventually.

The Flash Crash

Can it happen with SPY? Less likely, but it CAN happen. It is called a **Flash Crash.** It is a very quick, very deep fall in stock prices and then a recovery within an extremely short period of time, usually minutes.

Typically, it happens due to 'black box' trading and high-frequency trading. Black box trading is where the orders are computer-generated. The computers will have rules like: if the stock drops below $50 then sell immediately. Of course, when it does the stock price starts to go down triggering a lot of other computers to do the same. Combined with high-frequency trading where computers transact a large number of orders in a fraction of a second you get sudden drops – and usually a rapid price recovery as well.

OK, that explanation is very simplified, but you get the idea. The movement is not in response to any bad news, simply the computer algorithms triggering each other and then them all getting in on the party.

The first flash crash I actually experienced was in May 2010. I was in France at the time and happened to be watching the market as it happened. The Dow Jones dropped over 1,000 points, then rose back to its previous value *within 36 minutes*!

Watching it on the screen I was completely transfixed and wondering what was going on. I thought that an asteroid had hit, World War III had started, or there had been a huge terrorist attack. Luckily, it was none of those. Just computers being computers.

But I had to go and have a restorative vin rouge to calm my shaking nerves!

The Takeaway

It is easy to avoid a margin call: don't borrow money for investing. So, just in case I haven't been clear:

DON'T EVER BORROW TO INVEST

Market Makers

The concept of options being created is one that many people – including traders – don't get. As we mentioned before, options are not made or set up by the stock exchange. They are made by traders who decide to write them.

That doesn't mean, of course, that there is a free-for-all. It operates within a framework. The stock exchange sets up the strikes and expiry dates and then the market makers and the traders do the rest. We have just introduced another concept, the 'market maker', which is something that you do not need to know about to do ITM, but it will help with your overall understanding of the market.

A **market maker**, sometimes called a **liquidity provider**, is someone (usually a firm) licensed and authorized by the stock exchange to provide buy and sell prices for a stock or an ETF. The stock market needs market makers because otherwise when a trader wanted to buy an option there might be no-one ready to sell it to them, or when they want to sell their option there might not be any buyers. This is where the market maker comes in; they provide liquidity so that you can always buy and sell your options.

Market makers **must** offer a bid and ask price so that traders can always buy and sell. The bid and ask prices will be different, and this difference is called the 'spread'. This is how market makers make money. They buy at a lower price than they sell. The spread is usually mandated by the stock exchange. There can be different levels of spreads, with sparsely traded stocks having wider spreads than very liquid stocks like SPY which has a tight (small) spread.

Market makers are not involved in every transaction. Most of the time stock exchanges operate on an order-driven basis where a buyer's bid price meets a seller's ask price. You can put in a buy at any price, the same with a sell. But if it is not within the spread, it is unlikely to get filled right away. However, if the market moves up or down then your order may get filled.

When you put in an order, you specify how long the order is open (active). The choices are usually:

> ➢ Day only.
> ➢ Good until canceled.
> ➢ Fill or kill.
> ➢ Immediate or cancel.

The first two are self-explanatory, the other 2 not so obvious.

Fill or Kill (sometimes abbreviated as FOK) means that the order has to be filled in its entirety within a few seconds or the whole order is 'killed'. If you had, say, put in an order for 50 SPY shares then all 50 would have to be filled (bought) right away or none at all and the order canceled.

Immediate or cancel, means that the order has to be executed immediately, but it doesn't have to be completely filled Unlike FOK, a partial fill is possible. In our example, if 30 shares were filled right away then the other 20 would be canceled.

You can also specify **All-Or-Nothing** (AON) orders. This means that the order has to be filled in its entirety and can remain open until that happens. This is used to avoid the situation where you get a small parcel of thinly traded stocks.

Teasing the Market Makers

Market makers' bid / ask prices are automated, and this can be used to your advantage when trading illiquid stocks or indexes. It's also quite amusing if, like me, you have a warped sense of humor and enjoy the feeling that you have beaten the system in some small way.

Some exchanges, like the Australian Stock Exchange (the ASX), have very illiquid option markets, and many option chains are full of zeros – no bids, no asks. Many traders conclude that in that case then they can't buy an option because there are no options for them to buy and there is nothing that can be done about it. Wrong. There is. You can tease out the market makers and buy your option at less than the ask price you are going to force them to provide. It's rather fun. Here is how to do it.

If you find that the option that you want has no bid / ask (i.e., they are both 0), don't despair. Use one of the many option price calculators (just google to find one) to work out what the fair value of the option is. Let's say it is $10. Then enter a buy order at something well below the calculated fair value, say $3. Then watch the screen closely. Market makers are obliged to provide a bid / ask, but this may only be for a short time, maybe 20 seconds, that's why you have to watch like a hawk.

The market makers must respond with a bid/ask. When it comes up it will be something like Bid: $9.50 Ask: $10.50. If you then adjust your bid to just over the halfway point, like $10.01, then it will get automatically accepted, saving you $0.49 on the transaction. That's how the computer algorithm seems to work.

This is something I worked out by trial and error. I have spoken to other traders about it but no one else seems to be aware of that technique. We don't need it for ITM, but it gives you an insight into how things work and why you can always be sure of being able to buy and sell your options.

Chapter 8 Highlights

The major points in Chapter 8. Don't Trade Angry! are:

➢   Buying DITM options gives us leverage so that we get a better return than buying SPY stock.

➢ Our rules for choosing options are:

❖ Is it DITM?

❖ Is the effective price less than 1% away from the current price?

❖ Is it long dated? (a year to expiry is ideal)

➢ Margin calls are bad news; don't borrow to invest.

➢ Don't trade angry! The market doesn't have it in for you so don't try to get revenge. It never works.

And finally, some wise words from Paul Samuelson:

Investing should be more like watching paint dry or grass grow. If you want excitement, take $800 and go to Las Vegas.

◆ ◆ ◆

Chapter 9. Stay in or Sell?

Bull markets don't go on forever so big question is:

***When we are in the market and things are starting to look bad do
we get out? Or do we stay in and ride out the downturn?***

Before we look at the practical steps of when and how to get out - or not -
it is important that you know what to expect. Not just in practical terms, but
also in how you are going to feel about it emotionally. All people are
emotional, some more than others. You need to know how **you** are going to
feel in these situations, and what you are going to do in response to these
feelings.

You can't NOT feel – emotions are beyond our control. Just try not to get
frustrated while you are on hold listening to 'your call is important to us'
repeated endlessly! We can't control the emotion, but what we CAN do is
control our response to it. Definitely easier said than done, but you CAN do

it.

Years ago, when I was managing big IT departments, I used to have this quote under my computer screen where only I could see it:

If you are distressed by anything external, the pain is not due to the thing itself, but to your estimate of it; and this you have the power to revoke at any moment.

It was written by Marcus Aurelius, a Roman Emperor, almost 2,000 years ago. It reminded me that when I felt irritated, angry, frustrated, apprehensive. or any other emotion, that while I may not be able to change the situation, I could change the way I felt about it any time I wanted.

I would ask myself *will I remember what I found so annoying in 1 year's time? Will I even remember that I felt annoyed?* The answer was pretty well almost always 'No', and this helped me put things in perspective.

A shorter version of the same aphorism is:
You don't have to turn this into something. It doesn't have to upset you.
You will have emotions about trading; everyone does. You will feel fear and greed, anger and hope, frustration and even boredom. As humans, we are emotional beings. We can't help it, that is just the way we are. But you have to learn to manage these emotions so that you don't respond by doing anything silly that will cost you money. Just like I did in the last chapter when I was angry and determined that the market was going to give me my money back!

The best traders are the ones who can put their emotions to one side and look at the situation dispassionately.

It's also a good thing to continually ask yourself 'what if I am wrong?' and make sure that you can live with the consequences if you are. You are not always going to be right. No-one is!

Emotions and the Market

The stock market is not a 'thing'. It is made up of people, who are making decisions about what to buy and sell. As we saw earlier, humans make decisions based on emotions, and then justify their decisions with logic. When traders buy and sell, they are doing so because of their feelings, mainly fear, greed, hope, excitement, anxiety, boredom, and frustration. Traders are subject to emotions just like everyone else, perhaps more so as they are often playing a high-stakes game.

Traders like to belong. They have a need for acceptance into the 'clan'. They don't want to be the odd one out, the one that is acting differently from the pack. They like the safety in numbers and doing what everyone else thinks is a good idea. That way, they don't get criticized. Instead, they get a lot of approval, mainly from others who are also seeking approval. Of course, there is no safety in numbers. Not at all. The market doesn't care what you think or what anyone else thinks. ***The market will roll right over you if you are wrong, no matter how many people agree with you.***

When you grasp that the market is just millions of humans playing a high-stakes game, you see trading and the stock market in a completely different light. You realize that it is all about human psychology. As we said before, it is impossible to say with any accuracy what an individual trader will do, but you can work out with quite a high probability what the market, made up of millions of individual traders, is going to do. It's like medical statistics. You can't tell if a particular individual will develop cancer, but you can say that if you have 100,000 people then around 350 of them will develop cancer within a year.

Your Emotions

So that's everyone else in the market. What about you? To be successful in the market you have to be able to manage yourself and your emotions. That's not easy. In fact it is one of the hardest things about trading. It has taken me years to be able to hear or read something diametrically opposed to what I think (and am acting on) without feeling a stab of fear in my heart and doubt about my own abilities entering my head. But to be successful you must be able to put your emotions in the back seat and look objectively at what you have been reading.

You will find out that people love telling you why what you are doing won't work. Or can't work. Or shouldn't work. Or they ask: if *it is that simple, why isn't everyone doing it?* Goodness, if I had a dollar for every time I have heard that my trading accounts would easily be double what they are now!

People will tell you, with great relish, of someone they heard about, who played the stock market and they lost their shirt. Not just their shirt, but their house, car, their retirement account, in fact, they lost everything and ended up in debt, and other dire stories. You have to be strong and confident that you know what you are doing to be able not to be affected by this. It is hard. Often you doubt yourself in the face of 'experts' telling you how things are and what is going to happen next. Then remember that experts usually get things wrong, as we saw in an earlier chapter. You have to be able to put what they are saying to one side and concentrate on doing what you are doing.

I am not saying that it is easy. Whenever I see the headline **Market Crash Imminent** or hear an expert advising to **Sell and Move to Cash Immediately**, I still get a twinge of anxiety. But I have learned to control my actions by reflecting on who is saying it, why they are saying it, and if it matches my own observations.

I am not saying that I am oblivious to it. I'm not, and neither should you be. Listening to the prevailing feeling about the market is an integral part of being a trader. The quote by Templeton is something always to keep in mind:

Bull markets are born in pessimism, grow on skepticism, mature on optimism, and die on euphoria

This is so true. My estimate of where we were in mid-2019 when I wrote the first draft of this chapter was that we are transitioning from skepticism into optimism. There were still many negative headlines and articles warning of danger ahead, but you couldn't get over the fact that SPY had been making new highs, as was QQQ (the Nasdaq ETF). I did not think that we are into euphoria but keeping an eye out for the euphoria phase is something we, as traders, must do.

For most of 2020, we were on a roller coaster caused by COVID 19. After initially discounting reports of the new virus, the market suddenly decided at the end of February that there really was a problem and proceeded to drop 34% in 3 weeks, the fastest drop in history. Then surprisingly, it started to rise again sharply, and continue up until had almost made up the losses by the beginning of June. Now, there were signs of euphoria everywhere. News on the virus and economic front was dire, but the market was blithely ignoring it and carrying on its merry way. Until June 11th when it dropped 6% in one day. It bounced off support at 300, then retraced to test it again on the 26 June, then proceeded to move up again.

During the rest of 2020, the market moved up with two smallish downturns in September and October. In 2021 it continued upwards, with a bit of a downturn in September, then back on up again to finish the year with a new high at 477. The bull market seemed intact. But was it euphoria?

What Euphoria Looks Like

I have seen 3 of these euphoric phases in my lifetime, in 1987, 2000, and 2006-7. Each of them was characterized by the same symptoms, and they all ended badly as you know.

The first euphoric phase was in 1987. I was young, and not involved in, or interested in, the stock market. At the time I was a lecturer and noticed that the staff room conversations were all about the stock market. Being the mathematics & computing section, it was a predominantly male staff, and everyone seemed to be into it. The talk was all about what they had bought, how much money they had made and how much money they were going to make. Flushed with their successes, they were borrowing money so they could make even more money.

As practically the only person not involved, I could look at it from an outsider's point of view. What I could see was a sort of mass hysteria in people who really didn't know about the stock market. It was only recently they had become interested, and none of them had traded for more than a few months. They were all acting on tips and 'inside information'.

There is a saying: 'a rising tide lifts all boats' which is particularly appropriate in the euphoria phase. As the stocks rose the lecturers all thought they were terribly smart. Financial geniuses, really. The stock market was easy; everything goes up! You can buy anything! And the more money you can put into stocks the more money you make, so let's borrow as much as we can. What could possibly go wrong?

Well, as you know things DID go wrong. Badly. The stock market crashed in October 1987. On 'Black Monday' the Dow lost 22.6% of its value in one day! The aftermath was not pretty. The staff room was a pretty dismal place for a while. People had lost lots of money, and a lot of that money was borrowed money.

In the second euphoric phase in 1999. I had been interested in the stock market for a couple of years but was only trading in a very small way. At the time I was managing a large IT department, and I noticed the same symptoms. People were all talking about tech stocks, like Microsoft and Amazon, and how their prices were shooting up, and, of course, how much money they had made. Tips and recommendations were flying around. I heard the phrase 'this time it's different' bandied around.

Tech stocks didn't need earnings or market share like 'real' stocks – they just needed to be tech stocks. If they had a '.com' in their name people clamored to buy them. The valuations became outrageous – the price to earnings (P/E) ratio on the Nasdaq (which is mainly tech stocks) reached 200. Compared with a historical average P/E of about 15 this was huge. In 1999 the S&P rose 19.5% but the Nasdaq rose 85.6%.

It was people's behavior driving it. People's emotions. What we were seeing was the euphoria of people who had never been in the stock market before, and that let you know that it was going to come to a sticky end. There were lots of stories about people giving up their jobs to be day traders and making a fortune. Everyone knew someone, or knew someone who knew someone, who had done it.

In March 2000 the party ended with the start of the 'Tech Wreck'. The Nasdaq lost 78% of its value over the next 18 months. Again, I witnessed the aftermath of a bubble, and again it wasn't pretty.

The third euphoric phase started in 2006. I was managing another IT department, and the same thing happened. At the time I was well into the stock market, going to seminars, subscribing to newsletters, and actively trading stocks and options. I noticed that the talk in the department was all about stocks. Everyone was buying, or going to buy, stocks. Everyone had tips and recommendations. There were stories about so-and-so who had thrown up his job and was day trading full time. Others knew someone who had bought a holiday home on the beach with his stock market profits. People were borrowing to invest, and this was being encouraged by the banks.

I recognized euphoria. I had seen it before. I stayed in the market, but with growing unease. There were adverts for day trading courses, and newspapers were running online stock market games. It was everywhere, and it was all people seemed to talk about.

Then three things happened on the same day, in August 2007, that made me get out of the market. On the way to the airport the taxi driver started giving me tips about stocks. Then, in the airport lounge I read a newspaper and there was actually a headline saying: ***This Time It's Different.*** The article was about how the stock market could never crash again because CDS (credit default swaps) had removed the risk. I didn't understand what the article was saying, but I immediately recognized the headline, and that made me nervous.

The article itself worried me because I could not understand what it was getting at. It seemed like gobbledygook, and I figured if I couldn't understand it probably the guy who wrote it didn't understand it either. I turned over the page and there was a full-page advert for a one-day seminar that would teach anyone to be a day trader, no experience necessary. That was the last straw. I could no longer ignore the signs. We were definitely in euphoria.

I had to act on my conviction, and so I sold all my positions. Not in a panic, but over the next few days. And then I sat back and watched as the stock market rose. And rose. And kept on rising. I felt very silly, especially as everyone was crowing about how much money they were making, and there I was sitting on the sidelines. I really started to doubt myself, but I resisted the temptation to get back into the market.

As it turned out, I did lose around 2 months of gains that I could have made. But that's all. In mid-October, the market started turning down. And down, into the second-biggest crash ever. I was lucky that I was out of the market and my accounts didn't lose anything more than a couple of months of profits. But I know people who were wiped out, who lost all their savings, their retirement nest egg, and their house. Crashes are not pretty, and they devastate people's lives.

They Don't Ring a Bell

We know that the stock market is just lots of traders who are affected by fear and greed, just like everyone else. They also exhibit a herd mentality and tend to do what everyone else is doing. What we have to do is stand back and watch the behavior of the masses. Just so that we are clear, here are the symptoms to watch for:

> ➢ Headlines and articles about the stock market are practically all positive
> ➢ Bad news tends to be ignored by the market
> ➢ Stocks have high valuations
> ➢ Lots of adverts for free courses about trading the stock market
> ➢ Lots of adverts about systems guaranteed to identify stocks that are going to go up
> ➢ People you know are buying stocks for the first time
> ➢ You hear stories about people who have borrowed to invest in stocks
> ➢ Taxi drivers start giving you stock tips
> ➢ You read, or hear someone say 'This time it's different'

If you google 'market top' you can read lots of articles on how to recognize it, but they are mostly technical indicators and usually indicate that the decline has already started. Remember that 'bears jump out the window', so declines can be swift and terrifying.

When you see these signs, it does not mean bale out of all your positions immediately. It means that we are in the Euphoria stage. It means you need to watch closely for any other signs that the market is going down because it probably is. And now we have to decide what to do.

Stay In? Or Sell?

There are 2 ways we can deal with a market downturn:

➤ Sit tight and tough it out.
➤ Sell and wait for the correction/ bear market to be over then buy in again

Let's look at the pros and cons of each of these actions.

Sitting tight may be the wisest way if you have the luxury of a long-term approach. Stock markets tend to go up long term (as we have seen), and to date all corrections and bear markets have come back and exceeded their prices from before the correction.

Hanging in there waiting for the market to recover may be a good approach - if you only knew how long the recovery was going to take. Which you don't. Nobody does. Normally it is months, but it could take years. It has in the past.

If the downturn is going to be a minor dip, then the best strategy is to stay in – but the problem is, of course, that we don't know whether it is going to be a minor dip or a full-blown bear market.

Staying tight through a bear market can be devastating to your account – and your sanity! For example:

➤ If we had bought into the market in September 2000 (at its high) then we would have had to wait until 2007 to get back to that high.
➤ If we had then decided to sit tight through the next bear market, we would have to wait until 2013 to reach the same high.

In other words, if we had bought in 2000 and stayed in the market we would have to wait until 2013 before we were in profit. Not many people would have the patience to wait 13 years to start showing a profit. I know that

I certainly would not.

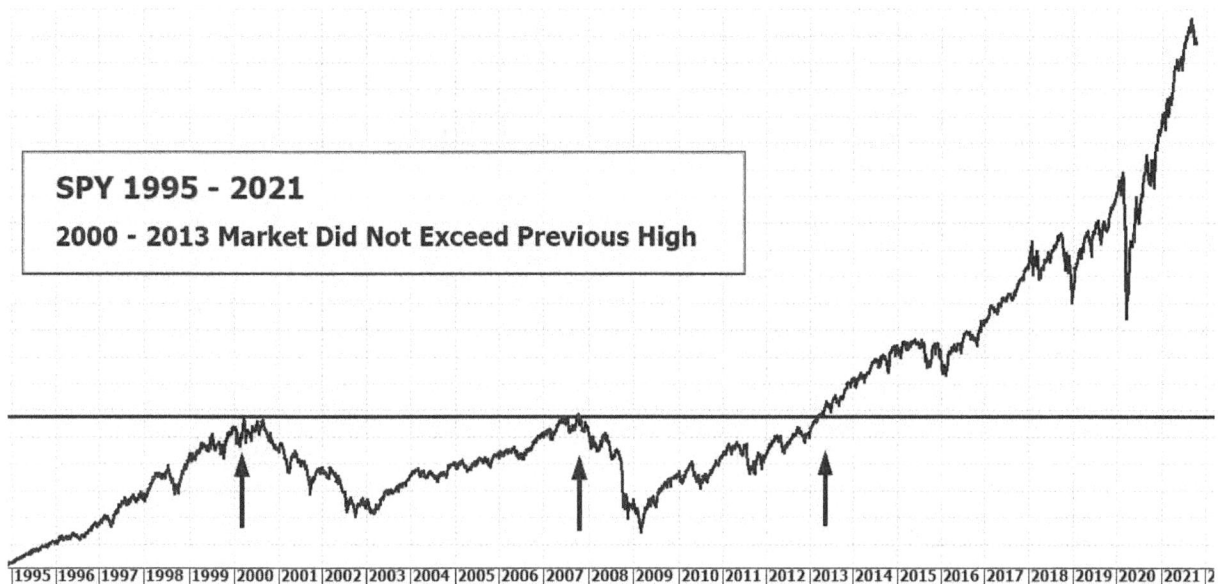

SPY 1995 - 2021

2000 - 2013 Market Did Not Exceed Previous High

On the other hand, staying in the market proved to be the better strategy in all the other downturns, both the secondary bear markets and the corrections. Getting out on the death cross and then waiting for the golden cross means that we sometimes have to buy in at a higher price than we sold. The difference is not usually hugely significant, but it is still very annoying.

That's why you need a long-term perspective if you are going to sit tight. This is your decision, no one else can make this for you, as only you know your timeframe and your tolerance for pain. The good bit about staying in the market is that you don't miss the recovery when it comes. And it will. It always does. But, as they say, they don't ring a bell at the bottom!

Selling and waiting for the bear market to be over is wisest if you have a shorter perspective, or if you simply can't bear the pain of the market going down and then the suspense of waiting for it to recover. If we look at the downturns in the graph above, we will see that we would have made large profits simply by being able to buy our positions back at much lower prices.

- ➢ 2002/3:
- ❖ Out: Sell at $145
- ❖ In: Buy back at $78
- ➢ 2007/9:

- ❖ Out: Sell at $146
- ❖ In: Buy back at $68

But how to decide when to get out and when to get back in? ITM has 2 clear signals, one for getting into the market and the other for getting out. Before we look at these signals, let's just clarify our choices when we see an OUT signal. We can

> ➤ **Sit tight,** knowing that if it is only a small dip or correction we will perform better, but if it turns into a bear market, we will perform very much worse.
> ➤ **Get out,** knowing that we will be safe from major losses, but we may have to buy back in at a slightly higher price when we see the IN signal.

It seems that getting out is the wise choice if we want to stay safe, but we must remember that there have only been 4 times in the last 30 years when the OUT signal has warned us of a real bear market. The other times it warned of a correction or a dip. If it was simply a correction or a dip, then we were getting out when it would have been better to stay in.

Still, I think that erring on the side of safety is the wise thing to do. Plus, if you stay in the market then you can't do the ITM bear market strategy as you need your capital to do that and you can't use it if it is tied up in a bull trade. And if you read *In The Money: Bear Market Strategy* then you will see that the bear is definitely worth trading.

ITM OUT: The ITM Death Cross

If you decide that you are not cut out for the sitting tight strategy, you need to know when to get out and when to get back in. What other signs should you look for? Checking the charts (we'll look at how you do this later in the chapter) and in particular, the SPY chart, can give you a clue to the market top. Not because there is any magic in what I am going to tell you, but simply because other traders THINK that there is, and they act on it.

When they see these signs, they tend to think that bad times are coming and dump their positions. The computers join in and voila! A self-fulfilling prophecy.

We looked earlier at moving averages on stock charts, in particular, the

SMA or Simple Moving Average. Well, most traders place great faith in the:

> ➤ 50-day SMA
> ➤ 200-day SMA

The theory is that when the price starts trading below either of these SMAs then it is time to get out of the market. And many traders do, triggering a decline that builds momentum and can turn into a serious slump. There are different levels of slumps, depending on the size of the decline:

> ➤ 10 – 20% is known as a **correction**
> ➤ More than 20% is known as a **bear market**

When you are looking at a stock chart you will see that the 200-day SMA is smoother than the 50-day SMA. In other words, it fluctuates less so it is easier to see the tide, not the waves.

You will also see that when the stocks fall below it, they tend to keep going down – but not always. If we use that as a signal to get out, we will be getting out when we don't actually need to.

The ITM solution is to use the crossing of the 200-day SMA by the 10-day SMA on the downside. That's the 'Death Cross' that we learned about in a previous chapter. The name itself is enough to scare traders out of the market! In the chart below, you can clearly see the death cross during the covid scare in early 2020. A 10/200 Death Cross would have kept us safe, and got us out in:

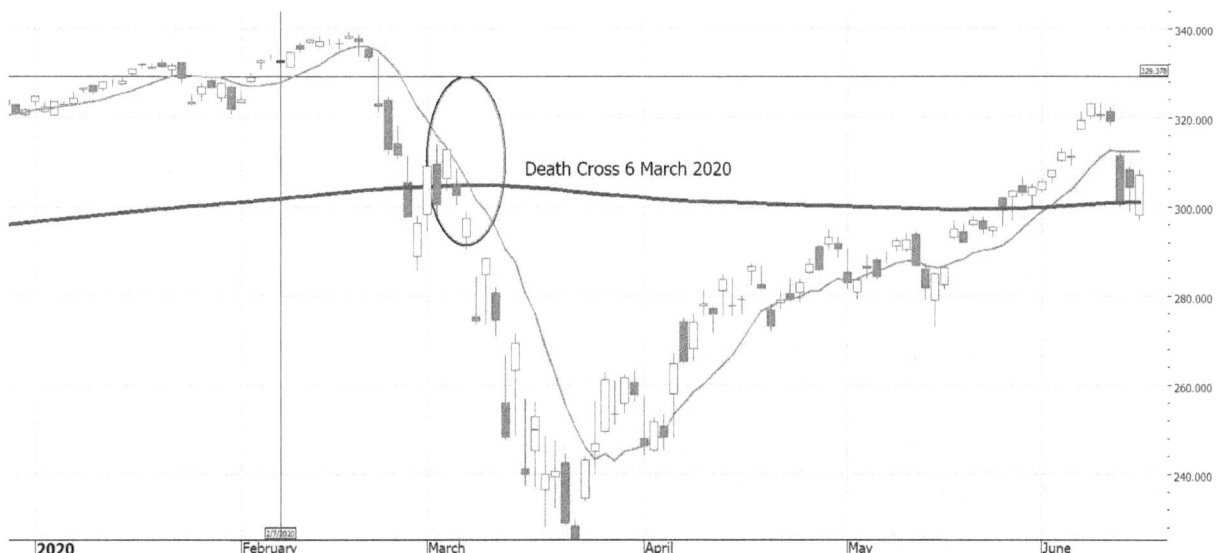

➢ 14 November 2007 (Bear market, bottoming March 2009 (GFC)
➢ 4 August 2011 (Correction bottoming in October 2011)
➢ 21 August 2015 (Correction bottoming September 2015)
➢ 16 December 2015 (Correction bottoming February 2016)
➢ 24 October 2018 (Bear market bottoming December 2018, see footnote)
➢ 6 March 2020 (Bear market, bottoming 23 March 2020)

You can see on the chart on the next page that the death cross would have got us out before all the major crashes going back to before the GFC.

Technically, the Death Cross would also have got us out in June 2010, November 2011, and a couple of other times when no correction ensued.

However, if you look at the chart of that time you will see that in these cases the market is going sideways, and all SMAs are converging. It is quite hard to tell if and when they cross as they are so close.

In this situation the best approach would have been to sit tight and to wait until the situation became clear and either the cross was confirmed or the SMAs pulled away from each other.

SPY Chart 2007 - 2021
Death Crosses

Bear Traps and Bull Traps

Trading is not an exact science, as you will have worked out by now. As they say, ***they don't ring a bell at the bottom***. If everyone knew when to get out of the market and when to get back into the market, then everyone would be rich. But everyone isn't rich.

When markets are going up (bull markets) or going down (bear markets) there are, unfortunately, traps along the way. They are called (rather colorfully) bear traps and bull traps.

- Bear markets often pause on the way down and have a rally and go up, then carry on going down. This is a **bull trap** because it catches the bulls.

- Bull markets often pause on the way up and have a sell off and go down, then carry on going up. This is a **bear trap** because it catches the bears.

Remember the tides and the waves? There are some big waves even when the tide is going out. There are some little waves when the tide is coming in. It is simply the nature of the market.

Bear traps happen in a bull market. Bull traps happen in a bear market. They are mirror images of each other. If you are in a bull market where prices are trending upwards and then prices decline it can mean one of two things:

➢ The trend is reversing, and prices are going down (the tide is changing) OR
➢ It's just a hiccup and prices will resume going up (it was just a freak wave)

If you think that it means the trend is reversing (the tide is changing) and sell your positions but actually it isn't and keeps going up (it was just a freak wave) you have been caught in a bear trap.

Conversely, if you are in a bear market and there is a temporary increase in prices, and you sell then you have been caught in a bull trap.

Naturally, we want to avoid getting caught in any kind of trap, bear or bull, that's why we are going to have simple, objective signals like the Death Cross.

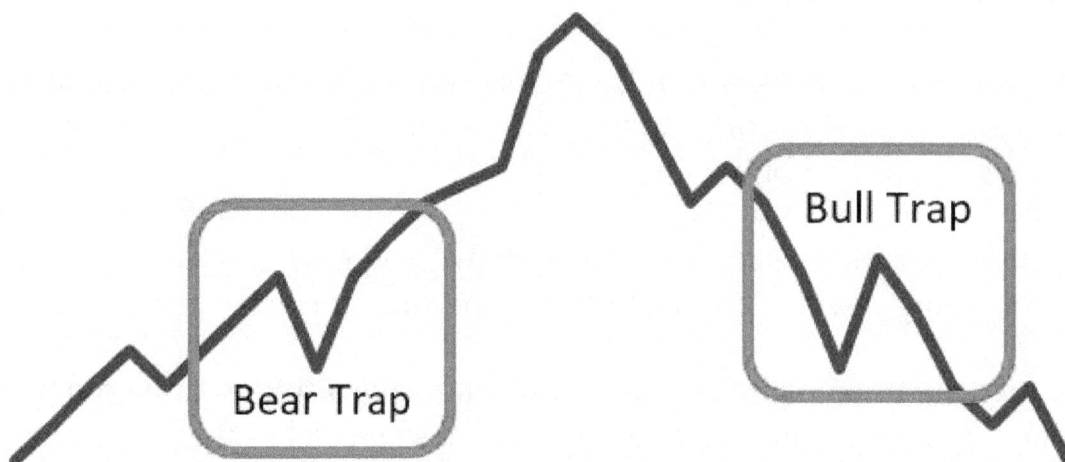

Short Sellers

Short sellers are often blamed for bear traps and bull traps. They don't cause them, but they can exacerbate them. As well, short sellers are frequently demonized and blamed for market crashes. During a crash there are calls for short selling to be banned, and sometimes it is. Some European countries (Austria, Belgium, Greece, France, Italy, and Spain) banned it in March 2020 (the covid bear) only to reinstate it 2 months later.

Short selling works like this: if a trader thinks prices are going down, she can sell shares *she doesn't actually own* hoping to buy them back at a lower price. How can she sell something she does not own? In effect, she borrows them from her broker, and of course, there is a fee involved. Brokers have to make money somehow!

She can sell the borrowed shares and then later to close the position she has to buy the shares back (buy-to-cover) and give them back to her broker. If the share price has gone down, then she makes a profit. If it has gone up, then she makes a loss.

Short Selling Example 1

Elise thinks that ABC which is trading at $100 will go down. She borrows 200 shares from her broker and sells them. And she is right! A week later the price falls to $80 per share. She buys them back and returns them to her broker. She has made a profit of $20 on each share, and she had 200 shares, so she has made a $4,000 profit. What a genius!

Short Selling Example 2

Sarah thinks that ABC which is trading at $100 will go down. She borrows 200 shares from her broker and sells them. But she is wrong! A week later the price rises to $110 per share. She buys them back and returns them to her broker. She has made a loss of $10 on each share, and she had 200 shares, so she has made a $2,000 loss. Not quite such a genius!

With short selling, losses are unlimited because the price could go up astronomically. Shares do from time to time. Alternatively, it could drop to close to zero. Either of these scenarios is possible and can involve you in heavy losses. The message here? Short selling is dangerous. Don't do it! In fact, many trading accounts don't permit you to do it unless you get a special rating.

Scrambling for Cover

Why do short sellers get blamed for bear traps and bull traps? Typically, when they see their positions going against them, they scramble to *cover their positions*. This means they buy them back before the positions move anymore and they lose more money.

If there are a lot of short sellers, then there is a lot of activity, and it looks like there is real buying pressure which makes the situation worse. You can find out how many traders are shorting stocks and which stocks they are shorting by Googling 'top 10 shorted stocks' or something similar.

What does this mean for your getting out and getting in signals? The safest is to choose an objective measure like a Death Cross as a get out signal. The problem is when to get back in again. Our questions now are:
  ➢ How long do we stay out?
  ➢ When do we get back in again?

The Golden Cross

Let's say we decided not to sit tight and we got out of the market when we saw the Death Cross. We now have to look at the signal we can use to get back in again. As we've seen, they don't ring a bell at the bottom. Trying to work out when the market is going to stop dropping and start going up again is hard. If it was easy no one would lose money. If you buy back in while it is going down it's called, for good reason, trying to *catch a falling knife*.

Let's say that we saw a 10/200 Death Cross and sold because we didn't want to lose money. Because our options are DITM we are not losing any time value.

There is nothing to stop us from buying them back anytime if we happen to be wrong and it was just a temporary blip when we mistook a wave for the tide. We can wait it out, and then buy back in when we think the worst is over. But how are we going to know that?

Luckily there is an indicator that we can use. If we take the opposite of the Death Cross, where the 10-day SMA moves up across the 200-day SMA we have what is called a 'Golden Cross'. Should we use that as a signal that the worst is over, and it is time to get back into the market?

This is a good idea, and a very safe one, but there is a problem. The Golden Cross is what we call a 'lagging indicator'. It tends to lag behind where the market is now and describe what has happened in the past not what is happening now.

The Death Cross is, of course, also a lagging indicator, but because bears jump out the window (the market tends to drop quickly), the Death Cross appears somewhat earlier in the downturn. Because bulls take the stairs (the market tends to go up slowly), the Golden Cross tends to show up rather later in the piece, often quite some time after the recovery has started. This is good in that you can be more confident that the recovery is really happening, but the downside is that you can miss out on the early gains which tend to be substantial.

Let's look at what would happen if we had waited for the 10/200 Golden

Cross to get in after the 6 downturns we have just looked at. The Golden cross happened:

> ➢ March 2008 (GFC) – Golden Cross 5 Jun 2009 – gain missed 39%
> ➢ August 2011 downturn- Golden Cross 5 Jan 2012 – gain missed 16%
> ➢ August 2015 downturn – Golden Cross 2 Nov 2015 – gain missed 12%
> ➢ January 2016 downturn – Golden Cross 14 Apr 2016 – gain missed 12%
> ➢ December 2018 downturn – Golden Cross 6 Mar 2019 – gain missed: 18%

We can see that the 10/200 Golden Cross keeps us safe by making sure that we don't get back into the market too early, we are waiting until we are quite sure that the tide has turned. On the downside, we miss out on the gains between the bottom of the market and the time of the Golden Cross.

In other words, we have missed the turn of the tide and the tide is well in before we set sail again. Let's look at the Golden Crosses on our chart with the Death Crosses.

SPY Chart 2007 - 2021
Death Crosses

The reason for this late entry is because market downs are more sudden and generally more pronounced that market ups and this reflects in the volatility of the moving averages. Bear markets don't generally last as long as bull markets. You will find widely varying figures if you Google this because although everyone has a standard definition for a bear market, there is no agreed definition of a bull market. Bull markets, on average over the last 90 years, last over 4.5 years or 8 years depending on your definition. Bear markets, on average, last 14 - 18 months.

The 10/200 Golden Cross is most effective when there is what is called a V-shaped recovery. That simply means that the market goes down very sharply but then rises again very sharply, because on a chart it looks like a 'V' shape.

What we don't want is to get back in and then have the market drop on us again. That can happen as it did during the GFC (Global Financial Crisis). In December 2007 there was both a golden cross and a death cross within a week! Following the ITM rules you would have got out, and then back in again almost right away. You would not have lost any time value and very little money as you would have bought at $147.91 and sold at $145.07, less than a 2% loss.

It is very hard to create simple rules about the market. It's a bit like trying to teach someone to ride a bike. You know how to do it but explaining to someone else how you do it is difficult. There is only so much you can tell them. At some stage, they have to get on the bike and figure it out for themselves, and probably have a few spills before they are competent. But – and it's a big but – if you try this in the stock market you can go broke before you figure it out, so we need some simple rules.

Rather than use support/resistance lines and other indicators let's stick with our moving averages and crosses. Let's say that we have seen a 10/200 Death Cross and have sold our option positions. We watch, and in a few weeks, we see a 10/200 Golden Cross. Time to get back in again, so we buy back our options (or different ones if the market has moved a lot). This is the danger time when you have to monitor the market, every day if possible. How to do this? Luckily it is easy – and free!

Monitoring the Market

To see when the death cross or the golden cross happen you need to look at the SPY chart. To see the chart, you can either buy a charting package, or use one of the excellent free resources online. The free ones have improved immensely over recent years, and for the ITM strategy, there is really no need to actually buy anything. The free ones are more than enough for our needs. To find them, simply google 'stock chart SPY interactive'. Finance.Yahoo.com has an excellent one, so I will use that as an example.

When you click on the link a chart opens up. You can choose what is on the chart and how it looks. You can change the time frames (choose a daily chart), adjust the axes, and choose what kind of chart you want (choose a candlestick chart). You can also put indicators on, so you can graph the moving averages you need. The Indicator drop-down box is at the top left-hand side, arrowed in the above chart.

Choose the 10-day and 200-day simple moving averages (SMA) and it promptly graphs it for you so that you can see the death or golden cross you are looking for.

There are lots of other indicators you can try if you want to. Other indicators that I use are the MACD (Moving Average Convergence / Divergence) which I discuss in the Bear Market book, RSI (Relative Strength Index), Volume and On Balance Volume. You don't have to use these for ITM, but you may want to have a look at them to see what they do. Or not.

It's your choice! If you want to see how any of them work just google – you will get heaps of information.

There are also excellent drawing tools, so you can put in trend lines and support / resistance lines. Seriously, you can spend hours playing with this stuff. I do, but then I am a bit of a nerd about it. However, it is not necessary. As long as you can see when there is a 10/200 death cross and golden cross that is all you need.

Should I have Sold?

Let's look at how this would have played out in real life using the 10/200 death cross to get out and the 10/200 golden cross to get back in again.

Downturn	Sell	Low	Buy Back
2007/9	$145.54	$68.11	$94.55
2011/12	$120.09	$109.93	$128.04
2015	$197.83	$187.27	$210.38
2016	$208.03	$182.86	$204.67
2018	$273.62	$234.34	$277.42
2020	$297.46	$222.95	$308.08

You can see that apart from 2007/9 when we benefitted a lot, we were buying back at the same or slightly higher than we sold. At first glance it looks rather foolish to have gotten out, only to get in again at a higher price. And most of the time it is, that's why staying in the market produces good results and is a viable option if you can take the interim pain. But we have to watch out for what is called a 'black swan' event.

Black Swan Event: The Global Financial Crisis

A **black swan event** is an unpredictable event that comes as a surprise and has either a major effect or is shocking. The term 'black swan' comes from the belief that everyone had, for hundreds of years, that all swans were white. After all, why wouldn't you think that?

Every swan anyone had ever seen was white, so they 'knew' that all swans were white. Just like we 'know' that elephants are grey, not pink.

But then in 1697 the explorer Vlamingh discovered black swans in Australia, which rather destroyed the idea that they were all white. It was unexpected, unforeseen, and quite shocking. It required major changes in the science of ecology and zoology. Hence the term 'black swan' to describe this kind of event.

And the biggest economic black swan event in the lifetime of any adult alive now is, of course, the Global Financial Crisis (GFC) of 2008. That was the most dreadful crash, the worst crash since the Great Depression 80 years before. There was carnage on the markets. People panicked and dumped their stocks, causing the market to plunge even further.

Traders were shell-shocked. Companies went bankrupt, others were taken over, and there was a banking crisis. Traders on margin went bust. Retirement funds were reduced to less than half. It was not a happy time. People were wiped out, their savings were gone, and many were left in debt because they have been using borrowed money.

The obvious question is: *would our ITM signals above have kept you safe?* Well, actually, yes, they would have. As we saw above our signals would have avoided losses and we would have been able to buy back at considerably lower prices. We would have sold at $145.54 and then bought back in again at $94.55, over $50 less. Nice.

What would have happened if we had sat tight? Well, we would have eventually made up our losses, but we would have to have waited several years. The market high of $156.23 in October 2007 was not made up until March 2013. That's 6 years of pain! The market then, of course, went on to double over the next 6 years. Much nicer.

What About Covid?

There is a fair bit of debate about whether COVID was a black swan event or not. There is an argument that it is not, because we have been warned about epidemics and pandemics (worldwide epidemics) and have had several in recent years.

In the last 20 years we have had other pandemics: Zika, Ebola, MERS-CoV, Swine Flu, and SARS. Based on this, then Covid is not unprecedented or unforeseen.

However, the response to this pandemic has been quite unlike any other event, with countries worldwide shuttering up their economies and ordering people to stay home. Perhaps the response to Covid is the black swan event.

It is hard to put the whole Covid episode in perspective as it has not finished yet. There is a realization that Covid is not going to disappear, and that at some stage we will have the learn to live with it. Different countries have different approaches and international travel is not back to pre-covid levels. However, things seem to be more predictable and less scary than they did in early 2020.

What To Look Out For

We don't expect another GFC, but then 'black swan' events are never expected. You should keep an eye on the market, just glance at the headlines and check what the S&P is doing.

What you are looking for is:

> The mood of the market – were we in euphoria? If so, then the downturn is likely to be bigger and nastier than if we were in any other phase.
> Is SPY starting to drift lower? Not on individual days (waves) but over 2 or 3 weeks (tide).

Both of these indicators mean that you should be careful and be watching for your 'Get Out' signal. Let's distill what we have been talking about into a few simple Getting Out and Getting In rules:

➢ **Sell:** When you see a 10/200 Death Cross then sell. When? As soon as it is confirmed. Markets drop more quickly than they go up so waiting for even a few days may cost you dearly. Once the SMAs have clearly crossed and there is 'white space' between them sell. If the SMAs meet but don't actually cross wait a day or so to see what is happening. If they don't cross but start to move away from each other then that means that the signal was not confirmed so you don't sell.

➢ **Stay Out:** Until you see a 10/200 Golden Cross. When you see that, it's time to buy back in. Again, make sure that the SMAs have actually crossed, and you can see white space between them before you buy back in.

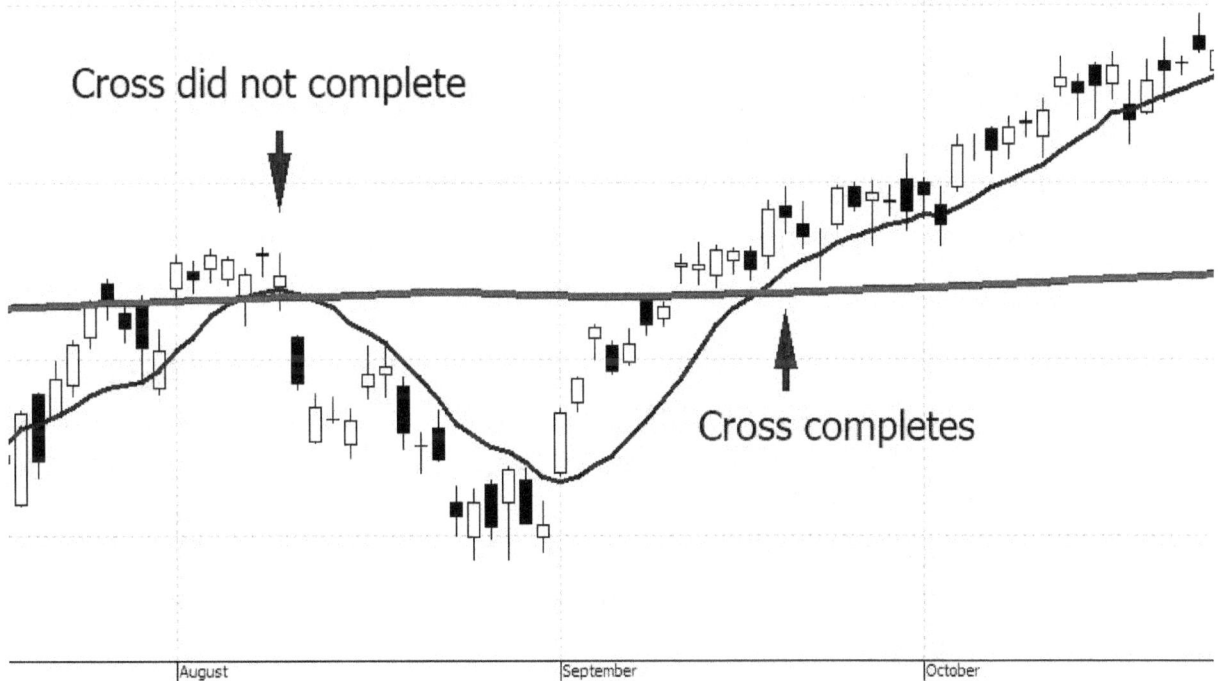

The above chart gives an example of a completed cross and incomplete cross.

Using the ITM signals in this way you will stay safe. The worst thing that can happen is you stay too long out of the market and miss out on some profits. But that is far preferable to losing your capital!

ITM aims to keep it simple and give you a few easy rules that will keep you safe. The most important thing to do is not to lose your capital because then you are out of the game. Remember Warren Buffet's 2 rules:

> ➤ Rule 1: Never lose money
> ➤ Rule 2: Never forget Rule 1.

Now, I am not a great Warren Buffett fan. I find his actions and his advice too often at odds with each other. For example, he personally lost about $23 billion in the GFC. Does that sound like someone following his own rules?

Rolling Your Options

There is one last thing we need to know before we are ready to start because, unlike diamonds, options are not forever. They have a limited life, and we need to know how to handle that.

Let's say you have started. You are in the market, you have bought your options, and everything is going beautifully. That's wonderful. You check your account every week, and it is going up nicely. Apart from depositing more funds when you can there is very little to do other than keep an eye on things.

However, there is still a little bit of 'housekeeping' you need to do from time to time, at least once a year. As you know, options have expiry dates, and you don't want to be holding them at expiry because you don't want the hassle of actually taking delivery of the underlying shares and then selling them. It's not a big deal if it happens because you can sell them right away. It is just easier to avoid that hassle and any costs involved by selling your options before expiry.

As we are buying DITM options with very little time value we don't have to be worried about losing money as time passes. We do not, of course, want to continue holding DITM SPY positions after the expiry date so we have to **roll our options.**

Rolling out means that you replace your expiring position with an option that has a later expiry date but the same strike. So, for example, if you sell your 240 Jan 2023 call and buy a 240 Jan 2024 call then you are ***rolling out***.

This is easy to do and can be done any time before the expiry date. A week or two is ideal. Because there is only intrinsic value the price of your new options will be about the same as the old ones.

You may, however, also want to **roll up**. This is rather like taking profits and freeing up some cash for you to reinvest. This is how you can turbocharge your profits. Here is how it works.

Let's say that you bought the 240 Jan 2023 call when the SPY was $400. Let's imagine that over the next couple of months SPY has moved up quite strongly and is now $440. To free up some of your profits you can choose a new option with a higher strike price which will be cheaper.

For example, if you choose a 265 Jan 2023 Call it will be $25 cheaper than the $240 one (how? $265 - $240) so you would free up $2,500 cash (options contracts are for 100 shares, remember?) If you sell your 240 Jan 2023 and buy a 265 Jan 2023 you are *rolling up*. The strike is different, but the expiry date is the same.

You can both **roll up and roll out** at the same time by choosing an option that has a later expiry date AND a higher strike price. If, for example, you sold your 240 Jan 2023 and bought a 265 Jan 2024 then you would be rolling up AND rolling out.

Of course, you don't have to wait until the end of the year to either roll up or roll out. If the SPY has moved significantly you can roll up at any time, freeing up some cash from your profits.

Roll Type	OLD	NEW
Roll OUT	240 Call Jan 2023	240 Call Jan 2024
Roll UP	240 Call Jan 2023	265 Call Jan 2023
Roll OUT and UP	240 Call Jan 2023	265 Call Jan 2024

What to do with the profits you have freed up? *Leave them in your*

account. This is really important if we are going to get you wealthy. Do NOT take them out and go shopping! We're building up your wealth, remember? Once you have enough profits in your account you can buy another DITM option, and this gives you more leverage so that you can watch your profits grow even faster.

Footnote re bear market 2018.

There is debate about whether the sudden drop in the share market in December 2018 was a bear market, albeit a very quick one. It is frequently listed as not being a bear market because the Dow only dropped 18.8%, which did not reach the threshold of 20% required for a bear market. But, as we have seen, the Dow is not representative of the market as a whole, being composed of only 30 stocks, and these being weighted by market capitalization.

The S&P 500, on the other hand, is made up of 500 stocks and represents 80% of the market so is a much better representation of what actually happened. SPY (the SPX ETF) was trading at $293.58 on the 20th September 2018, and dropped to $234.34 on the 24th December 2018. This is a 20.18% drop which is clearly over 20%, hence it could be classified as a bear market.

Remember earlier in the chapter I advised always to check who is saying it and what is their motivation for saying it? The mistake of using the Dow rather than the S&P 500 is an elementary one, one that anyone who had checked where the statistic came from would immediately recognize. So why do they do it?

Could it be that it is more newsworthy to bang on about the longest bull market ever, conveniently ignoring the obvious fallacy? No one is going to click on news items about a bull market that is only 1 year old!

Chapter 9 Highlights

The major points in Chapter 9. Stay in or Sell? are:

➢ The four stages of a bull market: pessimism, skepticism, optimism, and euphoria

➢ When faced with a market downturn our options are to either:

❖ Sit tight – this is OK if you have a **very** long-term focus.

❖ Sell and buy in again when the worst is over.

➢ Our signal to get out is the 10/200 SMA death cross.

➢ Our signal to get back in again is the 10/200 SMA golden cross

➢ Black swan events happen, but not often.

And finally, some wise words from Edwin Lefèvre, the original Wolf of Wall Street in Reminiscences of a Stock Operator

If a man didn't make mistakes, he'd own the world in a month. But if he didn't profit from his mistakes, he wouldn't own a blessed thing.

Chapter 10. We're in the Money!

Now we have learned all about how options work, and how to do the ITM strategy. The next question is obviously: is it worth it? What returns did ITM make over the last 30 years?

In the first edition of **In The Money: Bull Market Strategy**, I had backtested to before the GFC; for this second edition, I backtested an extra 13 years, right to the start of SPY, almost 30 years ago. And what did I find?

The ITM results over the last 30 years since SPY started at the beginning of 1993 are good. So absurdly good, in fact, that I could imagine readers thinking that I had massaged the data to get them. To be fair, after seeing the backtesting results, I had a tough time believing them myself. I was convinced that I had made a mistake somewhere. To check there were no mistakes, I redid the figures several times. I started from scratch each time, redoing the downloading of data and crossmatching between sources, pouring over charts, and checking and double-checking figures. However, no matter what I did, the results kept coming out the same and annoyingly good.

I had already decided that if I wanted to show that the ITM strategy worked it was imperative to be completely transparent and show all the details of the backtesting so that anyone could check the figures for themselves.

I had originally intended to put them in an appendix (as I did for the bear strategy book) but decided that it would make for very boring reading and put up the price of the book as printing costs and delivery costs for the eBook depend on the number of pages. Instead, I decided to publish them on the website, HeatherCullen.com

The trades go right back to the first day of trading of SPY in 1993. Every single trade during that time is detailed, along with the reasons for getting into and out of each trade. They all comply with the ITM strategy rules as laid out in previous chapters. The result of each trade is shown whether it's good, bad, or boring.

The most important thing is that the effect on the account balance is clearly shown so that you can see exactly how the account grew over the years.

The lists of trades in the backtesting are not exactly riveting reading, so don't feel that you have to wade through all the trades, but if you want to check my figures then feel free to knock yourself out!

Just be aware that SPY historical data sets are not always super 'clean'; there are sometimes minor discrepancies. When I say minor, I mean a few cents difference in the closing prices for a few of the earlier dates, but there is nothing of import that would materially change the overall results.

SPY Bull Strategy Backtest

The rules that were used for the backtesting are exactly as outlined earlier in the book but let us recap them here. The IN and OUT rules for reading SPY with the ITM strategy were quite simple:

> - **OUT Signal**: 10/200 SMA Death Cross
> - **IN Signal**: 10/200 SMA Golden cross.

As well as this there were rules on what options to buy. The buying parameters were:

> - **DITM**: A Deep in the Money Option
> - **Long-dated**: up to a year to expiry
> - **Effective price:** less than 1% above the current price

In backtesting, an options strike price of 60% of the current SPY price at that date was used, which history shows is always well within the +1% range. For example, if SPY was trading at $200 then a strike of $120 would be selected. So, to be clear, the backtesting parameters were:
> - **Buying** DITM options that were 60% of the current SPY price, one year to expiry.
> - **Rolling UP** (to maintain 60% level) and **rolling OUT** (later expiry date) at the start of every year.
> - **Rolling UP** at any time if the option strike dropped to less than 50% of the current SPY price (to maintain the 60% strike level.)

All prices are closing prices and the historical data can be found and downloaded from several places. If you wish to download the data set, then google 'Yahoo historical SPY' and you will find all the data going back to the start of SPY.

Closing prices, not intraday prices, were used in the backtesting.

The options pricing (premium) in the test is based on the closing price of SPY and based on the following parameters:

> - **Buying:**
> ❖ Time value of 1% assumed (i.e., the effective price is 1% above current the SPY price)
> - **Selling:**
> ❖ More than 90 days to expiry – time value same as for buying

❖ 90 days or less to expiry – assume that all time value has expired.

These assumptions err on the side of safety. They give a slight overestimate of what the trade would actually cost when buying, as at 60% of the current price we usually come in well under 1% time value. It also underestimates what we would get on the sale of the option, as at 90 days out any time value has not decreased significantly at this level.

The good thing about making these rules is that we will know that the backtesting results are underestimates, and are not inflated in any way

This ensures that the actual ITM results are significantly better than our backtesting results, but I wanted to make sure that there were no accusations of cherry-picking or massaging the results.

We entered the trades the day **after** the IN signal was visible and exited the day **after** the OUT signal was visible. This is to ensure that the IN or OUT pattern (the death cross or golden cross) has actually been completed before entering the trade.

If we wait until we can see white space between the SMAs then we know they have actually crossed rather than just touching each other. If they were just touching but didn't actually cross, then we waited another day or until there was an unambiguous indication that they have actually crossed.

We saw this diagram of an unconfirmed cross and a confirmed cross earlier in the book and it is worth revisiting here so that we are absolutely clear about what is meant.

You can see that on the incomplete cross there were several days when the SMAs were touching but did not go on to actually cross. In the completed cross there is white space between the 2 SMAs.

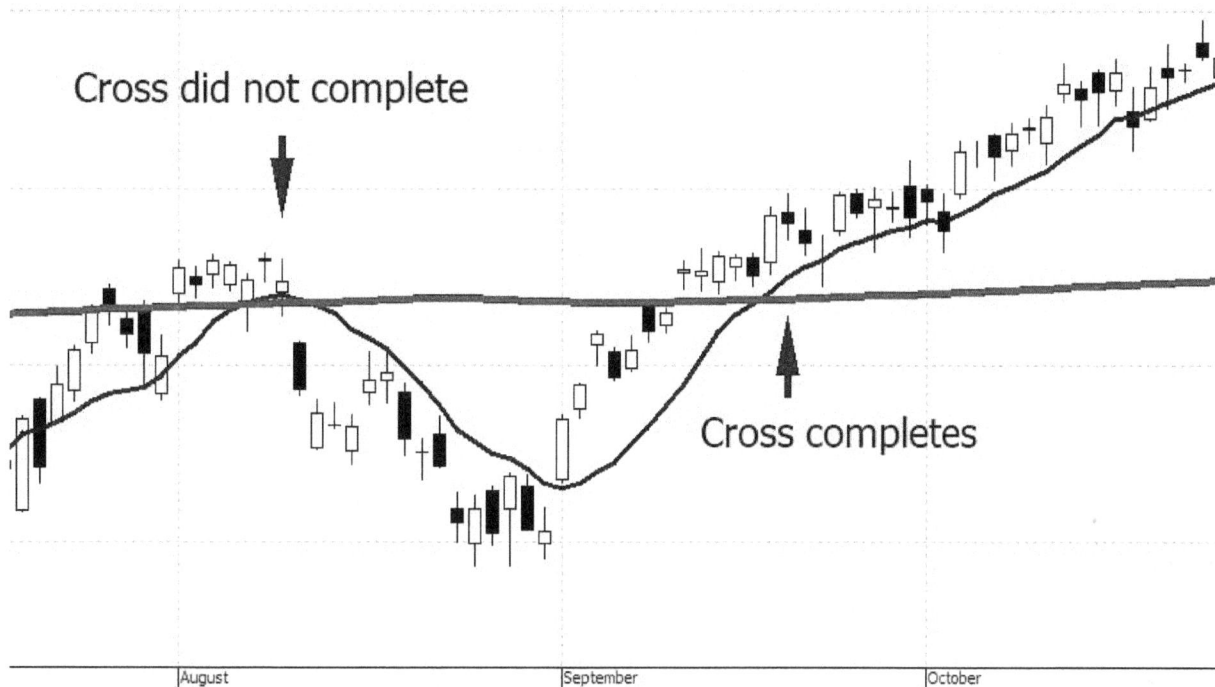

To be clear, if we are going to enter a bull trade it is a 3 day process:

➢ **Day 1**: SMAs touch.
➢ **Day 2**: SMAs have crossed, and white space is visible
➢ **Day 3**: enter trade.

We enter on day 3 because we have to wait until the market is closed for day 2 to make sure that the cross has been completed. Markets sometimes change dramatically in the last 30 minutes of trade, especially if it is a significant date, so entering on day 2 may be jumping the gun somewhat. It is better to wait for confirmation.

All of these rules used in backtesting are exactly as set out here. The figures are all detailed so that you can check that the backtest is accurate and the results have not been 'fixed' or 'massaged' in any way.

What was the Market Result?

The first thing to check, of course, was what the market performance had been so that we know by how much ITM beat it. Checking the historical data we see that in 1993, SPY was trading at $43.94, around one-tenth of where it is today.

For the following calculations assume that you started with an account of $10,000 in 1993. If you had bought SPY shares, then the calculation is easy:

➢ $10K could buy 228 SPY shares at $43.94 (closing price 29 January 1993)
➢   Today each share would be worth $474.96 (closing price 31 December 2021)
➢ Your SPY shares would now be worth $108,291

In other words, your SPY shares would have gone up by almost 1,000%. Nice!

However, your result **would actually be better than this** because just looking at the value of the shares is ignoring the dividends you would have received during that time.

That is one advantage shares have over options: with shares you get dividends but with options you do not. While the yearly average SPY dividend is small (1.94% average over the last 25 years) reinvesting this over 30 years makes a significant difference.

If you had not taken out the dividends but instead reinvested them then your account would now be worth $160,981 almost 50% greater than just holding the shares. An even nicer result.

This is what normally happens if you invest through a broker: if you tick the 'reinvest' box they will automatically reinvest for you, so it is a set-and-forget portfolio. Alternatively, if you wish, you can easily do it yourself. When the dividends are paid twice a year then check to see if you have enough cash in your account to buy extra shares and then do that.

This SPY reinvested dividends total ($160,981) is the real market performance we are trying to beat.

So, we have seen that just buying and holding SPY shares and reinvesting the dividends gives us a nice, solid return. That is what we are trying to beat. Let us see how ITM went.

The Advantages of Leverage

As we will see shortly, ITM beat the market easily, and by a very large margin. How can we do this by only using the leverage we get from options at 60% of the current price? Because apart from the leverage, our OUT and IN rules keep us out of the downturns that can seriously damage our wealth.

If you bought and held SPY shares then there were some years, like 2009, when you would have lost 36% of your account balance. If you drop by 36% then you need more than a 36% gain to get back to where you were. To show you what I mean, let us take an example:

➢ Your account was worth $20,000
➢ It dropped 36%.
➢ Your account is now worth $12,800
➢ You need an increase of 56% to get back to $20,000

This shows how damaging big dips can be; if your account dropped 50% then you need a 100% increase to get back to where you were.

This is why people who tell you *It's time in the market, not timing the market* are so misguided. They are not realizing what impact drops have on your account balance. They are simply looking at the yearly returns and figuring that a 50% drop can be regained by a 50% gain. You can see that it does not work like that, and they should know better.

A significant part of ITM's performance has been simply keeping us out of major market declines. During the last 30 years, we got the OUT signal 23 times, and we were out for an average of 103 days each time. That does not give the whole picture of course; sometimes we were out for as little as 7 days and twice we were out for almost 18 months. The times we were only out for a brief time were false alarms: the market was just having a dip and did not go into correction or into a bear market. This happens when the market is undecided and going sideways.

The two times we were out for a long time were the two big bear markets, 2001-3 and 2008-9. Getting out saved us a world of pain and protected our capital, contributing to the outperformance of ITM when compared with the market return.

ITM Bull Strategy Results

OK, ready for the ITM results? If you had invested $10,00 in January 1993 and followed the ITM rules, then your account would now be worth $1,475,952. Here it is graphically:

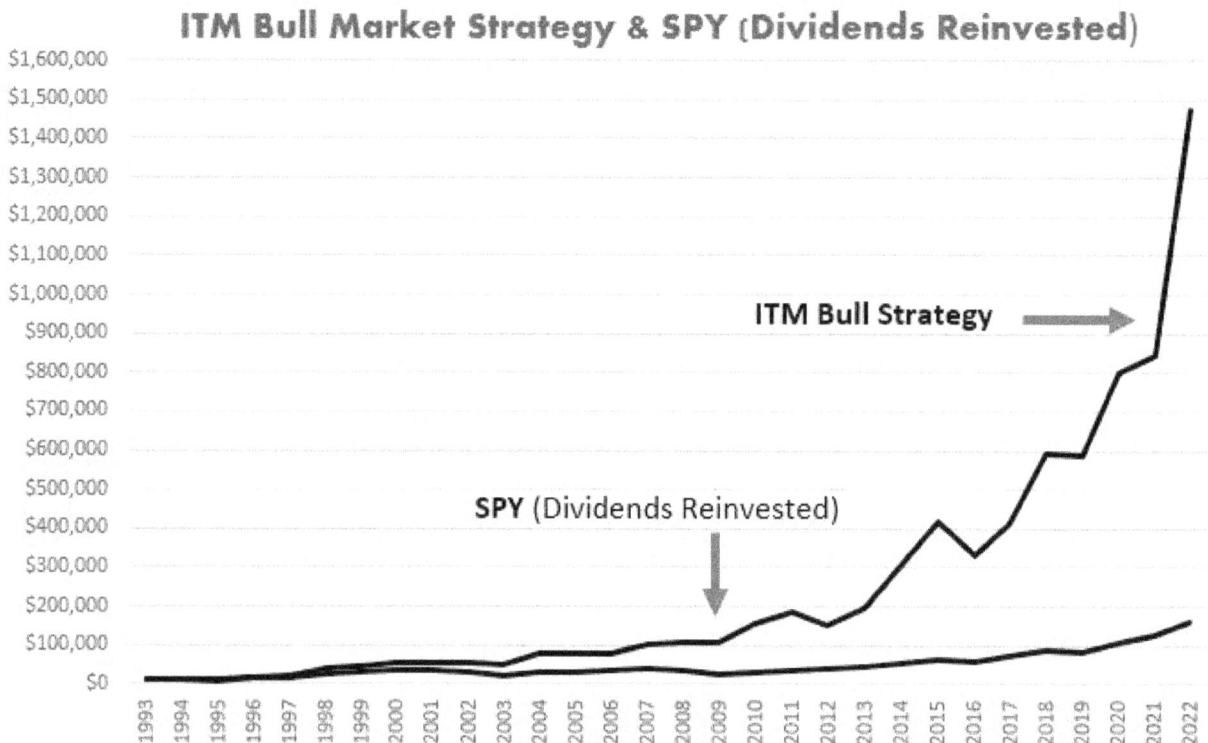

ITM Bull Market Strategy & SPY (Dividends Reinvested)

You can see why I did a double-take when I saw the results, then checked and rechecked – the difference is quite amazing. Almost ten times the market return!

You can also understand why I did not put the results near the front of the book. They look too good to be true. However, it was by exactly applying the rules from *In The Money: Bull Market Strategy* going back to January 1993 that these results came about.

I can honestly say that if someone had presented me with this graph, I would be very skeptical. This is why all the trades are published on the website, so that you can check the results for yourself if you wish. If I had been a reader, I am fairly sure I would have checked them for myself, so do have a look if you are not convinced.

Of course, the ITM journey wasn't always a bed of roses; there were years when SPY beat ITM quite convincingly. We know that the ITM Bull strategy is best in a bull market.

When the market is trending sideways it does not perform very well at all because if both moving averages are almost horizontal then some signals will be false alarms. In this situation ITM tends to whip us in and out of trades, often losing money in the process because we may have to buy back at a higher price than we sold.

You can see in the graph below that in the first few years it would have been hard to keep the faith with the ITM Bull strategy, especially when, in 1995, ITM dipped quite alarmingly below its starting price.

It was not until 1996 when the bull market really started that ITM started to perform well and its performance start to pull away from the SPY shares. Until then, you would have to bear three years of trading with a negative result at the end of it, which would unnerve most people, including me.

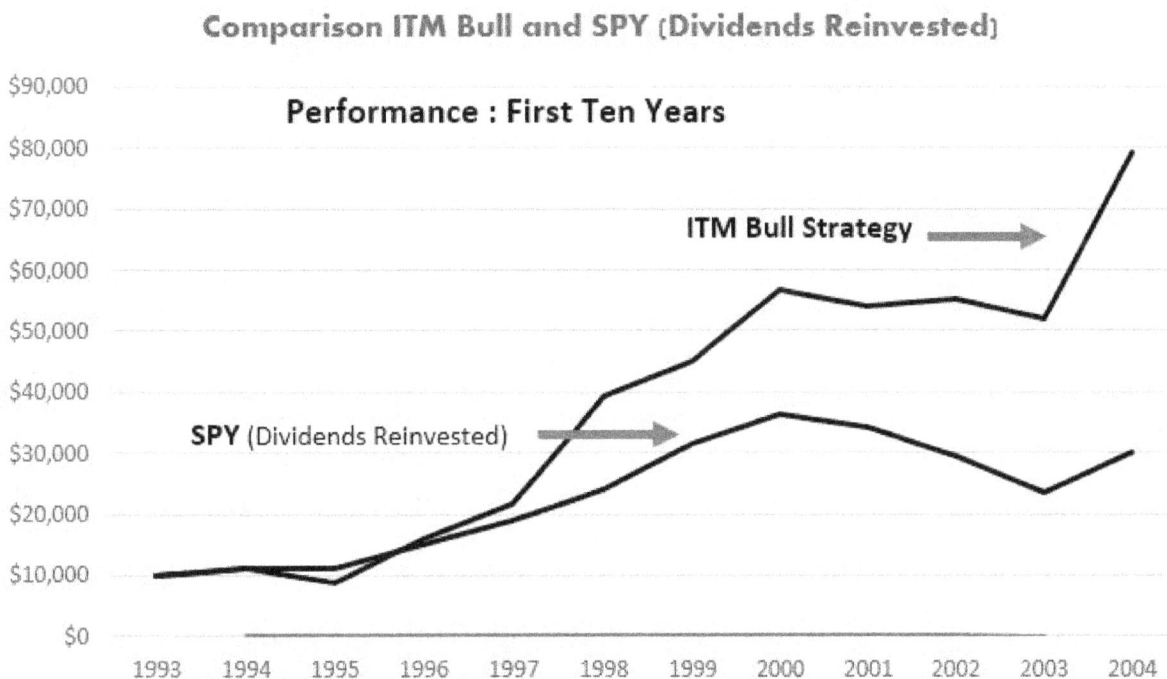

Comparison ITM Bull and SPY (Dividends Reinvested)

Performance : First Ten Years

ITM Bull Strategy

SPY (Dividends Reinvested)

The ITM Bull performance started increasing when the market started trending upwards quite strongly, so between 1996 and 2000 ITM established a significant lead over SPY. You can also see that in the downturn starting in 2000 (the 'tech wreck') ITM got us out of the market so that unlike SPY we did not lose a lot of our account balance, placing us in a good position to take advantage of the eventual upturn when it happened.

So, a word of caution about ITM Bull. It has worked really well over the past 30 years because it is a bull market strategy and we have been mostly in bull markets over that time. It keeps us safely out of the worst of any downturns, but what it is not good at is handling a sideways market. In a sideways market, it tends to get us in and out of trades too frequently and this can deplete your account.

ITM Bear Market Strategy

While the ITM Bull strategy backtesting results are impressive, combining it with the ITM Bear Strategy has produced results that are even better, increasing the ITM returns by a multiple of three.

The bear market strategy is the book **In The Money: Bear Market Strategy**, and it is recommended that you read it before any bear market starts so that you are prepared and know what to look for. All bull markets end – as do bear markets.

Bull and Bear Results

In a strange sort of way, I rather wish that the results had been less impressive. This stock market performance is not the norm and is way ahead of what market gurus and financial experts produce. It seems unlikely that someone from outside the industry, with no finance qualifications or Ph.D. in financial analysis, could analyze the data and come up with a strategy that gets these results. But that is what has happened.

There is no getting around it: these are the results. The figures are correct. All the trades conform to the rules. Everything is detailed so that you can check for yourself.

I can't pretend that the results are not wonderful. They are. And I think they are tremendously exciting and a way for 'ordinary' people to make extraordinary returns.

Chapter 10 Highlights

The major points in Chapter 10. We're in the Money are:

➢ Over the last 30 years and starting with $10,000 in our account, then today our account would be worth:

❖ $161,000 if we made the market return with dividends reinvested.

❖ $1,476,000 if we used the ITM bull market strategy.

➢ ITM made these returns by:

❖ Leverage – using options that were 60% of the current SPY price

❖ Maintaining that level of leverage by rolling up

❖ Avoiding major downturns – getting out of the market when there was an ITM OUT signal

➢ The Backtesting results are detailed on https://HeatherCullen.com / backtesting

And some words from Mellody Hobson to remind us that if we don't take the first step we'll never get there:

The biggest risk of all is not taking one.

◆ ◆ ◆

Chapter 11. ITM for Small Accounts

As SPY increases, and it has increased a lot over the past years couple of years, so does the price of SPY options. This can make it hard for people with smaller accounts to implement ITM because a SPY option with an effective price less than 1% more than the current price and a year to expiry can be more than $10,000.

One way to reduce the cost of the option is to choose a nearer expiry date, say 6 months. However, as we are choosing options with little or no time value then this does not have a huge effect on the affordability. As well, there is a downside in that we have to roll more frequently, although with brokerage fees being negligible these days this is not the financial consideration that it used to be.

Even choosing a nearer-dated option may not be enough for smaller accounts, so I have researched and backtested a strategy specifically for this situation. ***This strategy is not meant to replace the ITM strategy***; it is aimed at enabling people with smaller accounts to enter the market and hopefully build up enough capital to be able to do the full ITM Bull and Bear strategies.

It may also be done as an additional strategy if you are doing ITM. If you have spare cash in your account but not enough to afford another DITM option, then you can use this strategy as a sideline until you do. Because the premiums are considerably less than for SPY you can buy a DITM option for much less. To make things easier to read let's give a name to this new strategy: **ITMS** for **ITM Small.**

S&P 500 Growth ETF

We are going to use a different underlying instrument: SPYG. Like SPY, this is an ETF and it started more recently in September 2000. It is made up of stocks from the S&P 500 selected because they show the strongest growth characteristics. The SPY holds 500 stocks; SPYG is smaller and holds approximately 300 stocks.

The SPYG stocks and the number of stocks vary. They are selected because they outperform on three growth factors:

➤ Sales growth.
➤ Earnings change to price.
➤ Momentum.
Currently SPYG top 10 holdings are:

➤ Apple (AAPL) 13.8%
➤ Microsoft (MSFT) 12.1%
➤ Amazon (AMZN) 7.2%
➤ Alphabet (GOOGL) 4.4%
➤ Alphabet (GOOG) 4.1%
➤ Tesla (TLSA) 3.8%
➤ NVIDIA (NVDA) 3.3%
➤ Meta (FB) 2.7%
➤ Home Depot (HD) 1.4%
➤ Adobe (ADBE) 1.2%

As you can see, it is very heavily weighted to technology stocks. If you compared it with the Nasdaq 100, you would see that there is a lot of overlap. In fact, eight of the top 10 SPYG stocks are also in the top 10 Nasdaq 100 stocks.

But SPYG has the one great advantage we are looking for: it is cheap, less than 20% of the cost of SPY. This means that the options are proportionally cheaper, and so it will take less capital to buy them. Traders with smaller accounts will be able to start the ITMS strategy if their account balance is approximately $3,000.

SPYG does have one great disadvantage when compared with SPY; *the SPYG options only go out 6 months*. This requires us to trade more frequently, as we need to roll our options before or at expiry. This means we will be trading at least twice a year, and more often if we get an IN or an OUT signal. Apart from that the options market is good, with lots of strikes and relatively small spreads.

So, the good news is that the options are comparatively cheaper; however, nothing is cheap if it doesn't make us money, so the first thing to do was to check by backtesting the ITM strategy on SPYG. The backtesting went right back to its inception in September 2000, just at the height of the dot com boom.

Backtesting parameters and criteria

Needless to say, I approached this backtesting of ITMS with a sense of déjà vu rather than unmitigated delight. I seem to have spent an enormous amount of my life backtesting, creating spreadsheets and studying charts. But if I am going to write about and recommend a strategy then the backtesting has to be done. No choice. Nose to the grindstone.

The differences between SPY options and SPYG options mean that we cannot use exactly the same rules for using ITM on both. As we mentioned, SPYG options only go out 6 months, so we have to trade more often than we do for SPY. For the backtesting, I standardized this as rolling on the first trading day after 1st January and 1st July.

The strikes start at less than half the current price and at that level, and 6 months to expiry, we can buy an option at 60% of the current SPYG value with an effective price quite a bit less than 0.5% more than the current price. This is approximately the same as for SPY options for the same 6 months expiry.

So, let's check that our ITM parameters and criteria can be adapted to work for SPYG.

The IN and OUT rules for reading SPY with the ITM strategy were very simple:

> OUT Signal: 10/200 SMA Death Cross.
> IN Signal: 10/200 SMA Golden Cross.

In both cases, the trade dates are always the day *after* the signal is visible. This enables us to check that the IN or OUT pattern (the death cross or golden cross) has actually completed before entering the trade.

We wait until we can see white space between the SMAs so that we know they have crossed rather than just touching. If they are just touching, then we wait another day or two until we have an unambiguous indication that they have actually crossed.

Just to make sure that you are clear let's look at the diagram of the complete and incomplete cross yet again:

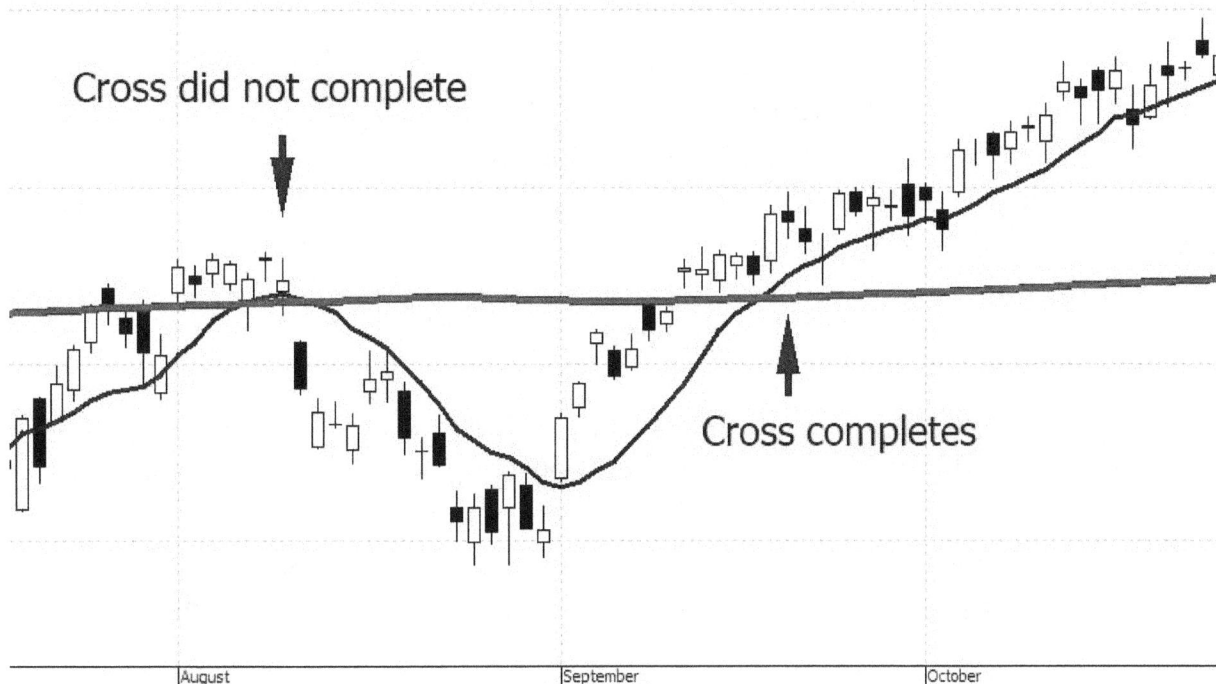

To recap, if we are going to enter a bull trade it is a 3 day process:

- ➤ **Day 1**: SMAs touch.
- ➤ **Day 2**: SMAs have crossed and white space is visible
- ➤ **Day 3**: enter trade.

As for ITM, closing prices were used, not intra-day prices. This is why we enter on day 3 because we have to wait until the market is closed for day 2 to get the closing price. Markets sometimes change dramatically in the last 30 minutes of trade, especially if it is a significant date, so entering on day 2 may be jumping the gun somewhat. It is better to wait for confirmation.

There is account maintenance that is to be carried out every 6 months in January and July:

- ➤ **Roll OUT** to a new expiry date.
- ➤ **Roll UP** to the highest strike that fits within the buying parameters

As for ITM, buy additional options when enough cash is freed up. The trading parameters for selecting and buying the options are:

- ➤ 6 months to expiry
- ➤ The effective price is less than 0.5% above the current SPYG price.

For the backtesting I have used a strike price of 60% of the current price, rounding at the .75 mark as follows:

- $10.10 would be rounded down to a strike of $10
- $11.75 would be rounded down to a strike of $11.
- $12.85 would be rounded up to a strike of $13.

At that level, price history shows that calculating an option price halfway between the bid / ask gives us an effective price 0.1% above the current price. To ensure that we are underestimating the results from ITMS, for testing I used an effective price of current price +0.5%.

This overestimate will give us more confidence in the results as we will know that in real life, they would have been better. For the backtesting, if the option was less than 40 days to expiry when the trade took place then the 0.5% time value was removed from the sale price. This ensured that we overestimated our buying prices and underestimated our selling price.

Because of the frequency of the trades (there are 94 separate trades over the 20 years) I did not want to put them in an appendix. It would only push up the price of the book as every page increases the price, whether on paper or an eBook – yes, Amazon charges me for 'delivery' of every eBook! I also thought that few people would want to wade through them anyway.

That said, I wanted the results to be available and transparent, so I have published the backtesting on my website, here's the link:

HeatherCullen.com / backtesting

It is all there; every trade, the reason for getting in or out and the effect on the account balance.

ITMS Results

As for ITM, we need to compare the ITMS results with the market. Again, we will use the S&P 500 with dividends reinvested, as our benchmark. Although ITMS can be done with a smaller account, I have used a starting account value of $10,000 so that comparisons between the strategies are easier.

So how did ITMS perform? Rather well. Take a look:

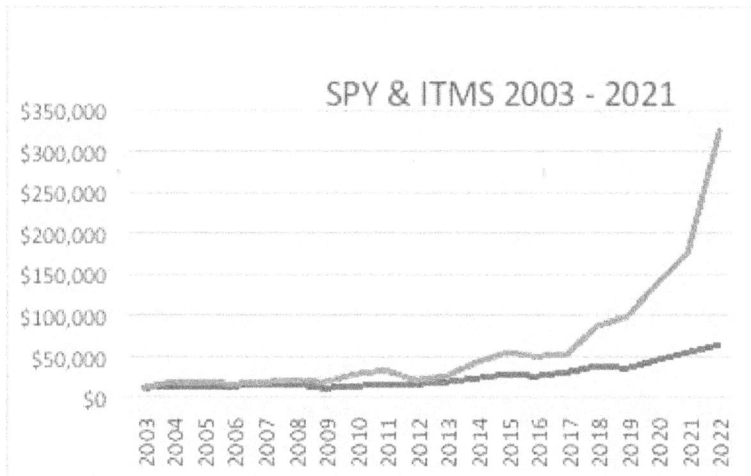

SPY & ITMS 2003 - 2021

You may also notice that the graph does not include the first two years of SPYG's existence. This is because the entry criteria were not met as there was a bear market going on.

You can see that the ITMS results beat the market quite convincingly, around 5 times the market return. You will also notice that it took a while for that to happen. For the first 10 years there was not much of a difference.

In these ten years, ITMS outperformed the market but not by a lot. This is because during the years 2003-2012 the market was not trending upwards; ITM and ITMS are bull market strategies and are suited to trending markets.

The chart shows that the difference in performance started during the GFC. The ITM rules kept us out of the worst of the downturn, and so we did not dip as much as the S&P 500 did and that was the start of the ITMS advantage. Check it out:

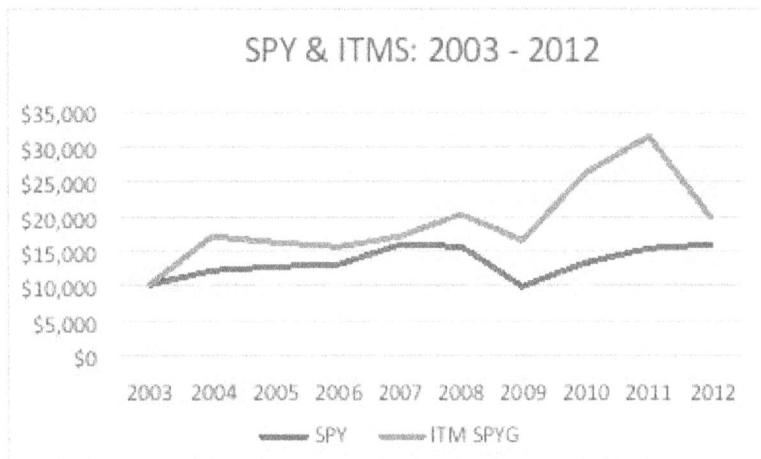

SPY & ITMS: 2003 - 2012

ITMS Rules

To recap, the rules for ITMS are as follows:

- ➤ **Underlying** asset: SPYG, the S&P 500 Growth fund.
- ➤ **Signals**
- ❖ IN signal: the 10 / 200 SMA golden cross.
- ❖ OUT signal: the 10/200 SMA death cross.
- ➤ **Buying criteria** for options:
- ❖ 6 months to expiry.
- ❖ Effective price less than SPYG + 0.05%.
- ❖ Strike approximately 60% of current price.
- ➤ **Maintenance** January & July
- ❖ Roll OUT to 6 months expiry
- ❖ Roll UP if a higher strike still fits within the effective price criterion.
- ❖ Buy additional options if enough spare cash.

As for ITM, you can monitor the market using one of the many free charting packages, like Yahoo (see Chapter 9 for details).

Volatility

This new strategy, ITMS Bull, is not a replacement for ITM Bull but is aimed at enabling traders with smaller accounts to get into the market. It is not as robust a strategy as ITM simply because of the difference in the volatility of the two ETFs.

We looked at volatility in an earlier chapter and defined it simply as price movements over a specified period for either stocks or ETFs, or even the entire market.

➤ **High volatility** means that the stock has large swings in its price.
➤ **Low volatility** means that a stock's price doesn't move around a lot

Stocks with high volatility are generally considered **risky** because the price is less predictable. If it is up one day down the next, then it is perceived as less safe. Whether high volatility is something you like depends on what kind of trader you are.

Some people, like long-term investors, avoid volatile stocks. Others, like day traders, seek out volatile stocks because they can profit from the price movements. If a stock or ETF has low volatility, then people feel more confident about buying it because there is less likelihood of nasty surprises.

The volatility of a stock affects the option price:

➤ If a stock has high volatility, then its options will be more expensive because there is a greater chance that the options will be in the money by expiration.
➤ If a stock has low volatility, then its options will be cheaper because traders can predict with more certainty where the price will be by expiry.

There are two types of volatility:

➤ **Implied volatility,** which is the market's expectation of a likely movement in price, calculated from current option prices.
➤ **Historical volatility,** which measures how much the price has deviated from its average in the past.

The Volatility Index

The **VIX** is the CBOE (Chicago Board Options Exchange**) Volatility Index,** sometimes known as the 'fear index'. It is a measure of the expected volatility of the US stock market and based on the S&P 500 index.

The VIX is calculated using the weighted prices of put and call options for the next 30 days, and so measures how much traders think the S&P 500 will fluctuate. Because it is based on actual prices it is measuring exactly how much traders are willing to pay for the time value in options.

We can graph the 90-day volatility of SPY and SPYG on the same scale. Looking at the two graphs, the first thing to notice is that the SPY line is much smoother than the SPYG line. We can see that when the market is relatively stable then there is not a huge difference between them, both sitting around 0.2.

However, when the market fluctuates and becomes more volatile then SPYG is affected much more. For instance, during the covid crisis in 2020 SPYG almost reached 0.6 whereas SPY only just got over 0.4. In general, market movements have a greater effect SPYG, much more than on SPY.

SPY Volatility

SPYG Volatility

This is why I am recommending that as soon as you can then buy SPY options rather than SPYG. Use SPYG as a sideline flutter if you like, but the real game is to get into SPY.

Whatever you do, don't be swayed by people, usually temporary traders, trying to get you into one of the most safe-sounding but dangerous strategies on which many temporary traders have come to grief. ***Leveraged ETFs.***

Leverage and Leveraged ETFs

You will often see reviews of **In The Money** that say scornfully that the same results could be achieved by buying a leveraged ETF. This is annoying because it is quite wrong, as I will show. It shows a basic misunderstanding of what a leveraged ETF is. I understand that it can be tempting to listen to these voices because they sound as though they know what they are talking about, but really it is the fast track to becoming a temporary trader. However, these people can sound quite convincing, and there is the added attraction that you can do it with smaller accounts, so let's go through what leveraged ETFs are and how they work so that you don't fall into that trap.

Firstly, lets discuss leverage. **Leverage** in investing is often taken to mean buying on margin, but that is not what ITM does. Not ever!
We use options to give us leverage because it is much safer than borrowing money.

When we use DITM (Deep In The Money) options they give us leverage, meaning that when SPY goes up 1% then we go up more depending on the strike we have bought.

Let's check out some examples (with nice easy figures). If SPY is trading at $100 and we buy 3 call options, all deep in the money. Keeping it simple with no time value, only intrinsic value, we buy:

➢ $40 Strike at a cost of $60
➢ $50 Strike at a cost of $50
➢ $60 Strike at a cost of $40

Each option controls 100 shares of SPY. If SPY goes up 5%, and the share price increases $5 to $105 then:

➢ The $40 strike is worth $65
➢ The $50 strike is worth $55
➢ The $60 strike is worth $45

The options have gone up by the same amount ($5), but our initial outlay was different with the higher strikes costing less than the lower strikes. This means that the percentage increases are different:

➢ The $40 strike has increased by 8.3% (How? 5/60)
➢ The $50 strike has increased by 10% (How? 5/50)
➢ The $60 strike has increased by 12.5% (How? 5/40)

With a strike at 50% of the current value, your leverage would be 100%. If SPY goes up 2% you will go up 4%. If SPY goes up 10% you go up 20%. If you buy a strike at 60% of the current value (which is what the backtesting is based on) then your leverage is 125%.

SPY emulates the performance of the S&P 500 (SPX) with no leverage. If SPX goes up 1% then SPY goes up 1%. Here is where **leveraged ETFs** come in. These are ETFs that seek to deliver **multiples** of the SPX performance. They are referred to 2X and 3X ETFs.

➢ A **2X ETF** is aiming to return **two times** the SPX Return. If SPX went up 5% then a 2X ETF would go up 10%
➢ A **3X ETF** is aiming to return **three times** the SPX Return. If SPX went up 5% then a 3X ETF would go up 15%

Two of the biggest 2X leveraged SPX ETFs are:
- ➤ SPUU - Direxion Daily S&P500 Bull 2X Shares
- ➤ SSO - ProShares Ultra S&P500

And two of the biggest 3X ETFs are:
- ➤ SPXL - Direxion Daily S&P500 Bull 3X Shares
- ➤ SSO - ProShares UltraPro S&P500

There are also inverse ETFs, which seek to provide multiples of the opposite return of an index, again either -2X or -3X, for example:
- ➤ SDS – ProShares UltraShort S&P500 (-2X)
- ➤ SPXU – ProShares UltraPro Short S&P500 (-3X)

   Warning: Leveraged ETFs have very different results to ITM.

It sounds at first that the leverage that you get from these ETFs is the same as we get using DITM options. That is the trap that many temporary traders fall into, but in practice it is a very nasty 'gotcha'. There is a clue to this trap in some of the ETF names like Direxion ***Daily.***

The important thing to note is that these ETFs are NOT designed for long-term investing, but rather ***they are aimed at day traders***. To achieve their multiplier on one-day returns they are 'reset' daily. They use shorting, swaps, futures contracts, and other derivatives to get their leverage. ***Because of the daily reset they can very quickly diverge from the index they are trying to track.***

It is often thought, especially by temporary traders, that leveraged ETF results are easy to understand. What could be simpler? SPY goes up by 2% they go up by 4% or 6%. Unfortunately, buyers of leveraged ETFs are often in for a nasty surprise. A 2X ETF may return 2% on a day when the SPX rises 1%, but that's where it ends. You cannot expect it to return 30% in a year when SPX rises 15%. They don't work that way. Let's have a look and see why.

EXAMPLE 1
Let's take a 10 day period where the market is basically flat, going up and down 10% in one day (unlikely, I know, but keeping the math easy). Here is what happens to our leveraged ETFs:

Start	$100			
Day	Day change	ETF	2X ETF	3X ETF
1	10%	110.00	120.00	130.00
2	-10%	99.00	96.00	91.00
3	10%	108.90	115.20	118.30
4	-10%	98.01	92.16	82.81
5	10%	107.81	110.59	107.65
6	-10%	97.03	88.47	75.36
7	10%	106.73	106.17	97.96
8	-10%	96.06	84.93	68.57
9	10%	105.67	101.92	89.15
10	-10%	95.10	81.54	62.40
RETURN	0%	-4.90%	-18.46%	-37.60%

You can see that the market dropped almost 5% over the 10 days – but look at the performance of the leveraged ETFs. It is MUCH higher than double or triple. They are clearly not tracking the index over time, otherwise their returns would be -10% (instead of the actual result of -18%) and -15% (instead of -38%).

EXAMPLE 2
Let's take a more realistic 2% per day move with the up days and down days next to each other.

Start	$100			
Day	Day change	ETF	2X ETF	3X ETF
1	-2%	98.00	96.00	94.00
2	-2%	96.04	92.16	88.36
3	-2%	94.12	88.47	83.06
4	-2%	92.24	84.93	78.07
5	-2%	90.39	81.54	73.39
6	2%	92.20	84.80	77.79
7	2%	94.04	88.19	82.46
8	2%	95.92	91.72	87.41
9	2%	97.84	95.39	92.65
10	2%	99.80	99.20	98.21
RETURN	0%	-0.20%	-0.80%	-1.79%

The actual performance of the ETFs after only 10 days is 4X and 9X, not the 2X and 3X some traders are expecting. Interesting, isn't it? If this is what can happen in just 10 days, imagine how the performance could diverge after 100 days or a year!

Are you starting to see why leveraged ETFs produce so many temporary traders? So, some words of advice:

Leveraged ETFs are dangerous. Don't use them.

The U.S. Securities and Exchange Commission has even put out a warning about them, just google 'SEC investor warning leveraged ETFs' to find it.

My recommendation? I'm with the SEC. Steer clear of leveraged ETFs. I have seen people get wiped out by them and it's not pretty. They thought they were safe and that they knew what was happening, but they weren't, and they didn't. Be smart and avoid them. Don't join the ranks of the temporary traders!

Chapter 11 Highlights

The major points in Chapter 11. ITM for Small Accounts are:

➢ SPYG is an ETF made up of growth funds within the S&P 500, and its shares are less than 20% of SPY (which means their options are also much cheaper).

➢ ITM has been backtested on SPYG and the strategy is called ITMS (S for smaller accounts). ITMS can be used by people wanting to get into the market but find the cost of SPY shares too high.

➢ ITMS can be used by traders until their account is large enough to trade SPY options.

➢ The leverage that you get with ITM is dependent on the strike price. 100% leverage is obtained with a strike 50% of the current price.

➢ Leveraged ETFs are for day traders; they are not suitable for long term investing.

➢ Leveraged ETFs quickly diverge from the underlying asset because of the daily reset.

And some words from Robert G Allen:

How many millionaires do you know who have become wealthy by investing in savings accounts? I rest my case.

◆ ◆ ◆

Chapter 12. Keeping Your Balance

Keeping your head when all around are losing theirs is hard. Very hard, but essential to your survival and success as a trader. It is important to manage yourself and your environment to make it as easy as possible. If we separate your environment into your immediate environment (family, friends, and colleagues) and the general environment (TV, news, websites) we can get a better handle on how to control it.

I recommend that you don't talk about your trading. I don't mean that you should lie about it, but don't volunteer information. If you say that you trade and the other person doesn't, she is not going to be able to talk to you with any understanding of what you are doing. If the other person does trade, then the chances are that she is a 'temporary trader' and will tell you about the stocks she is buying and how wonderfully well they are doing – or not. This only confuses your thinking. I suggest that you keep it low-key.

If you are asked directly if you trade, then have a couple of answers ready so that they come naturally. Mine are: ***Yes, a bit, but not stocks or currencies*** (that usually leaves them confused and the conversations end there) or ***Yes, a bit, but I mainly trade index options not stocks.*** About here most people move right on because they don't understand what else I could be trading or know what an index option is. People generally don't want to show their ignorance by asking.

If you do get further questions they will probably be about money: how much you have made and how much you are making. I would suggest that is probably none of their business, but you don't win friends by saying that! I recommend that you don't talk in money terms.

Instead, talk about percentages. Say *I made 30% last year* or *I am up 20% in the last 6 months* or whatever the figure happens to be. Don't talk actual dollar figures.

Let Compounding do its Work

In other words, don't talk about money. Apart from anything else, it does your head in. You have to be able to partition trading money from everyday money, and think of it in a different way.

For example, I am as likely as the next person to balk at paying $10 for a coffee. But at the same time, I don't turn a hair at buying or selling $100K worth of options. Comparing the two doesn't make sense and you have to learn that. You need to keep them separate.

When you look at the SPY and see that it has gone up 1% in the day then you know that you are up 2% or 3% depending on your strategy. Resist the temptation to translate that into dollars! Let's say you have been doing ITM for a year and you started with $10K then your account is now worth $19,000. A 3% gain overnight is $570. Nice! But resist the urge to go out and spend the $570 that you have just made. Leaving it in the account and adding it to your total makes the next 3% even bigger – next time it would be $587.

Compounding really does work, so leave your money in your account and let ITM do its work.

Dealing with Losses

The thing that REALLY does your head in is, of course, the days when the market goes down. And it does go down, even in a bull market. Remember the waves and the tide? Checking your account and seeing that you are $570 down may trigger the immediate response *Damn! I've just lost $570!* and ruin your day. My own accounts are a lot larger than they used to be, and I sometimes have to deal with what are, to me, quite huge daily losses. To keep my sanity after a large drop in the market (and to keep my head clear for thinking) my strategy is to not look at the accounts.

I always check the market indexes every morning and evening on a different website in any case. If the indexes have gone down, I can work out in my head what percentage my accounts have gone down. *And that's where I leave it.* There is no point in making yourself miserable by looking at the actual dollar figure.

Instead, I reflect on the day last week when I made even more than today's loss. I didn't run down the road waving my arms and yelling *Woohoo! I'm a genius!* I just smiled in a Cheshire cat sort of way and got over it. Do the same with losses. Make a scowling face at yourself in the mirror, then get over it.

I cannot stress enough the importance of keeping your day-to-day money head and your trading money head separate. If you start measuring your trading by what it would buy, then you can easily lose the plot. Keep your eye on your goal. Your goal is $500K in 5 years? Great. That's what you should think about and focus on.

Your general environment is slightly easier to control. You can decide not to read stories with lurid bullish or bearish headlines and decide not to go on a chatroom or read other traders' recommendations. I definitely recommend that you do both of these things! You can't avoid reading the headlines if you are already on the website or have picked up the paper. But you CAN choose not to read the article, and instead reflect on WHY the journalist wrote it. Are they after clicks? Is it to be different from the article yesterday? Is this journalist a well-known bear? What were their previous articles about? Remember, no one clicks on a headline that says **Market Looks Pretty Normal Today.**

However, do keep an eye on the headlines. Negative headlines you should treat as a positive sign that the market is still not completely in the optimism phase. When the headlines about the stock market start becoming all positive then that is the time to be wary. We may be entering the euphoria phase and have to prepare for a coming bear market.

Who Should You Listen To?

You can't live in a vacuum, and I am not recommending that you do. You have to keep an eye on the world around you and how it affects the market. We are not talking about relatively small adjustments. Yes, if the CEO of a major company dies suddenly, we can expect that the stock will go down, but this is unlikely to affect the whole market. Try to differentiate between events that affect the whole of the market and events that affect only a particular stock or a sector.

For example, as we all know September 11, 2001, was a day when a terrible tragedy happened. It seemed that America was under attack. People were bewildered about how this could happen in the middle of New York and frightened of what might happen next. This horror and uncertainty would clearly have affected the markets and could have triggered a market meltdown. It was feared that people would panic and dump their stocks. Both the New York Stock Exchange (NYSE) and the Nasdaq did not open for trading that day and remained closed until Monday the 17th of September.

When it reopened there was an immediate sell-off, although it ended up being a white-candle day (the close was higher than the open). By Friday, however, the S&P 500 was showing a loss of 11.6%. Subsequently, it only took until the 3rd of October before the S&P 500 was back to pre-9/11 levels. Devastating as the attacks were, once the market realized that this was a once-off event and unlikely to be repeated it continued on its trend. In other words, it was a horribly big wave, but it didn't affect the tide.

Handling the Dips

While the overall ITM and ITMS results are impressive, not every year is a winner. You can see that there are some quite major dips. Between 2015 and 2016 for example if you were following ITMS your account value dropped from $54,301 to $48,445. That's a drop of 11%.

If you were following ITM then your account would have dropped 26% from $416,333 to $333,635 which is a drop of almost 20%. Looking at it another way, that's a loss of almost $100K! No one can look at that with equanimity.

Our problem was a market that was going sideways that had a couple of very sudden dips but didn't progress to being a bear market. ITM quickly got the money back and by the end of 2017 had surpassed its earlier high and then some. However, you still would have had to deal with the psychological pressure of having 'lost' $100K.

You could have consoled yourself by reflecting that your current balance was more than it was two years ago and more than double what it was four years ago.

However, human nature being what it is, probably you would have berated yourself for not having gotten out when you were in front. You would have thought of all the things you could have done with that money – the holiday, the new car, the house renovation – and feel depressed. It's only human. I do it too although I try (not always successfully) to limit my wallowing in misery to a day at most and then get back on track. But I have a technique that works for me that you may want to try.

I call it my 'smug index'. I know when I am smug because I update my wealth spreadsheet more than once a day, just for the pleasure of it. This is one of my warning signals.

When I feel smug about the way my trading is going, I check through my accounts. For the ITM accounts, I check that I am trading in accordance with the rules and that I haven't missed any signals. I review my non-ITM accounts for any risky positions. Yes, I still play with OTM options and try other strategies, but only with 'play money' in 'play accounts.' I get out of anything that is too leveraged or short-term.

I remind myself of the last time I was feeling smug, and shortly afterward the risky trades went against me. Then I was annoyed with myself that I hadn't acted sooner and thought about all the cool things I could have done with that money and then beat myself up. Which is, of course, a complete waste of time. We can all be brilliant traders in hindsight.

However, if your ITM accounts are all in order but you have still lost money (as in the 2015 / 2016 situation) you have to manage your emotions and the best time to do that is before the situation happens. You need to work out what level of risk you are willing to take. Here is a suggestion.

As a way of making it easier to sleep at night if you are worried about losing money then *as your account grows, take some of the leverage away*.

For example, when your account gets to be worth $500K or $1 million, whatever to you seems large enough to know that losing 20% or so would be hard for you to deal with, consider whether it would give you peace of mind to take away some of the leverage.

An idea could be to put half in straight SPY shares and use the other half for the ITM strategy. The amount you allocate to leveraged and non-leveraged positions can be adjusted depending on your account size, and you can fine-tune this level until you feel comfortable.

This way part of your portfolio is relatively protected but can still share in the upside, and the other part has the leverage and can still get the great returns. Your account will not make the level of returns that you would with a fully leveraged account, but possibly you will feel calmer and not worry so much about a downturn and the associated losses. There is always going to be a trade-off between leverage and the size of losses.

In this way, you can 'protect' a higher percentage of your funds as your account grows. The amount that you squirrel away into unleveraged investments depends on your own situation – both your account balance and your ability to withstand portfolio pain.

Please note that I am not a financial adviser, and this is general information only. You should discuss anything specific to your situation with a qualified financial adviser who can give you professional advice.

Protective Puts

Another way that people protect their portfolio is by using **protective puts**. Puts are used in the ITM Bear strategy (ITMB) and are covered in detail in the Bear Strategy book. For this section, however, all we need to know are the basics.

Put options are just like call options but in reverse. Instead of getting the right to **buy** at a strike price we get the right to **sell** at the strike price. Just as we buy a call option hoping that the price will go up, we buy a put option hoping the price will go down. Call options increase in value as the underlying stock goes up but put options increase in value as the underlying stock goes down.

Let's take an example to see how it works. If we have a SPY put option with a strike of $350 then we have the right to sell 100 SPY at $350. If SPY was currently trading at $400 then we definitely would **not** want to exercise our option. Why would we want to sell SPY for less than it is currently worth? We wouldn't, of course. On the other hand, if SPY was trading at $300 then we would love to sell it for $350.

Most people buy call options because they are bullish but being bearish is not the only reason people buy puts. Traders may be buying them as a hedging strategy. That's what is known as a **protective put**.

If you have a stock in your portfolio that you intend to keep for a long time you can guard against the price dropping past a certain point by buying a put option with a strike at the point you don't want it to drop below. It's a bit like an insurance policy on your stock holdings.

For example, let's say you had 100 Apple shares which are currently trading at $143. You are planning to keep them for the long haul but are worried that the price might go down. You don't want to lose more than 10% of your investment so you look at buying a put with a strike of $130 (Why? 10% less than $143, rounded). This protects you, because if AAPL drops below $130 then you have the right to sell them at that price.

However, this protection comes at a price. The put premium can be expensive. The price of a $130 strike one year to expiry costs $10.30, which is approximately 7% of the value of the stock. This is a large overhead for one year's protection, and, of course, you will have to buy it every year that you own the stock. This adds up, eating away at the value of your account and any profits you have made.

Another disadvantage of protective puts is that if the stock rises strongly over the year, then your protective put is not protecting any of that increase. For example, if AAPL rose 25% to $180 your protective put only protects you against price drops below $130 which is now 28% below the current price. To protect the new valuation, you would have to expend more funds to buy a new put with a strike 10% below $180 and sell your $130 put at a considerable loss as it would have gone down a lot in value due to the rise in the underlying stock (AAPL).

Protective puts sound good in theory, but in practice they are not so great. It's like buying insurance with a way-too-high premium. Sometimes it makes more sense to self-insure.

Taxation

Everyone's tax situation is different, and I am certainly no tax expert. I have received some reviews and emails that complain I don't think about the tax situation. I have to say that they are absolutely right: I ***don't*** think about the tax implications at all when I am trading.

I never go into a trade thinking about how it will affect my tax bill. I figure it is my job to make the money and it is a tax expert's job to guide me in how it should be handled taxation-wise.

That doesn't mean that my approach is right for you. I recommend that if you are worried about making too much money then you should consult a taxation specialist to see how you should handle it and if you should modify your trading strategy.

Turbocharging your returns

If you want to turbo charge your returns, there are some extra strategies that you can implement.

Rolling Up. You may want to roll up more often to get better leverage. If the market has moved up 10% or more, then don't wait until the start of the next period. You can roll up anytime to a higher strike, as long as it fits within the parameters. The extra funds that you release can be used to fund more DITM options or one of the next ideas.

Buy SPY shares. If you don't have enough cash in your account to buy another DITM option, rather than have it just sitting there doing nothing buy SPY shares. If SPY continues to go up, then you will reap the benefit. These can be easily sold when you are ready to buy your next DITM options.

Flutter on an OTM option. OK – a warning here: *this is a high-risk strategy* (as you know) so only do this with a VERY small percentage of your portfolio, never more than 5%. Be prepared to lose the lot – you know the odds! However, it is good fun, and you may just strike it lucky.

Choose an OTM option, say 4 – 6 months to expiry and around 10% more than the current price – and make sure that you are using 'play money'. You can decide to sell if it increases by 25% or 50%, whatever seems like a good return to you, but whatever happens always sell it at least 30 days before expiry. Remember time decay? You don't want it to happen to you.

Commit to adding funds. By adding even $100 per month you hugely increase your account balance in the long term. When I was doing the backtesting I experimented with adding in small amounts like $10 a week and was amazed at the effect on the final results. If you like playing around with spreadsheets I encourage you to do it. It will probably give you the motivation you need to make the commitment.

Where to get these funds? Here are some ideas. Every MONTH the average American spends:

- ➢ $92 on coffee
- ➢ $250 on restaurants
- ➢ $313 on appearance (OK, women only!)
- ➢ $123 on fitness (gym, classes, supplements)

When you add this to the fact that Americans each year spend $32 billion on pizza, $80 billion on lottery tickets ,and $62 billion on cosmetics you will probably have a few ideas on where you could get these extra funds!

Now, I am not suggesting that you turn your life into a no-fun zone. Not at all. I can't do it, so I can hardly suggest that you do it. Being miserable now so you can be happy later is a mug's game. You don't want to be gloomy and despondent while you are building your wealth, you want to be happy and excited and looking forward to all that lovely money!

So, don't go for self-denial. Don't eliminate something that is important to your present-day happiness. If you need a cappuccino in the morning, if missing out on it would ruin your day then that's NOT what to cut out. Look for something else. You want to identify some expenditure that is a ***meh – I can do without that!*** and choose to cut that out to save the money you need for your wealthy future.

For me, it was going out and buying coffee ***on my own***. although I will freely admit giving it up was easy for me because I was working from my home office and could make myself a coffee at any time. Even now, when I can easily afford all the coffees I want, I still have a bit of a block on buying myself a nice latte unless I am with other people when somehow, it's OK. Humans are weird. OK, maybe it's just me!

A Word about Dividends

In practice, if you had been holding SPY shares then you would have received dividends every year. That is the one unfortunate thing about options: you don't receive dividends. Only shares receive dividends. However, I am always dismissive, perhaps too dismissive, of dividends mainly because I have never received any worth having.

For example, recently I got a dividend of $2,000 on some SPY shares I was holding instead of cash. That sounds nice – but they were worth over $450K. Not a great rate of return. Not even 1%! Likewise, on QQQ (the Nasdaq ETF) I got a dividend of $384. For shares that were worth almost a quarter of a million dollars that seems pitifully small.

I tend to ignore dividends as sources of wealth or income. I suggest that you do too. Look on them as a welcome occasional windfall. There are far better ways to make money!

Dumb Things People Will Say To You

Keeping your balance (yes, it's a pun, couldn't resist!) means that you have to stay strong in the face of people telling you that you are wrong and that ITM can't possibly work. Lots of people will try to tell you their thoughts about the market and convince you that they are right. Here are some of the things you are likely to hear most:

You haven't lost money until you sell

This is so obviously wrong I don't know where to start! What they mean is that you haven't **realized your loss** until you sell – but you have definitely lost money. The asset, whether it's a house or a car or an option, is only worth what someone will actually pay for it, not what you would like them to pay for it. You may think that your house should be worth $1 million, but if no one is prepared to pay more than $500K then it isn't worth $1million whether you sell it or not. Basically, people who say this are deluding themselves that something is worth more than it really is.

Dollar-Cost Averaging

This theory is that investing the same amount of money in a share on a regular basis (like every month, or every quarter) regardless of the price will help you ride out downturns in the market. Yes, it does average out volatility. But let's face it: some stocks are dogs and buying them when they are 'cheap' is the quick way to the poorhouse.

Dollar-cost averaging is supposed to take the emotion out of buying decisions. It also, unfortunately, takes the thinking out of it as well. Financial advisers love nothing more than having clients who just buy regardless of what is actually going on, and how the stocks are performing. Money for jam!

You can't go wrong with blue-chip stocks

Actually, you **can** go very wrong. Stocks in the Dow, for instance, are generally considered 'blue-chip', but we saw in a previous chapter how many 'market darlings' in the past are no longer in favor.

Above is a chart of GE (General Electric), once one of the bluest of blue-chips, and trading at almost $460 twenty years ago. Today, it's below $100. Imagine if you had stuck with that blue-chip stock for 20 years waiting for it to go up!

Diversification is Key

You will often see financial advice to diversify by putting money into different investments. For example, invest some money in blue chips, some in small-cap stocks, some in emerging markets, some in commodities, some in currencies, and so on. The theory says that one area may go down while another may go up. To me, this looks like a sure-fire way to make sure that you don't outperform the market.

I subscribe to Andrew Carnegie's approach:

The way to become rich is to put all your eggs in one basket, and then watch that basket carefully.

In any case, we are already diversified simply by using SPY as it represents the top 500 stocks listed on stock exchanges in the U.S.

Buy cheap options – one is bound to be a 10-bagger!

Cheap options are cheap for a reason: *the likelihood of them expiring in the money is low*. Sure, if you buy 10 or 100 of them the chances of getting one that increases 10-fold is 10 or 100 times higher. That sounds good. Until you look at the effect on your account balance.

Let's say you start with $1,000 and invest $100 in each of 10 cheap options. Nine expire worthless, but one of them is a 10-bagger! Hooray! Or not. Your 10-bagger is now worth $1,000 – but your others are worth nothing. So, you are exactly back where you started. Not the smartest strategy.

Dumb Things That I have Done

Now, I am not saying that I have never followed some of the above advice. I have. In my time I have done a lot of dumb things. I have read hundreds of books about the stock market and been on many courses and seminars, some of them costing a lot of money. I have followed any number of crackpot theories and trading strategies.

Invariably, I have ended up losing money – sometimes a bit, sometimes a lot. But hopefully, after reading this list you can avoid them, because losing money hurts, and worse, it can take you out of the game.

Elliott Wave Theory

I thought that this was going to be great given my idea about the market being about waves and tides. Unfortunately, I found that Elliott Wave only works in hindsight. It knows where things are now, but it is not good at predicting where they are going. After reducing my account by 25% in a few months I decided to give it up.

Sector Trading

There are different sectors in the stock market like energy, consumer discretionary, health care, and technology. Sector rotation trading is moving your stock investments from one sector to another depending on the stage of the economic cycle.

For example, in a recession cyclicals and transports do better at the start, then technology and then followed by industrials. As a recovery starts, basic materials and energy are more successful. I traded this way for a few months after the GFC and I can report that I missed out on a lot of the recovery gains and managed to lose money when the market was trending up strongly.

CFD (Contracts for Difference)

This is where you speculate on very short price movements in a stock without actually owning the stock. CFDs are illegal in the US partly because they are not under the control of regulated exchanges, and partly (I assume) because they are dangerous. They are legal in many countries like Australia, France, Canada Germany, and Japan.

There may be some successful CFD traders out there, but I have never met anyone who has been doing it for more than a few months. The successful ones (if there are any) are vastly outnumbered by temporary traders who have lost their shirts. My last experience with CFDs was using them to trade Bitcoin. Not smart. I lost 90% of my stake within 2 days. Not fun.

Momentum Trading

This is a strategy where you buy stocks that are rising (i.e., they have momentum) and sell them when they have peaked. If you have a crystal ball that tells you when a stock is going to go up and when it has peaked, then this should work just fine for you. My crystal ball was useless. I lost money.

Value Investing

This is where you look for stocks that are (or seem to be) trading at less than their intrinsic or book value. In other words, the stock *should*, in the opinion of the trader, be worth more so they think that they are buying the 'on sale' at a discounted price. This is what Warren Buffett is famous for, but he buys companies not just stocks. A seductive theory, one that I have never found made me any money plus it takes a lot of time.

Currency

A fun, fast-moving way to lose all your stake. I did. Luckily, I only play like this in small accounts where it doesn't matter too much if I blow it up. Play if you like – it's fun - just make sure you only use play money.

Swing Trading

Basically, this is buying and selling stocks with a short time frame of a few days to a few weeks. No magic. Just stock picking which we know doesn't work.

Asymmetric Trading

This is where you take a risk that the profit is bigger than the risk taken. For example, if you risk $500 for the chance of making $5,000 that is asymmetric. If you risk $500 to make $500 then this is symmetric. Traders look for downtrodden stocks with the hope that they will come up again.

Here is one of my asymmetric trades on Dry Ships (DRYS) once a market darling. As The Wall Street Journal noted, Dry Ships Investors lost 99.99% of their investment between November 2016 and July 2017. I'm still waiting on the payoff, which won't happen now because the company has been taken private.

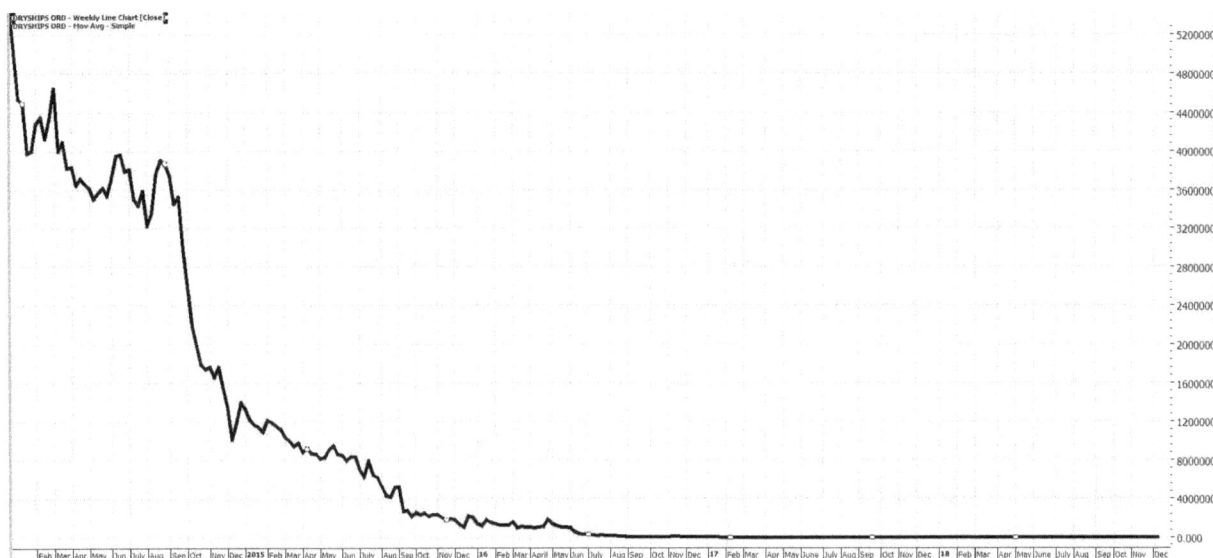

On all of these strategies I have lost money. Never enough to wipe me out, but enough to cause quite a lot of sleepless nights. I have paid for numerous websites and newsletters, way too many to name, but have never found any that have consistently made money. I have read many, many books, but have never found any of the 'trading secrets' to be reliable ways to make money.

The best book that I have read on the stock market and trading was written almost 100 years ago. It is 'Reminiscences of a Stock Operator' by Edwin Lefevre. It is based on the life of Jesse Lauriston Livermore, the original Wolf of Wall Street (he was also called the Great Bear of Wall Street.) He is widely regarded as being one of the greatest traders who ever lived.

The book is remarkable. Fascinating and wise, it is cited by many famous investors as being crucial to their success. I totally recommend that you read it for the insights it gives into what makes the market, and people in the market, tick.

So, in summary . . .

. . this is the journey I have been on for the last twenty five years. Hopefully I can spare you having to go through the same journey. It was frequently nerve-wracking and often frustrating, but it was always fascinating. I just couldn't seem to give it up even when it looked like I would never make any money from it.

Working out the ITM strategy was a game changer for me. Yes, I still play with other strategies, but most of my positions are in DITM options on either SPY or QQQ (the Nasdaq ETF). I keep quite a few small accounts where I experiment with different strategies, and hopefully will find another one that works just as well.

But in the meantime, I wish you all the good fortune in the world in your trading and on your journey to being wealthy. I hope that you really enjoy it.

Getting Started

Nothing happens unless you take action, so here is your action plan. Everything you need to carry out these steps has been covered in the book, but it is probably a good idea to reread the relevant chapters before you carry out the steps.

➢ **7 Steps to Getting Started:**

❖ if you already have an account and are familiar with buying and selling options then start at step No 6.
❖ If you do not already have an account then google 'best brokers 2022' and choose one. Practice on the demo platform until you are sure that you know how to buy and sell an option.

➢ **Ongoing Maintenance**

❖ Login to your account at least weekly
❖ Check HeatherCullen.com/Blog to make sure that there have been no Out signals or check the SPY / SPYG chart.
❖ If you are nearing expiry then you will have to roll OUT to a later expiry date
❖ (Optional) if your option is too DITM (less than 50% of the current price) then roll UP to a higher strike.
❖ When you have free cash in your account then buy a new DITM option.
❖ (Optional) if you have free cash but not enough for a new DITM option then buy SPY shares.

Over to you – take action!

7 Steps to Getting Started

1. ➤ Choose broker (Google)

2. ➤ Open an account

3. ➤ Deposit funds

4. ➤ Enable account for options

5. ➤ Practice on demo platform

6. ➤ Find SPY/SPYG options chain

7. ➤ Choose DITM option & buy

Ongoing Maintenance

1. ➢ Check balance and positions
2. ➢ Deposit extra cash
3. ➢ Chart / blog OUT signal?
4. ➢ Near expiry? Roll Out
5. ➢ Too DITM? Roll UP
6. ➢ Cash left? Buy DITM option
7. ➢ Not enough? Buy SPY shares

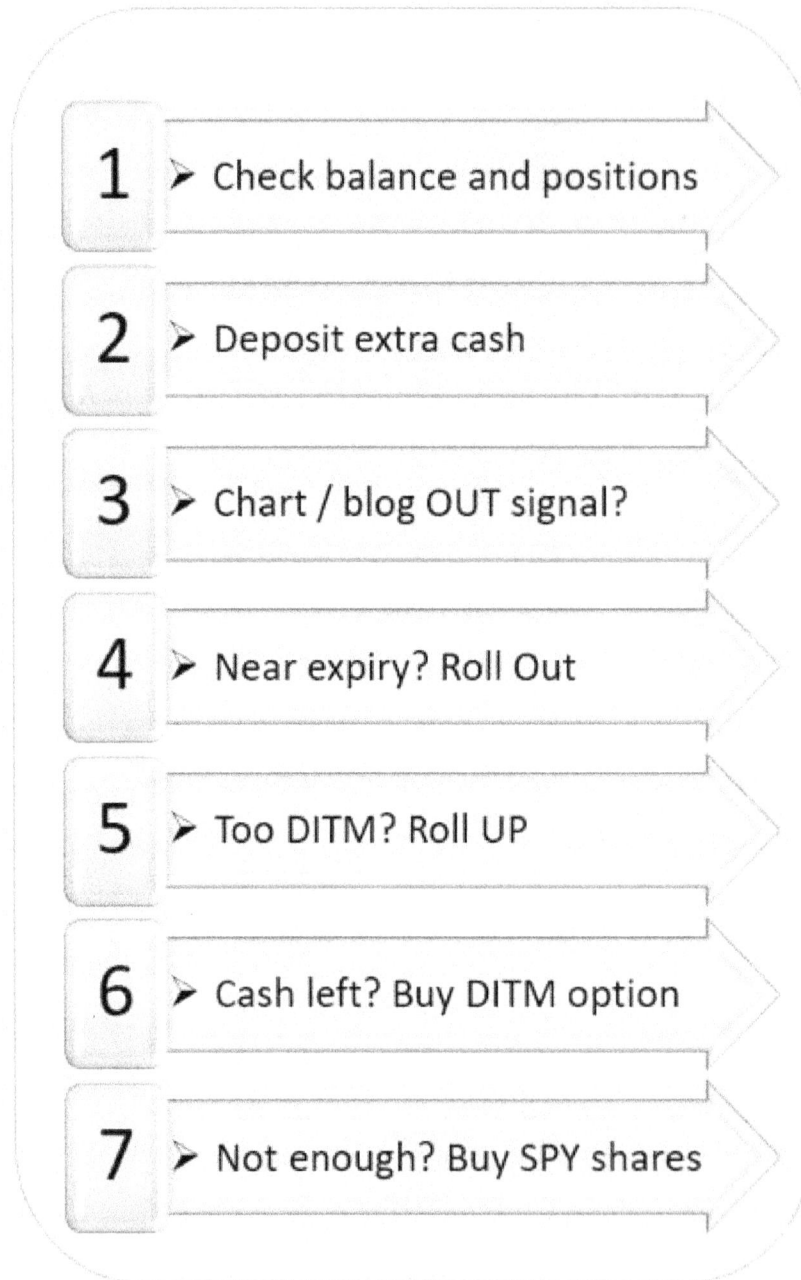

Entering the Market

I am often asked about timing the market entry and what entry signals I use. The simple answer is that I don't. I am not very successful at picking good entry points. That's one of the things that you can do very well in hindsight!

If I have decided to get into the market, then I get in. Every time I have waited for the price to come down it hasn't, and I have been left kicking myself for not getting in at that price. Of course, the opposite happens as well: I get into the market and the next day it has dropped a bit. You just can't predict the waves. The takeaway? You don't know what is going to happen tomorrow. Just do it.

You can't predict the waves, only the tide.